THE COWBOY

THE COWBOY

His Characteristics, His Equipment, and His Part in the Development of the West

Philip Ashton Rollins

Skyhorse Publishing

Skyhorse Publishing books may be purchased in bulk at special discounts for sales promotion, corporate gifts, fund-raising, or educational purposes. Special editions can also be created to specifications. For details, contact the Special Sales Department, Skyhorse Publishing, 307 West 36th Street, 11th Floor, New York, NY 10018 or info@skyhorsepublishing.com.

Skyhorse® and Skyhorse Publishing® are registered trademarks of Skyhorse Publishing, Inc.®, a Delaware corporation.

www.skyhorsepublishing.com

10 9 8 7 6 5 4 3 2 1

Library of Congress Cataloging-in-Publication Data

Rollins, Philip Ashton, 1869–1950.
The cowboy : his characteristics, his equipment, and his part in the development of the West/by Philip Ashton Rollins.
p. cm.
Originally published: New York : Charles Scribner's Sons, 1924.
ISBN-13: 978-1-60239-081-2 (pbk. : alk. paper)
ISBN-10: 1-60239-081-9 (pbk. : alk. paper)
1. Cowboys—West (U.S.)—History. 2. Cowboys—West (U.S.)—
Social life and customs. 3. Frontier and pioneer life—West (U.S.)
4. Ranch life—West (U.S.) 5. West (U.S.)—Social life and customs.
I. Title.
F596.R75 2007
978'.02—dc22

2007015962

Printed in the United States of America

CONTENTS

CONTENTS

ILLUSTRATIONS

PREFACE

The American cowboy, by reason of his picturesqueness, has been a frequent subject for the dramatist, the novelist, the illustrator, and the motion-picture photographer.

All these producers have been limited by the technical requirements of their arts, and have stressed the cowboy's picturesqueness to the exclusion of his other qualities. They have done this so definitely and attractively as to create an ostensible type which rapidly is being accepted by the American public as an accurate portrait of the now bygone puncher.

The portrait is often charmingly presented, but it is not accurate. The cowboy was far more than a theatric character. He was an affirmative, constructive factor in the social and political development of the United States.

Consequently he deserves to be assured more kindly treatment by ultimate history than presumably he will receive unless, while the testimony of eye-witnesses be still procurable, such testimony be gathered and recorded.

Mr. Emerson Hough's "The Story of the Cowboy" supplied evidence of this nature, and was so delightfully readable that it alone should have proved sufficient; but nevertheless the "movie man" still continues his work of smirching the cowboy's reputableness. Wherefore it is incumbent that additional eye-witnesses should follow Mr. Hough onto the witness-stand, even though their testimony be given in a form far less interesting than was that which he employed.

The writer, during a series of years before the fateful one of 1892, was upon the open Range, and was brought into intimate relationship with many of its people. In 1892, that year of Wyoming's "Rustler War," he was in Wyoming and in close contact with participants in that adventure. Since 1892 he has been more or less frequently in the one-time Cattle Country.

He makes no pretension of having discovered the West, any part of it, any person in it, or anything relating to it. But in this book he has earnestly striven to record truthfully what Western ranchmen, in the ordinary course of their business, said within his hearing and did before his eyes, and thus to recount accurately the every-day life of the old-time Range.

He has restricted himself to what he actually saw and heard, except in the cases of four classes of matter.

The first of these classes is comprised of the description of events which occurred prior to the decade of the eighties. To various standard histories, notably that of Bancroft, to numerous old-timers talking at the ranch-table or beside the camp-fire, and to the several printed reports by live-stock commissions, the writer is indebted for the material which he has used.

The second class is made of such of the illustrative anecdotes as relate to adventures with the Indians. These, although hearsay, came from unimpeachable sources. They were severally given to the writer by the direct word of mouth of Major Frank P. Fremont, Tazewell Woody, John Yancey, and, above all, of that great scout, James Bridger. A whole new world was opened to a very youthful "tenderfoot" when in 1874 Mr. Bridger told him of Kit Carson.

The third class, the references to the distances ridden by Leon and by Aubrey, is taken from Haydn's "Dictionary of Dates," and Captain J. L. Humfreville's "Twenty Years among Our Hostile Indians," this last augmented by Captain Humfreville in conversation.

The fourth class consists of the assertions as to the probability of pursued men's "doubling back" upon their courses. These assertions are the result of frequent conversations held years since upon the subject with various of the Indian scouts.

Because the book represents a sincere attempt to provide some future historian with reliable statements of fact, it contains no imaginative material beyond that specified in subsequent paragraphs of this Preface.

All the people mentioned in the book did and said just what the book attributes to them; and, with the single exception of "Mr. New Yorker" in Chapter IV, all the names ascribed to people mentioned in the book were the actual names of such people.

The names which, on pages 181 and 231, are ascribed to ranches are fictitious.

The writer owes a very real debt to his friend, Howard Thayer Kingsbury, who, loaning his keen sense of historical perspectives and his nice appreciation of literary forms, made various suggestions, all of which have been followed, and who also pricked some virulent literary blisters.

The writer is much indebted also to his friend, John H. Bradford, who, experienced on the cattle-range and versed in the accurate use of English, made corrections in the manuscript.

This Preface closes with a duplication of the appeal wherewith the final chapter of this book concludes.

P.A.R.

THE COWBOY

CHAPTER I

THE BEGINNINGS OF RANCHING

ORIGIN OF RANCHING, OF ITS EQUIPMENT AND TECHNIC—"WILD HORSES"—"WILD CATTLE"—
"INDIAN PONIES"—BEGINNING OF RANCHING BY AMERICANS—OVERLAND TRAIL AND ITS USERS—
DEVELOPMENT OF RANCHING—TEXAS TRAIL—VARIOUS DEFINITIONS—RAISING OF CATTLE AND
HORSES COMPARED—"FREE" WATER AND GRASS—OPEN RANGE—SELECTING LANDS—FENCES—
USE OF OPEN RANGE—RANCHING'S INCOMPATIBILITY WITH FARMING—SOURCES WHENCE
RANCHMEN RECRUITED—CHARACTER OF RANCHMEN—ENGLISH CONTINGENT—FINANCIAL
CAPITAL—EXTENT OF RANGE.

To the Mexicans the American cowboy owed his vocation. For his
character he was indebted to no one.

He obtained from Mexican sources all the tools of his trade, all the
technic of his craft, the very words by which he designated his utensils, the very animals with which he dealt; but, as one of the dominant
figures in the development of the United States, he was self-made.

His saddle, bridle, bit, lariat, spurs, and specialized apparel were not
designed by him. He merely copied what for generations had been in
use below the Rio Grande. The bronco that he rode and the steer that
he roped, each reached him only after they, in self or by the proxy of
their ancestors, had come northward across that river.

Long before the cowboy's advent and in A. D. 1519 and the years
immediately succeeding it, the Spanish invaders of Mexico took thither
from Europe small lots of horses and cattle. These horses were assuredly
the first the American continents had seen since the geological Ice Age,
when the prehistoric native horse became extinct; and these cattle very
probably were the first upon which those continents had ever looked.

From these imported beasts descended the vast herds which eventually overspread the grazing lands of Mexico, and with countless hoofs
pounded the plains of America's West.

This wholesale multiplication from the initial fifteen military char-
gers and the original little group of long-horned Andalusian cattle was a
matter not of a day, but of years that well-nigh spanned three centuries.

Nor was this overflowing into the present United States a causeless
thing. It was planned and supervised by dark-skinned, wide-hatted
men to whom Cotapaxi, Montezuma, and, withal, "mañana" were
familiar words.

To understand this movement and its incentive one must turn back
for a moment to that year 1519 and its Spanish invaders. The latter promptly resolved themselves into Mexican settlers; and, as with
successive generations they numerically increased, they, generation by

1

generation, spread and in part crept northward. Each migrating settler took his live stock with him as he moved. At the end of three hundred years the Rio Grande had long since been crossed, and there were firmly established in the southeastern part of present Texas numerous ranches, each covering an enormous acreage and asserting ownership over the great herds that habitually grazed upon it.

The owners of these ranches obtained from them no commercial profit, for the reason that there was no available selling market for their animals. These owners could make of their live stock no disposition beyond satisfying the scant requirements of the hacienda's dinner-table, of the local cobbler, and the neighboring saddle-maker, and also beyond insuring that every person on the premises ever would be provided with a riding horse. These requisitions withdrew so little from the herds that each year they markedly increased in size.

Throughout the stretches between the landholdings of the various ranches and throughout the peopleless country to their north were other horses and cattle, either themselves strays from then contemporary herds, or else descendants of strays from prior herds. These outlying animals gleefully led a life of saucy independence, were very numerous, and were claimed by no man. They were the so-called wild horses and wild cattle, having been thus misnamed by early explorers, who had failed to recognize them as issue of domesticated animals.

These wild cattle rarely wandered far above the northerly boundary of what is now the State of Texas; but the wild horses used all the plains as a playground, and were familiar with even the present Canadian border.

From such of these wild horses as were ensnared by the Red Man sprang the "Indian ponies," a classification that was fictitious in that it assumed the existence of a special breed.

The owners of these early ranches in present Texas were accustomed to burn or to cut upon their animals marks of proprietorship, but the indolence of the various owners let many of their animals escape this imposition. Thus intermingling with the inscribed animals were others which, being unmarked, did not patently disclose whether they were the property of a rancher or were mere visitors from the "wild" bands.

The methods and implements employed at these early establishments were so fully developed that, when years afterward America's West came into existence, it at first adopted these methods and implements in their entirety, and subsequently modified them only in so far as to brand more industriously, break and ride less cruelly, shepherd more carefully, guide both breeding and grazing, and establish sufficient selling markets. Incidentally, these later betterments in methods of breeding and breaking were due largely to Englishmen who, trained in stock-raising, had bid farewell to their home country and had cast their lot in with that of the plains.

But America's West had not as yet been born, and the Mexicans were the only ranchmen in present southeastern Texas until the year 1821.

In that year there began to trickle into that Texan section from the more easterly part of the continent a scant rivulet of pioneers who were of Scottish and English descent and of colonial American stock, who were quitting their homes in Mississippi, Alabama, Tennessee and elsewhere in the lower valley of the Mississippi River, and who were more or less aimlessly wandering westward. These pioneers, coming upon the Mexican establishments and well pleased with what they saw, settled amid the ranchers they had unearthed; learned to break and ride bucking horses; and, as the most important element of all, provided themselves with an ample supply of branding-irons. These irons so industriously were wielded amid the "wild" herds as well of horses as of cattle, and, if Mexican accusations be correct, so frequently were rested upon the sides of the accusers' unbranded animals that presently these once impoverished American pioneers found themselves in the class of "cattle kings." Then they in a desultory way sought for a selling market. They found none within reach, and, dropping thereupon into the easy-going life pursued by their Mexican neighbors, followed it until, long years afterward, a commercial outlet was secured.

They could not sell their animals, for the very simple reason that there were not within reach people to buy them.

To the south lay the waters of the Gulf. Westward were, at the map's bottom, Mexico with its sparse population and its excess supply of live stock; and, at the map's top, only more animals, mile after mile of uninhabited prairie, and then the scant Spanish settlements in far-away present New Mexico and California. Northward lay the great plains, peopleless save for the Indians. Only to the eastward might one reasonably look for opportunity to sell. But there was a wide interval between Texas and the settled portions of the East.

No railways as yet crossed that intervening space.

Nor could animals in quantity march across it. Although it was true that cattle and horses could be driven great distances, they could thus be driven only over territory wherein both nature and the local peoples consented to let them pass. Between Texas and the Mississippi River there was such unfavorable topography and such comparative scarcity of proper herbage as to forbid the transit of large herds. Nor could the beasts as yet elude this bunker by trudging northward to the latitude of benevolent east-bound trails, since hostile Indians, like myriad wasps, flitted to and fro across the route. Thus nature and man conspired to keep the Texan beasts impounded, to prevent Texan ranching from expanding into a national industry, and the Texan cowboy from becoming a national character. This impounding ceased when the Indians were suppressed, and their suppression was directly due to events which presently transpired in a more northerly section of the United States.

Wherefore these pages must for a while turn aside from Texas, leave it to rest for some years powerless for its cattle, and must devote attention to the Northern country and certain happenings there.

By 1848 the American farmers who were working westward through the Ohio Valley, Illinois, and Iowa had forced the northern sector of the westward frontier but little farther than the Mississippi River. Just beyond were trappers, hunters, traders, Indians, and also wild horses that had wandered up from Texas. These horses had remained largely masterless, as the demands of the equestrian Indians and of the few transborder white men had drawn comparatively little upon the supply.

In the fall of 1848 there came from the Pacific coast to the eastern United States word of the gold discovery at Sutter's Mill, and forthwith there plunged across the frontier a set of adventurous men. Some of them held their course toward California and its mines, either to reach their goal or to die upon the way. Others of them, allured by the agricultural richness of the soil, cut short their journey and settled on the route.

When the natural horsemen among these settlers first came face to face with the wild horse the Northern cowboy was in the making. When these natural horsemen discovered that commercially it was more profitable to capture and break the wild horse than to accumulate animals through the conventional breeding of more familiar stock, and that the market behind the horsemen would absorb their modest output, the initial Northern ranches began, and coincidentally the Northern cowboy was born.

These ranches were in their methods in no way different from those of southeastern Texas, for men trained in this latter section had drifted northward and given technical instruction.

But as regards comparative sizes of ownerships these Northern ranches, at the outset, had to content themselves with more modest holdings, inasmuch as the plains of their locality held fewer wild horses, and far fewer wild cattle than had obtained in Texas. This deficiency was soon in part corrected through domesticated cattle, which were procured from the pioneer farms to the eastward, and were turned loose upon the range.

Slowly the Northern ranchmen pushed westward; slowly because, on the one hand, they had to shove the hostile Indians ahead of them, and, on the other hand, they could not advance too far beyond the market at the rear. By 1860 no more progress had been made than that, in Nebraska, scattered ranches had crept out along the Overland Trail for one hundred and fifty miles west of the Missouri River, while in Kansas one hundred miles had been the limit of the movement.

Penned up in these establishments were the men who later, and because of the coming of the railroads, were enabled to fling across the continent, and, joining forces with the Texans, to fill the great plains with grazing cattle.

It was true that, still westward of the fettered establishments just mentioned, and far out upon the Overland Trail, were here and there a few brave settlers who, defying the Indians, conducted ranches whereon to grow supplies for sale to the occupants of the passing wagons. But these ranches were too scant in number and with too local a market to be considered as having been an integral part of the so-called ranching industry, the task of which was to supply the Eastern States and England. They really were refitting stations on the trail, rather than ranches in the sense that the "off the trail" West used the latter term. Nevertheless all honor to the pioneer settlers beyond Fort Kearney, to Pat Mullaly, Miller and Pennison, Dan Smith, Jack Morrow, and their Indian-harried live stock.

These men knew what was meant by the little sign occasionally displayed by the postmaster at Julesburg, Denver, Cheyenne, Virginia City, or wherever: "No Eastern mail to-day." They knew that somewhere on the plains were a smouldering yellow stage-coach, six dead mules, and some arrow-bedecked human bodies, and that presently upon the scene would be erected a candle-box lid inscribed with a date, a list of names, and the statement, "Killed by Indians."

However, these outlying pioneer settlers, because directly upon the trail, saw far more passers-by than did many of the later coming ranchmen who made their ultimate homes farther afield. There moved along the trail not only the Overland Stages, and for a time the Pony Express, but also a host of wagons. In the first half of the decade of the sixties, four thousand to ten thousand wagons were, save in mid-winter, always upon the trail.

These outlying pioneer settlers were ever within a short distance from a "station" of the Overland Stage, and at each such station news of doings in "the States" could be obtained from the occupants of the daily west-bound stagecoach during its halt, and at any time from either the station's employees or the voyagers in the "pilgrims' room," a shelter-room available to all passers-by on condition that they sweep it out after using it.

These stations, from ten to fifteen miles apart along almost the entire trail, furnished six fresh horses or mules to every stage-coach as it rattled in. The stages, "Concord coaches," carrying mails, baggage, express-chest, a "driver," a "conductor" or "guard," and as passengers nine "insides" and six "on tops" or "outsides," jolted from Atchison, Kansas, to Placerville, California, approximately nineteen hundred miles, in from seventeen to nineteen days.

The Pony Express in its short life raced from "St. Joe," Missouri, to Sacramento, California, upon a schedule of eight days, making the transit on one occasion in seven days, seventeen hours.

The Overland Trail, having formally started originally from Independence or Westport (fifty miles below Atchison), later from "St. Joe" (eighteen miles above Atchison), and finally and after 1861 from Atchison itself, ran northwesterly to Fort Kearney on the Platte River, meanwhile merging with the connecting, northerly trail from Omaha. From Fort Kearney the route followed the Platte's southerly bank to Julesburg, Colorado. There, sending off a side spur to Denver, it crossed the Platte, followed its north fork to Fort Laramie, and proceeded thence along the Sweetwater and through the Great South Pass. Then it forked, one branch leading to California by way of Fort Bridger, Great Salt Lake, and the Humboldt Basin, the other branch leading to Oregon by way of Fort Hall and the Snake and Columbia Rivers.

It was along this trail that the Northern ranchmen first pushed out into the Cattle Country; but by the year 1860 they, as already stated, had progressed but little.

By that same year Texas, still in shackles, had thrust a few driven herds through the Indians at the State's northern border, and so to market in the East; but it had been able to do no more than to dispose of mere nibblings at its live stock.

Now began the era of western railway construction, and, despite the damper of the Civil War, tracks commenced to push into Kansas and lengthwise of Nebraska. They reached Wyoming in 1867, and two years later had spanned the continent.

Through these railways the Indians presently ceased to be an omnipresent menace. The federal government desired peace and quiet for the colonists whom, it was anticipated, the railways would scatter over the plains, and so had its army sweep the Red Men into reservations. The major portion of the grazing country was soon made reasonably safe, though in various localities the Indians delayed decent behavior until the close of 1876. Even after that time they occasionally broke bounds and went upon the war-path, but these later forays were usually short-lived, and with limited field.

Through these railways the ranchmen were given not only immediate use of all the grazing lands of the West, but also instant contact with a consuming market of sufficient size. Experience had shown that to earn the maximum profit cattle could not march far in moving from pasture to the consumer. Although they could successfully be driven unconscionable distances to obtain succulent grasses, they, after achieving this food and having thus become portly, were economically poor subjects for a long trail. Their excess profits lay in their fat, and to turn this into unnecessary sweat was bad business. Hence the old slogan: "To the grass on the hoof. To the butcher in the train." This slogan, however, often was violated after market contact had been established, and while the railways were as yet unable to furnish sufficient tracks and trains.

So soon as the plains were opened there poured into their vast stretches men and animals from Nebraska and Kansas on the east, from Texas on the south. The inpouring of animals across the eastern border was short-lived, for the supply of surplus breeding beasts in that locality was limited. But Texas had no such handicap. Moreover, she from experience had discovered that the North was more generously watered than was the South, that the grasses of the continent's central and northern reaches were more fattening than was the forage of her own Texan prairies, and that her Texan climate, while omitting frigid weather dangerous to expectant mothers and their later offspring, and so tending toward a maximum number of births and a minimum number of infant deaths, militated against marked gain in weight by a maturing animal.

Furthermore, she from the teachings of the Northern ranchmen had learned that cattle could be sold by the pound, and that this method of selling was far more lucrative than had been the former Texan custom of selling by the head.

Wherefore she began, and for more than two decades continued, a northward procession which, though composed primarily of lowing cattle, attained majesty through its physical bigness and its social and political effect. From the time that this procession became well established, that is from and after 1866, a horde of cattle and their attendant horsemen annually marched up the route that, somewhat changing its course with successive years, was, in the southern latitudes, known at first as the Chisholm Trail, then as the Fort Griffin and Dodge City Trail, later as the Northern Trail, and, in the Northwest, was called the Texas Trail.

This procession, referred to in the Southwest as the Northern Drive, and in the Northwest as the Texas Drive, did not move in a single, compact mass, but was made up of numerous, independent, and widely intervalled herds, each composed of anywhere between a few hundred and ten thousand cattle. The parading cattle in 1866 numbered three hundred thousand; in each year thereafter, through 1871, progressively so increased that in the latter year over six hundred thousand made the trek. For some further years they held to very high numbers, but presently began to lessen. However, not until 1885 did they in any twelvemonth recede below the mark of three hundred thousand. Then the procession commenced to dwindle rapidly.

These marching animals, in part, trudged through weary, dust-clouded miles to the ranges of Nebraska, Kansas, Dakota, Colorado, Wyoming, Montana, Oregon, of even British Columbia, each lot of cattle there to tarry for months, or for a year or more, and eat to fatness. Each lot of cattle thus feeding might have been sold by its Texan owner to a Northern ranchman; or the Texan, still retaining ownership of the beasts, might graze them either upon lands which, as yet unpre-empted, were open to all comers, or else upon lands the right to use which he had hired from such Northerner as controlled them. When thus "fed up," these beasts, with well-covered ribs and as beeves of quality, moved on by rail to the abattoirs of Chicago, Omaha, and Kansas City, the junction points for the Eastern stomachs.

The paraders on the Texas Trail, in other part, once clear from Texas, headed for the nearest railway station, and there entrained, to fill forthwith at those same abattoirs a call for less excellent meat.

The nearest railway station was, in early days, the railhead, which, advancing with forward thrusts like those of a measuring worm, intermittently pushed itself farther and farther westward. The rail-head, until it had passed beyond the median line of the Texan Panhandle, was the magnet for all driven, railway-destined herds; and so, pending that transit, maintained unquestionable supremacy in notoriety. At each halting spot a town sprang up, had for a while in Eastern reputation virile competition with certain mining-camps for the palm of infamy, and then lapsed into the position of a mere way station upon the railway.

The Texas Trail was no narrow, trodden street. It rather was, for the major portion of its length, a wide zone along which the herders picked their way and guided their charges, according as conditions of grass and water demanded. This zone, however, at various places contracted almost to a mere road, for certain rivers and arid spaces had crossing spots that were particularly favorable. This trail at its southern end was composed of countless little paths, one leading from each ranch in Texas. These paths gradually drew together, welded finally into one broad route that, avoiding the forbidden area of Indian Territory, passed northward through the Texan Panhandle, or just outside its eastern border, and then frayed into innumerable divergent byways which kept on, here to the fattening ranges wherever situated, here to Omaha, there to Calgary, there to San Francisco, and, amongst themselves, to every spot upon the Northwest's map.

Up this trail passed the Texan stockmen with their inbred sectionalism based, in part on proud recollection of the Texan Republic, in part on inheritance from a restricted area of the Old South, namely Mississippi, Alabama, Tennessee, and their environs. At the trail's upper end these stockmen encountered and fraternized with the Northern ranchmen, who were gathering from the four corners of the continent, and from even beyond its shores. The fraternization caused each element so freely to give, and so fully to take, that there was crystallized a new form of public opinion, the so-called spirit of the West, and there came into existence two new beings, the Western rancher and the American cowboy. These latter persons not only definitely shaped public opinion throughout America's West, but also dominated for a quarter of a century in its government, and finally left upon it a social and political impress which, potent until the present day, may prove itself to be permanent.

Associated with these men, obedient to their leadership, taking color from them, and so also a factor in formulating the social and political system of the Range were such of the cowboy's fellow employees as, not being cowboys, were therefore of a station more humble than was his. These men of humbler station were the cook, the horse wrangler, the teamster, and the long-suffering individual who, as useful man or general worker, did countless odds and ends of tasks.

The men comprised in these new classes, the Western rancher and the American cowboy, and the men who, of humbler station, were associated with them may have retained their several preferences for Texas, Arizona, Montana, or wherever, may have retained their acquiescence to the ideas of their several home localities, but they had in common the spirit of the West, and they all understood the language of the West.

The Texas Trail was no mere cow-path. It was the course of empire.

So important a part did this trail play in the development of the Northwest, so relatively numerous were the Texans among this section's ranchmen, and so conspicuous were the Texans among this section's cowboys that some writers have been led not only to credit to Southern birth the major portion of the Northwest's white inhabitants, but also to assume the latter's immigration to have been effected on this trail, and thus to have proceeded in violation of the natural law which requires emigrants to travel for the most part upon parallels of latitude. In these averments these writers clearly have been in error. The Texas Trail was, as regards numbers of human travellers, far surpassed by the Overland Trail, and also by the Union Pacific and other transcontinental railways. Although Texans and other Southerners formed a very important element among the Northwest's ranchmen, there appears to be no reason to question the opinions orally expressed upon the point in the latter part of the decade of the eighties by several thinking Northwesterners who lived in widely separated localities, journeyed extensively, and had somewhat investigated the subject. These men unanimously agreed that the large majority of the Northwesterners were of northerly extraction, including northern Europe in this latter category.

While the hardy frontier ranchmen of the decade of the sixties and before deserve the homage due to pioneers, their aggregate businesses constituted an enterprise which had large commercial importance only in so far as it was path-finding and subsequently instructive as to methods. Accordingly, when speaking hereinafter of ranching and of ranchmen, reference will be made only to such as obtained or were operating in or after the early seventies, when the Western Range first might use wholesale financial terms.

Furthermore and in conformity with Range custom, the text will restrict the term "rancher" to members of the proprietary class, will, in "ranchmen," include employees as well as employers, and will endeavor to make as little avail as practicable of the word "rancher," for it was not of colloquial usage throughout the Range.

Although the term "ranchmen" thus included both employee and employer, it usually was differentiated to the extent that, while all men engaged in ranching were, as compared with the men of any other vocation, called "ranchmen," the latter as among themselves often limited the term to the class of ranch owners, designating the employees, according to their special functions, as cowboys, wranglers, etc.

"Rancheros," the Mexican border's synonym for ranchmen, was subject to like differentiation.

The word "ranch" itself had several and quite diverse meanings. Whether it appeared as "ranch" or in its earlier American form of "ranche," or in its Mexican border guise of "rancho," it denoted interchangeably either an entire ranching establishment inclusive of its buildings, lands, and live stock, or else the principal building, which usually was the owner's dwelling-house, or else that building together with the other structures adjacent to it, or else the collective persons who operated the establishment. The principal building, however, was more commonly specifically designated as the "ranch house," or, on the Mexican border, as the "rancheria."

Because man's necessity for food outweighed his need for travel, cattle-raising, from the beginning of American ranching, overshadowed in extent the raising of horses. Wherefore the majority of cowboys were associated primarily with the cattle industry and not with that of the horse. While it was true that some ranches raised in quantity both cattle and horses, almost all of the ranches specialized upon either one or the other of these animals. Notwithstanding this, all specialists in cattle maintained perforce horses in number generously sufficient for the transport of men and supplies.

So predominant were the cattle that the entire grazing area of the West customarily was called the Cattle Range or Cattle Country. A horse rancher would naïvely say: "I live in the Cattle Country. I've got a horse range there." He did not say this in any deprecating way, for, unlike the sheepman, he was never expected to apologize for his calling. On the contrary, he was a bit disposed to consider that his vocation gave him a standing a little better even than that which the cattleman enjoyed.

Horse ranches were relatively more frequent in Texas and Oregon than elsewhere, this because of the fact that the ranchmen of early days had found Texas, and to a less extent Oregon to be the sections most affected by the wild horse. Such of these men as devoted themselves to horse-raising settled where the wild horse could be found in quantity, and so gave to the locality a ranching trend which was apt to be followed by subsequently arriving ranchers, and this though their coming was delayed until after the wild horse had passed into captivity.

He had virtually disappeared by the close of the decade of the seventies, though, for years after that, small bands of unclaimed animals frisked about in the Texan Panhandle.

When the United States first acquired the West from France, Mexico and the Republic of Texas, all the grazing country except the relatively small acreage which was privately owned under titles of Mexican origin, belonged to the government, the lands in Texas, by the terms under which it entered the Union, belonging to the government of Texas, the lands outside the Texan borders belonging to the government of the United States.

Subsequently pieces were carved out in Texas for State allotments on account of local soldiers' bounties, in Texas and elsewhere for grants by State and federal governments to railways. The United States set apart still further portions of its domain for Indian reservations and military uses. But nevertheless all this subtracted relatively little from the vast extent of the public lands.

The great bulk of the grazing country as well within Texas as beyond its borders still awaited the prospective hordes of settlers who should absorb the almost countless acres by each settler's taking into his private ownership, as a grant from the government, the comparatively modest holding which, for Texan realty, was contemplated by Texan law, and, for property beyond the Texan borders, was prescribed by federal statutes. Until each particular tract thus passed into private ownership, it remained a part of the so-called "vacant" public lands, and was open, as was every other tract of such vacant public lands, to use by whoever cared to enjoy it. Thus all its grass and water were free to every comer.

Such were the so-called "free grass" and "free water" of Western history, a grass and water that in combination were flippantly termed "free air." The vacant, grazing-lands, because open to everybody, were dubbed the "open Range."

The phrase "open Range," as used colloquially, had various significances. It might mean the mere condition of being "open" to the public. It might mean a particular Western locality thus "open." It might mean, too, either the entire area of the Cattle Country, or else the collective people that inhabited it.

The phrase "the Range" also had differentiations in significance identical with these.

But for the existence of the open Range and the government's tacit consent to its use by ranchmen, Western ranching would not have been conducted on the bold, adventurous lines which history records, probably would not have expanded beyond the raising of small bands of animals by individual farmers; there would have been little opportunity for round-ups, and scant need for cowboys.

Had the various ranchers been called upon to pay fair value for the lands which their several herds of animals needed, few of them could have met the demand, and to the majority of these few would have remained little, if any, capital wherewith to purchase their initial animals. Furthermore, only in certain localities could very extensive single tracts surely be gotten in private ownership. They were obtainable with certainty only through purchasing from railways some of the alternate sections which had been governmentally ceded to the latter, and piecing them out by buying the intervening homesteads, or through purchasing Texan lands which that State previously had granted; although occasionally some one attempted an amassing by hiring numerous individuals to act as dummies, and either to make false homestead entries on many contiguous tracts or to buy from the State of Texas numerous coterminous parcels within that State's boundaries.

But, though the grazing-grounds legally were "open," they practically were closed to such ranches as did not have access to water. Accordingly each rancher preempted all the watercourses or springs he reasonably might hold, and stood ready to defend his claim to their rightful and exclusive ownership. These invaluable water outlets, these so-called "pieces of water," if not, as sometimes, purchased by the rancher from an earlier individual grantee, or from a railway, would be in the tract the government had granted the rancher under one or more of the laws above cited, and quite possibly also in adjacent tracts over which he had obtained control through the willingness of obliging cowboys to pose as intending settlers and subsequently to sell the landed birthright which the statutes had accorded them.

Thus few ranchers bothered themselves with the legal ownership of lands beyond such as either held the water or were the site of their ranch buildings, and many of the men did not go even so far as to acquire ownership of this latter site.

The rancher, when selecting a location for his establishment, gave almost as much consideration to the land's capacity for yielding winter shelter to his live stock as he did to the matter of the supply of water and grass. Ground interlaced by hills and hollows offered to the animals in winter not only patches of grass devoid of snow, but also screens from bitter winds. But, because as between shelter and water the latter was the more important, the rancher, if he could not find both of them conjoined, often was forced to content himself with lands well watered and well grassed, though with no defensive contours. Nothing could be in summer a substitute for water, though in winter the animals could somewhat quench their thirst by eating snow. Dangerous as were winter's storms in open country, they were not as perilous as were summer's droughts on arid ranges.

In conformity with the theory of the open Range, free grass and free water, no fencing was permissible by law except for the enclosure of lands held in legal ownership, though custom, despite the law, sanctioned additional fences, if in the immediate vicinity of ranch buildings or in the form of isolated corrals.

The proof of legal ownership was sometimes complete, but often it was a bit flimsy. It might be formal papers conclusively showing an honestly acquired and valid title. It might be a reference, if in Texas, to a local statute, or, if elsewhere, to one of the federal laws for encouraging settlement, the "Homestead," "Desert," or "Timber" Acts. It might be advice in Montana that the grass would be found to be better in Idaho or Arizona. It might be a terse request to "vamose the ranch," to "pull your freight," or to "git." It might be a gun. But the West was not disposed to cavil about the character of evidence. When it found a man in possession it might envy him, but it was apt to leave him undisturbed, and to "prospect around" for other and unoccupied property, optimistically assuming that the search would be short and successful.

In no whit did all these customs change after heavily capitalized corporations had absorbed many of the theretofore individually owned ranches. There were, as exceptions, lessees of Indians' lands in present Oklahoma, or occasional ranchmen who were scattered elsewhere and who actually owned the grazing-lands of which their herds made use. Some of these excepted men fenced their ground, but these excepted ranchers, save such of them as were lessees from Indians, usually had small holdings.

A rancher's animals grazed in the neighborhood of the water he controlled. The lands which these animals thus habitually used were called their owner's range in contradistinction from *the* Range, that is from the entire grazing country. If water in this rancher's locality were unstinted, the herds of several ranchers might intermingle on the feeding-grounds, incidentally each owner referring to the entire tract as his own range. The number of beasts supportable by even such a generously watered section was not unlimited, for the quantity and quality of grass were also determining factors. Accordingly Western custom prescribed that the ranchers, in the chronological order of their pre-empting the lands involved, should have right of pastoral satisfaction, and that no late-arriving rancher might graze his animals upon these lands unless all the animals of the earlier-coming ranchers were assured of ample fodder. Whatever late-arriving ranchmen, in contravention of this tenet, intruded upon an already filled range were met by a boycott whenever they sought assistance in the handling of their live stock.

This boycott was the one and only permissible violation of the Old West's otherwise jealously enforced precept: "Help thy neighbor as thyself."

By reason of the dependence upon water, ranchers who owned a large number of animals were, in some localities, unable to keep all of their beasts within a single tract, and so were forced to distribute these beasts among several independent and often widely separated ranges.

If, as in a semiarid country, one person were seized of all the scanty, local supply of drink, he might, from this mere ownership, enjoy the exclusive usage of mile after mile of herbage. Such a monopolist could keep this kingdom to himself, or else, by rental or gift, could allow to others access to the water, and thus ability to use the adjacent grass.

Many a rancher who, through control of water, was able to exclude other stock-raisers from the rancher's range could not bar out the farmer when years afterward the latter ultimately arrived. The farmer, when he came, found many spots where, by reason of the considerable size of the streams or lakes, the already established local ranchers had been unable to pre-empt the entire water body; and there, with a frontage which at the water's edge was wide enough for the intake of the farmer's irrigation ditches, though not for the watering of many animals, the farmer homesteaded. A second farmer would homestead at the first one's rear, and, by a ditch permitted across the first one's land, would lead water to the second farmer's place. Dry-farming could be practised with but little surface water, so that farms, once finding an agreeable resting spot, were apt to multiply. Ranches could not exist amid the farms.

The earliest ranchers and cowboys of the Cattle Country came directly from the initial Texan and the other frontier ranches, and from the frontier farms. Of the later recruits some were the sons of these pioneers, while the rest came from the farms, villages, and cities anywhere and everywhere in the United States and even in Great Britain. Aristocrats and plebeians, men from each and every business, profession, and trade, and the sons of such men appeared upon the Range.

The vast majority of the arrivals were represented by persons who moved West of their own volition, and primarily because of the lure of the Cattle Country. The small and presumably exceedingly small minority was represented by criminals whose proximate object had been to escape jail doors in the East, and who had turned to the Range as a mere hiding-place.

Many a young man, on his own initiative and for love of adventure, on medical advice and for hope of recovery, or on parental compulsion and for chance of reform, exchanged a metropolis for the bunch-grass and mesquite. The universities of the Atlantic coast and of Great Britain had, amid the sage-brush, a representation which was strong numerically, if a bit weak academically. It was this latter weakness that kept it from making any scholastic impression.

While the men of the Range were mainly of English or Irish descent or birth, and had, in frequent instances, claim to early American ancestors of Scottish origin, the Southwest added to its quota of such bloods numerous men of Mexican extraction, and a more than occasional negro, with here and there men of strain partly Indian. The great majority of all the men were American born. The largest single immediate source of the puncher was doubtless the section covered by Texas and western Missouri, for almost every ranch employed at some time a "Texas Ike" or a "Tex," and was familiar with the Missouri drawl.

The sticky clay of the South had prevented the building of good roads, and thus kept successive generations of Southern men out of wheeled vehicles and in the saddle, and so had developed the Southerner into an innate rider. Incidentally, a first-class rider like a particularly accurate shooter, was "born, not made."

The references hereinbefore contained to young men for whom was sought moral improvement did not mean to assert, or even imply, that such men, to any considerable extent, had been criminal in either achievement or intent. The most of them, in fact, had transgressed or promised to transgress merely ethical decency, and not formal law. The heinousness of almost all of these young scapegraces lay not so much in what they had done as in what conservative advisers of family warned that they might do. Liquor and undesirable affairs of the heart accounted for the presence of many, and here and there was one who in England had been socially sentenced to a disappearance until his people should succeed in paying his debts, and so wipe out a stain on a title.

Thus England's delegation was comprised not so much of the sons of business men and of the middle class as it was of the delightfully companionable, mildly reprobate, and socially outcast members of the gentry and nobility, these latter persons being, in part, self-supporting, in part, as "remittance men," dependent on moneys forwarded from overseas. These aristocrats withheld all mention of the titles which their elder brothers bore, passed under whatever names they themselves arbitrarily assumed, but could not permanently expunge from their manners the earmarks of gentle blood.

Sometimes a slip of the tongue disclosed identity. News of the result of an English university boat-race produced in Montana the spontaneous cry: "Thank God, we won!" An Easterner, present and unfamiliar with the Western code, asked a liquor-wrecked wrangler why he should have cared so much. The latter blurted out, before his excitement had died away: "Why, man, once I stroked that crew!" and then the mask fell to its old position.

The West contained more than one signet-ring, cut with ancestral arms and studiously hidden under a flannel shirt. Such a bauble at no time was revealed unless its owner joyfully had received from home advice that his sins had been forgiven, that the social coast was clear, and that he might return; or unless its possessor, about to "cross the Divide," with body amid the grama-grass, and with thoughts apportioned between the hereafter and some great country house in England, shamefacedly, hesitatingly, desperately was confiding to an uncouth attendant an heraldic seal, a packet of woman's letters, and an oral message. The contents of these death-bed commissions never were disclosed to any but the designated consignee, and faithfully and promptly were transmitted to their proper destination; the ring and letter packet in sealed wrapper, along with a laboriously indited screed in which the scrivener, after reciting that he had taken his pen in hand, accurately recounted every word committed to his charge by the excommunicate, and added, in preface and conclusion, the entire story of the outcast's Western life so far as it was known.

It was to the glory of the cowboy that he unfailingly fulfilled such trusts. It was to the joy of more than one English family that a scrawling missive from a distant puncher revealed a secret which had long been buried in a single and tormented breast, and, by the revelation, conclusively established that what mistakenly had been accepted as confession of turpitude had been, in fact, merely unfortunate application of haughty pride.

But England's representation was not all from her gentry and nobility. Her middle class, too, sent delegates. These latter were, in part, as fine a lot of men as ever lived, and, in other part subscribed for the *London Graphic*, in order to know the current doings of the then Prince of Wales, and so be enabled to relate anecdotes that intimated frequent association with him. In certain sections of Texas, during the final seventies and the early eighties, to people unfamiliar both with London and with America's West, it might well have seemed that all the most intimate male friends of the late King Edward VII had received his reluctant consent to their absence from court, and, for a monthly wage of twenty-five dollars, were herding sheep in Texas. The more insistent men of this latter type were sometimes referred to upon the Cattle Range as "belted earls."

The English delegation, as a whole, comprised in number a small percentage of the ranchmen, but it was conspicuous because of its social individuality and the largeness of its financial interest.

Whether a man began his Range life as a rancher or as a cowboy was predetermined by the extent of his finances. Men of college training tended, for this reason and also because of their usually indifferent riding, to fall entirely into the rancher class. Whether a man starting as a cowboy graduated into the rancher class depended on the same factors as ever have obtained in deciding whether one in any calling were to remain an employee or become an employer, the factors of brains, character, and luck.

The average cowboy on entering the industry did so with expectation that he would follow it during his entire working life, while for many of the ranch-owners, especially for such as were from collegiate sources, there was intended but a temporary connection during which there might be effected the desired improvement in character, in health, or in business initiative.

The financial capital invested in ranching represented, in part, the increment derived through years of frugality by men who had preferred a markedly increasing herd to the luxuries for which a portion of the animals might have been exchanged; in part, money ventured by men experienced in active business affairs of other sort and who had hope of considerable profit; and, in part, cash which steadily moved out to the chaparral, rabbit-brush, and greasewood from sources in the Eastern States, and particularly in England. This cash either betokened paternal endowments of the attempts at improvement, or else indicated conversions of gilt-edged securities by persons who, as yet in their twenty-second year, had but recently received from erstwhile guardians various first-mortgage bonds supposedly secure against loss.

Once ranching became a real industry its followers, in annually increasing numbers, spread westward, until, at the zenith of the business, their animals dotted the plains and foothills from central Nebraska to the mountains of the Pacific slope, from Montana to the Mexican border, and so occupied approximately one-third of the area of the United States.

CHAPTER II

RANCHMEN AND FARMERS

PROTECTIVE MEASURES—NEW MEXICAN AND CALIFORNIAN RANCHES—VARIOUS DEFINITIONS—BRONCO'S VARIOUS NAMES—IMPROVING QUALITY OF LIVE STOCK—DECADENCE OF HORSE-RAISING—PRICES OF LIVE STOCK—FARMERS' ADVENT ENDS RANCHING—RANCHMAN'S AND FARMER'S VALUE TO STATE COMPARED—DISPERSAL OF RANCHMEN ON ENDING OF OPEN RANGE—VARIOUS DEFINITIONS—RANCHWOMEN—"COWGIRLS"—ANTIPATHY TO SHEEP—ITS CAUSES AND ITS CESSATION.

THE ranching industry, once it had become established, was everywhere guarded, not only by State laws but also by stockmen's voluntary associations (these associations later largely supplanted, in their functions, by official stock commissioners) which in various States maintained inspectors, and as the horse thief's enemy armed and mounted Range detectives.

When Texas embarked in ranching, present New Mexico also had ranches which were of Mexican origin and as old as those of Texas. But at the outset of ranching as a national industry in the United States, New Mexico was too isolated for its establishments to be a participating factor. As ranching spread westward from its Texan-Nebraskan-Kansan birthplace, New Mexico eventually was reached, and its establishments were absorbed into the nationalized system.

California, too, had its ranches, many of them of Mexican genesis and coeval with those of Texas, some of them with vast acreage; but, while California's method of raising cattle and horses was the same as that of the country east of the Sierras, its civilization was different. The "Pacific sloper" and the plainsman were not actuated by identical tradition. Mines, farms, Oriental commerce, and San Francisco's metropolitan life had in California prestige such as prevented the local ranchmen from shaping that State's public opinion as their more easterly brothers did the local sentiment in their own bailiwicks. It is with these more easterly brothers that this book deals.

These more easterly brothers, whose westward limit was "timberline" upon the eastern side of the Sierras and the Cascades, were the "Westerners." The people who lived still farther west were not "Westerners" but "slopers," though such of them as had the right to do so might, if they wished, call themselves, instead, "Californians."

By selective breeding of live stock and the admixture of imported blood, the ranchmen gradually absorbed the former wild horse into a markedly more tractable and somewhat physically larger type, eight hundred pounds against the earlier six hundred.

21

The new product, nevertheless, did not wholly rid itself of its "wild" progenitor's Spanish name, although it went so far as to modify the spelling. However much the South might speak of "cow-horses," however much the North might mention "ponies," however frequently both South and North might betake themselves to slang and talk of "fuzzies" (Range horses) and "broomies" or "broom tails" (Range mares), there continuously cropped out, in either section, the original appellation. This was "bronco" (from Spanish "broncho," meaning rough, rude), though it often was contracted into "bronc" or "bronk," and also was interchangeable, particularly in the Southwest, with "mustang," and, especially in Oregon, with "cayuse" or, as sometimes spelled, "kiuse." Such interchange was the more apt to occur when a local purist in language was relieving his mind on the subject of his animal's moral infirmities. Texas, when speaking technically, restricted "mustang" to the unmixed wild horse, and limited "bronco" to such of these as were particularly "mean" in nature.

Like breeding and importation improved the cattle, which, though they doubled in weight and shortened their horns, but little bettered in temper.

It is said that upon the Range the interchangeable terms, "tenderfoots" and "pilgrims," were applied first to these imported cattle, and not until later were attached to human newcomers.

This breeding animals into better blood, this raising of so-called "graded" stock was, commercially, a great advance over the prior ranching methods, which had infused no new blood into the horses and the cattle obtained from Mexico. These Mexican horses may have been able to trace their ancestry back, through Spain, to the Arabian steeds that the Moors carried thither in the eighth century. These Mexican cattle may have been able to prove themselves kin of the thoroughbred bulls of the Spanish ring. But blood, save in isolated animals, apparently had degenerated.

A limited number of ranches, principally of English ownership, essayed the raising exclusively of thoroughbred cattle; but these ranches were so relatively few as not to be a commercially important factor, except to the extent that their blooded animals interbred with the commoner beasts of the Range, and so tended to "grade up" the commercial beef herd.

Practically no ranches had horses of thoroughbred racing strain.

In the twelve years commencing with 1875, the stockmen were at the height of their prestige. Then came the collapse of the horse market owing to the rapid substitution, throughout the country, of electricity for the horse as the motive power of street-cars. For years the traction companies had been the largest and most tolerant customers. They not only had bought in great quantity, but also had accepted animals which no one else would purchase.

Cable tramways already had somewhat threatened values; but the blow fell in 1887, when, at Richmond, Virginia, the initial American electric trolley-car began to move, although it was not until some four or five years later that this type of car came into general use. Everywhere upon the Range the price of an unbroken "top" or first-class horse sagged from twenty-five dollars to fifteen dollars and below, and the long-established valuation of fifteen dollars per head for untrained animals in lots of size was smashed to pieces. In eastern Oregon, for a short while, "just a horse" would bring at forced sale but a dollar and a quarter. In Dakota one rancher, the Marquis De Mores, attempted to slaughter and can horses as a food for European consumption.

This subject of prices suggests the fact that, throughout the life of the industry, "gentling," i. e., breaking, a horse added ordinarily ten dollars to the value it had had as an unbroken animal, and that, during the same period, "thirty-dollar steers" had the normal high mark in the cattlemen's good years.

Though the market for horses fell away, the demand for cattle continued unabated. Yet the open Range was nearing its end.

By the year 1887 all ranchmen had begun to feel the pinch of the wire fences which the immigrant settlers, under governmental protection, were putting about their newly homesteaded farms; farms homesteaded on what, until these fences, had been part of the open Range. The stockmen, with their threats, their wire cutters, and occasionally their guns, at times ejected the would-be farmer. But he had the government behind him; and patiently, slowly, surely his fences crept snakelike around the waterholes, isolated many sections of the grazing-lands, and killed the open Range by thirst.

These farmers hastened the result almost everywhere by bleeding through their irrigation ditches streams theretofore devoted wholly to the live stock, and also in certain States by a grim process of the law. They procured various legislatures to enact statutes requiring stockmen either to fence in their live stock or else to stand liable for their animals' destruction of the farmers' unenclosed grain-fields. Immigration had brought the farmer into political ascendancy, and he thus through law ordered the rancher to commit suicide.

The stockmen made their final show of forceful opposition in 1892, during the so-called "Rustler War" in Wyoming. United

States cavalry intervened; and the American cowboys there aligned in fighting array, representing all their brethren as well as themselves, surrendered ostensibly to the cavalry, practically to the farmer, and, as a dominant social and political factor, dismounted forever.

There still remain in 1922 large fenced ranches and large areas of ungirt grazing-land, the latter open to the public; there still ride in 1922 men who sit the buck as well as ever it was sat, but already in 1892 the stirring West-wide open Range, sick for many years theretofore with wire fence, had died as a national factor, as virtually a state.

The ranchmen of the open Range, although squatters on the land, and in the main intending but transient stay either of definite years or until enmeshed by prospective farmers' fences, were of economic value to the public. They converted otherwise unused grasses into living flesh during the time in which the West was awaiting the arrival of immigrant farmers who should people its plains, become permanent citizens, and put the lands to more profitable use. The State could well afford, until the ultimate settler arrived upon the soil, to suffer its use by the rancher. Though he added nothing to it, he took nothing from it beyond that the wild verdure was eaten, instead of annually dying and merging in the humus. Meanwhile his live stock brought some money into the State.

But when the permanent settler arrived the latter's substitution offered more. The rancher had raised no crops of any sort. Beef and horse-flesh had been his sole business and his bucolic horizon. His live stock, wholly dependent on wild forage, had required for the sustenance of each animal never less than an acre and a quarter, in the average locality approximately eleven acres, and in some regions as many as twenty-five acres. Consequently a single herd had occupied space available for several farms. The permanent settler planted fields, and by irrigation increased both the arable area and the grazing capacity. Within his fences were a few cattle which received attention such as would have been impossible upon the wide stretches of the open Range, and thereby the farmer's cattle far surpassed in quality their freer forebears. Before long the aggregate farmers raised annually more cattle than had all the ranchmen in any year. The farmer brought increased wealth to the State.

Then, too, through him the State gained in virility of citizenship. The various ranchers and their employees, owning virtually no soil and living on lands which in almost their entirety were property of government, had, save in the case of the Texans, but lukewarm allegiance to the particular political subdivisions in which their several ranches lay. The ranchmen, for the most part, while intensely loyal to the United States and to the West as such, were citizens of the Range rather than of any definite political subdivision. The various farmers, on the other hand, owned land, and from this mere fact of ownership became ardent partisans of the several States in which their lands were situated.

It was well that the ranchman of the open Range came. It also was well that he went.

While the Range was being slowly murdered and commencing some years before 1892, the ranchmen gradually remodelled their affairs; many of these men keeping an eye open for some new land of adventure, because ranching had assembled many true soldiers of fortune.

Such of the owners as were not wedded to the industry quit, one by one, and were absorbed into the manifold activities the world pursues; the wars in Cuba and South Africa offering in numerous instances a later respite from prosaic office work.

Of such of the ranchers as preferred to continue in the business, a few transferred their operations to Mexico, to Canada, or to Central or South America; while the rest, for the most part, relinquishing long-standing pretensions of sovereignty over public areas of tremendous extent, adjusting their minds to terms of hundreds or thousands in place of the corresponding former thousands, tens of thousands, and hundreds of thousands, either contented themselves with such frag-ments of open range as still continued; or else they converted a por-tion of their herds into lands actually owned and additional to the modest tract obtained by "filing" under the Homestead Law, wofully stretched a wire fence around their realty, and joined the class which they for years patronizingly had disdained, that of the stock-raising farmer. Occasional men with foresight, unusual ability, and large capi-tal had come, through years of piecemeal buying, into actual owner-ship of at least a large part of the lands they had used. These latter men continued to do as they had done; but, once the clear dominance of stock-raising had passed and other industries had appeared in quan-tity, the short-memoried public forgot its obeisance to these persons as cattle kings, and with some envy and great local pride pointed to them merely as millionaires.

The cowboys followed relatively the same course as did the owners.

Some of the punchers migrated to the ranges of foreign countries—Mexico, Canada, or wherever. Others stuck to the ranges of the United States, and, with minds filled with memories of big, bygone things, rode either amid the comparatively little free grass that still remained, or else behind the wire fences newly installed about their employers' ranches; and, in the latter case, as punchers, thus immured, became what they formerly had sneered at, "pliers men," so called from their tool for repairing the wire strands in fences. Or else, emerging in modest way as ranchers, they placed upon a homestead of one hundred and sixty acres a cabin and a few animals, which represented either possibly, but improbably, fruit of individual savings, or almost surely, and instead, a "stake" by appreciative former employers. Still others abandoned the cow-horse and landed in the army, in Alaska's mines, in San Francisco's shipyards, in Montana's banks, in Denver's shops, in the lumber mills of Puget Sound, in Chicago's factories, in New England's mills, or anywhere a suitable job was open.

A stake such as is mentioned above was an unqualified gift, while a "grub-stake," according to the usual significance of the term, required its recipient to pay to its donor an agreed share of whatever profit might accrue from the enterprise on which the recipient was about to embark, and for the furtherance of which the grub-stake was given.

However, each of these words might, on occasion, be used in a different sense, "stake" to denote either one's entire assets, or else the entire amount hazarded in any venture; "grub-stake" to denote one's food-supply, regardless of how obtained.

Upon the new and tiny ranch "staked to" our former cowboy, very likely a wife soon appeared.

In this book but incidental mention will be made of women. The reason for this scant consideration is that women were so relatively few in number in the Cattle Country as collectively not to have been an important factor in either its social life or the formation of its opinions. The Range described itself as a "he country in pants."

The great majority of the ranchers and practically all of the cowboys were unmarried. Marriage meant almost always for the man of gentle birth a return to the East, or to England, and usually for the man of more ordinary blood retreat from the open country and settling either in some town or upon a fenced farm near it.

There were, of course, from time to time at various ranches feminine guests, usually sisters, nieces, fiancées, but the number of ranches thus happily receiving was relatively very small.

There were, it is true, permanently living on numbers of ranches women, some of them of superior brain and far more than average moral force, but the direct influence of all ranchwomen was exerted only upon their immediate households. No outsider was given the privilege of intimate association; for, at the moment of his appearance, such women suppressed their bigger selves, retreated to the cookstove, and promptly set to flowing a stream of toothsome dishes, in order that the honor of the ranch might be upheld in rivalry with all other ranches, particularly those in which other females lived, and in order also that inmates of womanless establishments might appreciate the extent of their deprivations. There were a few ranches owned and capably operated by women, widows of former ranchmen. Even these women obeyed the custom which Range femininity imposed on all its members, and fled to the kitchen the instant a visitor had received his welcome. The women of the Range all sacrificed themselves to competitive housewifery.

The horse being the principal and often the only means of transit, many of these women and many of their daughters rode extremely well. Some of them equalled almost the best of men in horsemanship, though lacking the vitality long to sit a violent buck. The side-saddles and woollen riding-skirts used by most of the women, the modest divided skirts used by the few who rode astride, imparted to those quiet, unassuming, courageous females of the real frontier none of the garishness which that modern invention, the buckskin-clad "cowgirl," takes with her into the circus ring.

These "cowgirls" may be of Western blood and spirit, but their buckskin clothing speaks of the present-day theatre and not of the ranches of years ago.

In the heydey of the open Range the sheepmen were the pariahs of the plains. They and their animals were anathema to the ranchers of horses or cattle. The fact that legally the Range was as open to sheep as it was to horses and cattle availed nothing. Many a band of sheep, in wild stampede, leaped to death from the brink of a canyon, or in bleating fear huddled in a woods to await the arrival of encircling flames. Cowboys behind the stampede or at the edges of the forest were the sponsors, and they sent many a sheepman to a sudden and unrecorded grave.

There was real reason for this feud. The horse men and cattlemen were the pioneers upon the Range. They had settled themselves in places to their liking, had installed their herds about them, and were well content to regard themselves and to be regarded as local kings. Presently arrived the sheepmen, whose flocks with their busy mouths nibbled the grass to its roots; with their sharp hoofs chopped those roots so thoroughly that they died; with their constant travel necessary for the avoidance of disease within large flocks, their so-called "walk," carried their destruction mile after mile, and cut a wide, desolate road across the plain; and with their pungency either left upon the ground a scent which for many hours was apt to reach the nostrils of passing cattle and horses, or imparted to a water-hole a lingering taste and smell.

Whether it was in recognition of this war upon their food-supply, whether it was mere dislike for the searching odor and flavor, or whatever else was the cause, the cattle and the horses hated the sheep with an intense and constant hatred. It was not unusual for a bunch of cattle lazily streaming across a range to stop suddenly, to sniff, snort, and gallop madly away. Its leader had come upon the trail of a band of sheep. Horses were as wont to leave a spot so accursed, though their departure generally was less precipitate.

Some wandering shepherd would permit his flock to wade through a currentless pool, and for days thereafter the water would smell and taste of wool. It was only extreme thirst that led horses or cattle to imbibe water thus contaminated; and, so soon as they felt the drink's refreshing effect, they were very receptive of suggestions to stampede. Very possibly the nervousness which caused the stampede was left over from the former thirst, but ranchmen unhesitatingly blamed the wool.

The vendetta of the animals extended to their owners. In various localities, the ranchers of horses or cattle not only arrogantly announced that their regions were closed to sheep; but also, when so doing, were far from niggardly regarding the boundaries of the forbidden territory. Such pronouncements had to the feudal senses of these men the force of law, and stern punishment was meted to such as transgressed the arbitrary edicts. The sheep raisers eventually tended to immure themselves and their ill-smelling flocks within various segregated sections, which promptly attained in the eyes of the raisers of horses and cattle the social status of leper colonies. Then came the wire fences, the resultant ending of the open Range, and with that ending the cessation of dissension.

By the irony of fate recent years have proved that in various parts of the former Cattle Range sheep, not cattle, are the profitable tenants. Thus in the very country where wool once was hated save by a few harried citizens, it now is generally applauded.

CHAPTER III

DEFINITIONS AND COWBOY WAYS

VARIOUS TITLES FOR COWBOY—VARIOUS DEFINITIONS—NO TYPICAL COWBOY—USE OF PISTOL—DANGEROUS ANIMALS—BEAR-DOGS—LOCO-WEED—SHOOTING AT TENDERFOOTS' FEET—ITS INCENTIVE—CARRIAGE AND SHOOTING OF PISTOL—EXTENT OF LATTER'S USE—PISTOL NOT ALWAYS NECESSITY—BAD MAN, PSEUDO AND ACTUAL—PISTOL AS NOISE-MAKER—RIFLE, ITS TRANSPORT AND NAMES—CREASING AND WALKING DOWN MUSTANGS—VARIOUS DEFINITIONS—INTIMACY WITH HORSES—THEIR NAMES, COLORATION AND SECTIONAL DIFFERENCES—KILLING HORSES—SIGNALLING—KNIFE—LARIAT.

THE cowboy was not always called "cowboy." He everywhere was equally well known as "cowpuncher" or "puncher," "punching" being the accepted term for the herding of live stock. In Oregon he frequently was called "baquero," "buckaroo," "buckhara," or "buckayro," each a perversion of either the Spanish "vaquero," or the Spanish "boyéro," and each subject to be contracted into "bucker." In Wyoming he preferred to be styled a "rider." To these various legitimate titles, conscious slang added "bronco peeler," "bronco twister," and "bronco buster."

He was a cowboy or cowpuncher whether his charges were cattle or horses. There were no such terms as horse-boy or horse puncher.

Thus called a cowboy when his task was riding as an employee, he lost that title as soon as he became a ranch-owner; and, according to the kind of stock he raised, was termed a "horse man" or else interchangeably a "cowman," "cattleman," or "cattle man." While a cattle man and a cattleman were identical, a horse man and a horseman were not. Of the latter the first raised horses, the second was either a mounted person or one versed in horsemanship.

Curiously, though the word "puncher" was created but a comparatively few decades since, its derivation is now unknown unless it relate to the metal-pointed goad occasionally used for stimulating cattle when they were being urged to board railway cars.

While punching was thus the accepted term for the herding of live stock, it ordinarily was restricted to cattle, the term "herding" being used in connection with horses. A cowpuncher might "punch" or "herd" cattle, but colloquial English usually made him "herd" horses and would not let him "punch" them.

Sheep were merely "herded," and that by "sheep-herders," never by "cowboys."

Every cowboy of the novel or the adventure story fits squarely into one of the three species created by fictionists. He is portrayed in these several species as being necessarily clownish, reckless, excessively joyful, noisy, and profane; or else wolfish, scheming, sullen, malevolent, prone to ambush and murder; or else dignified, thoughtful, taciturn, idealistic, with conscience and trigger-finger accurate, quick, and in unison, and also in all these species as being assuredly freighted with weapons, terse in utterance, and picturesque in apparel.

In reality, there were no species, there was no type. Cowboys, as Bart Smith, one of them, said, were "Merely folks, just plain, every-day, bow-legged humans." Cowboys, like the rest of the ranchmen, were simply the men of a particular trade; were, as among themselves, as diversified in disposition as were and always will be other men; and, as a class, had from the followers of any other calling differentiation in but a limited number of subordinate though highly specialized attributes.

Fictionists to the contrary, the ranks of the cowboys, of all ranch-men, contained but few swashbucklers, particularly such as wore long hair. Those ranks were composed largely of men with character and heart, of men whom future generations well may regard with pride.

The writer of tales has made the "gun," "six-gun," "six-shooter," or "shooting-iron," as the West variously termed the pistol, more ubiq-uitous even than long hair, has imposed at least two of these weapons upon every storied cowboy, and at times has converted him into a veritable itinerant arsenal.

When one recalls that the gun actually carried, when one was car-ried, was the forty-five or forty-four caliber, eight-inch barrelled, single-action Colt's revolver, weighing two and a quarter pounds, and that its ammunition weighed something in addition; when one recalls also that the average cowpuncher was not an incipient mur-derer, but was only an average man and correspondingly lazy, then one realizes to be true the statements that the average puncher was unwill-ing to encumber himself with more than one gun, and often even failed to "go heeled" (armed) to the extent of "packing" (carrying) that unless conditions insistently demanded. These insistent conditions were, first, expectation of attack by a personal enemy; second, service near the Mexican border or in an Indian-infested country; third, a ride on the Range where there might be met human trespassers, or be encountered either animals dangerous to stock or stock hopelessly injured or diseased, temperamentally prone to assail man and beast, or so debased that, for breeding reasons, its elimination was urgent; fourth and finally, either a holiday visit to another ranch or to town, or else a formal call on a girl.

The gun not only was an integral part of full dress, but also was to the mind of the cowboy as effective on the female heart, and as compelling an accompaniment of love-making as to the belief of the young soldier has ever been the sword.

The fewness of women in the Cattle Country did not lessen man's wish to go a-courting. Any female could get a husband. An attractive one could choose from an army.

The animals likely to molest stock and so marked for slaughter included coyotes, bears, timber-wolves, mountain-lions, and stray dogs. Every strange and unattended canine found wandering on the Range was prejudged to have had murderous intent, and was sentenced and executed at sight. This, however, does not imply that the puncher might not have had his own pet dog wagging its tail at the ranch-house.

If this latter dog were small, curly, yellow, thoroughly mongrel in looks, but treated with profound consideration, it would sell, on the instant, for one hundred and twenty-five dollars, this being in amount over three months' pay for a first-class rider. All this would mean that the little brute was a "bear-dog," a cur trained to hold the grizzly bear by staying without the danger zone, yapping at Bruin's heels, and driving him to such irritation that, instead of fleeing, he lost his judgment, backed up against a tree and made a target for the rifle. Such a dog would have a countywide reputation, while a mere blue-ribboned thoroughbred would be frowned upon as a latent killer of calves.

The dangerous animals comprised, too, occasional horses, more numerous steers, and still more numerous cows, all seemingly deranged in brain, and all apt, without warning, savagely to attack their fellows, the ranchmen, or the latters' mounts.

These bellicose horses made their assaults by rearing, and with their front hoofs striking hammerlike blows. These warring cattle attacked another animal or a mounted man by "prodding" with their sharp horns, and assailed a pedestrian in either this same way or by trampling on him.

Part of these "locoed" brutes were victims of feeding upon toxic plants, the so-called "loco weeds" (from Spanish "loco," meaning mad), but others of the beasts had not so clear excuse for their insanity. Horses more often than cattle became addicts to the poisonous plants, and frequently spurned legitimate grasses when the illegitimate weeds could be obtained in quantity.

These weeds recently have been classified by scientists into three distinct species, of which one with purple flowers and hairy leaves and stems was in popular parlance indiscriminately called "purple loco" or "woolly loco." The other two species each had seed-pods that, when dried, rattled on being moved, and so gave to each of these species the colloquial and undistinctive title of "rattleweed." There were other popular titles; for, of these rattleweeds, one having blue flowers often was called "blue loco," while the other, having flowers of white, pink, or bluish-purple color as each individual plant preferred, and being devoid of a main stem, was termed either "stemless loco," or, according to the blossom's color, "blue loco," "purple loco," "white loco," or "pink loco."

The ranchmen, thus undiscriminating in the selection of names, made their botany still more confusing by employing the grammatic singular number instead of the plural, and thus referring to the collective plants not as weeds but as weed.

When whatever title employed included either the word stemless or the name of a color, the term weed usually was omitted from the title. Accordingly one would speak of a particular plant as "purple loco" or as "loco-weed," but not as "purple loco-weed."

These weeds, whatever their variety, usually contented themselves with imposing upon their habitual devourer a death from starvation, having first cruelly thinned their victim, injured its eyesight, its muscular control, its nervous system, and its brain; and sardonically having decorated it, if a horse, with an abnormal growth of the hairs in mane and tail, or, if of the cattle family, with an equally unnatural increase in the hairs upon the poor beast's flanks.

At times the vile weeds modified their process and sent an animal upon a run amuck.

These death-dealing plants injected two words into the dictionary, the words "locoed" and "rattled," the first as a synonym for crazy, the second as a synonym for crazy or excitedly confused.

The employment of the pistol either as a means of admonishing strangers' feet or inviting them to dance, or else as an instrument for snuffing barroom lamps occurred so extremely rarely as to have amounted to little more than the foundation for amusing legend, but it has become in the novel one of the cowboy's diurnal functions.

Persistent tradition is that, save on the Mexican border and in most infrequent instances at drunken frolics elsewhere, every stranger with whose feet this liberty was taken was either a tenderfoot so self-assertive as to merit some form of chastening or else a tenderfoot who, wholly innocent of this offensive quality, had stepped into the place just vacated by a self-assertive tenderfoot and so been, by an impatient audience, adopted as a proxy for the latter or his type. Assuredly many an Easterner touring in the West has at times allowed his suddenly startled interest to upset his manners, and has rubbed fur in the wrong direction. Many such a tourist, diverted by the cowboy's costume, has forgotten that within it was a human being. By many a tourist such punchers as he came across were in boorishness as blankly stared at and as openly discussed as though they had been monkeys in a cage.

As an example of this gaucherie is offered the following account of an occurrence, which, though containing unusually exasperating factors, makes clear illustration of the point.

One day, in 1889, there squatted in a circle upon the station platform at Pocatello five cowboys, who, bound eastward with a bunch of live stock, had paused for a bite of luncheon. Each of them displayed a puncher's full equipment, including "chaps" and gun. One of them, their foreman, Ed Peters, was an amazingly fine rider. The other men were almost of front rank. At the moment, the five punchers were doing nothing more "wild and woolly" than to eat canned peaches out of five cans, to include among the feasters a local, very wistful-looking little girl, and to affect great interest in her battered dolly's precociousness as prattlingly alleged.

There rolled from the southward into the station a train for "American Falls, Nampa, Baker City, The Dalles, Portland, and intermediate points. Stops here twenty minutes," but the cowboys' interest was absorbed by peaches and the owner of the dolly. From one of the train's Pullmans alighted two young and comely women, a self-confident cub male, and a stout, elderly, austere female.

The young women and the cub male, each carrying a camera and clicking their way among the station's populace of disdainfully inquisitive townsfolk and seemingly imperturbable Indians, came upon the cowboys. Click, click, click, this for a dozen times, and punctuated with "Aren't they interesting!" "Right out of a book!" "I think that one over there is the most picturesque." The punchers did not counter. They merely writhed and grunted and lessened their talk to dolly. Then the cub male authoritatively volunteered: "You men move into a straight line. The ladies want to take you that way." Ed Peters, one of the quickest shots on the northern Range, quivered, glanced at the cub male, serious-faced in his position of general manager, glanced at the young women, serious-faced in their perpetration of a nuisance, grinned, and ordered: "Let's git in line, fellers."

Quietly, save for the jingling of spurs and the scraping of feet, the men moved as requested, and resignedly were clicked standing, and then squatting.

The men had not yet risen in compliance with young cub's next dictum: "Say, this looks too peaceful. You men draw your guns and brandish them," when the stout female bustled up in answer to "Mother, come here. We've found five, real, live cowboys." Mother looked, sniffed, said, "I'll have to change my specs," looked again and uninterestedly observed: "Humph. Fancy. They're playing with a doll. And as for those hairy overalls, they suggest vermin."

Ed Peters shot out sotto voce to his companions: "My Gawd, ten minutes more of this! Not on your life." Then he rose to his full height of six feet three, doffed his wide-brimmed hat with courtly flourish, and commencing, with honeyed voice: "Beg pardon, ma'am, for speakin'," he continued, with a howl to his companions: "Whoop, playing with a doll and full of vermin! They wants our real selves. Rise up, you murderous devils, and raise immortal hell for the ladies."

The audience fled. The punchers bowed solemnly to their little guest, mounted, and rode out into the lava beds. And, as they started, there floated back Ed Peters' wail: "Oh, why didn't that old one wear pants! Why didn't it! Oh, if it had been a man!"

To the tale-writer and not to the historian is due the generally accepted tradition as to the uncanny speed and deadly accuracy of all cowboys' shooting. The fictionist, having heavily freighted his protégé with weapons, requires him to transport them in melodramatic fashion and to discharge them in theatric manner.

Carriage of the gun, not in a commonplace holster openly depending from a loosely hanging belt, but in a holster which was either swung low upon the front thigh and connected by a thong with the boot-top or the knee, or was hidden and harnessed on the breast, conduced to increased rapidity of fire. So did keeping the gun holsterless, attaching it at the end of a strap, and concealing it beneath the coat sleeve. So did firing from the hip and through the holster's tip, without pausing to withdraw the pistol. So did filing the latter's mechanism in such a way as to produce a "hair-trigger." So did completely removing the trigger and actuating the hammer either by a pull of the thumb of the hand holding the weapon, or else by a brushing back of the hammer with the palm or side of the other hand, by this last method "fanning" it. And so did carrying two guns, either each openly in a holster and hung from the belt, one on each side of the body, or else one openly shown in its holster and intended as a mere decoy to hold the opponent's attention, the other concealed and suddenly "flashed" when conditions demanded.

These variations from the normal were, in fact, not uncommonly employed by officers of the law, by bandits, all men who hunted other men, and were, in fact, sometimes in the presence of tenderfoots ostentatiously availed of by a tiresome, innocuous form of braggart, the ostensible but pseudo "bad man." But, in fact, they were very rarely made use of by the cowboy. The latter kept his solitary weapon at his side (his right or left side, according as he was right- or left-handed), butt to the rear, and in the clearly visible and commonplace holster above mentioned; and, when he wanted to shoot, merely pulled out the pistol and shot it. The cowboy, however, did take pains to use a holster, which, by being devoid of a covering-flap and of all protuberances, offered to the pistol speedy and easy egress. He took pains also to see that none of his clothing should ever intervene between his hand and his pistol's butt.

He did not touch the holstered weapon, or even, in the language of the novels, "feel for it," until he was prepared to explode the cartridge, for otherwise an absent-minded fingering of his weapon might occur at an inopportune moment, and thus give to an armed enemy good reason for firing the first shot. Moreover, the pistol was an instrument wherewith to shoot and not wherewith to make mere threats.

Incidentally, no old-timer, having "gotten the drop" on a man and wishing to disarm him, would for an instant have thought of asking the prisoner to do what some modern tale-writers have required of him, to "Hand over your gun, and do it butt toward me." The old-timer knew that butt first meant a finger dangerously near the trigger-guard, that a finger through that guard and a quick snap of the wrist would "spin" or "flip" the gun, that in the fraction of a second its muzzle would point forward. So the old-timer ordered his prisoner merely to drop the latter's weapon and to back away from the spot where it lay on the ground.

The cowboy shot, if he thought it necessary, and then without hesitation. When he shot, he shot with intent to kill; but his bullets rarely struck another man save for the shooter's self-protection, in the support of Western law, or in the punishment of a criminal who had deserved the hangman's rope. The cowboy may have disliked to have another person "ride him," or "run over" him, but the average puncher would not kill for the mere resultant pique, or in defense of mere personal pride.

However prosaic it may seem, one half of the West did not spend its time in either "getting the drop" or "pulling down" on the other half, or even in "looking for somebody." Nor did the puncher "notch" his pistol's butt. He had no killings thus crudely to be registered. But the West was far from having mushy softness. Any one disposed to think differently should recall, among other things, that line of thirteen human bodies dangling at the end of thirteen ropes one day at Virginia City, in Montana.

As compared with men the country over, the cowboy, to state a truism, was no better or worse a marksman than innate aptitude and the extent of target practice warranted. Nevertheless he materially advantaged himself by disdaining the short-barrelled, top-heavy, erratic pistol of the townsman, and by habitually using the long-barrelled, perfectly balanced Colt. It was by the faultless "hang" or balance of the latter weapon that the puncher's shooting reputation was made. The weapon's balance induced both accuracy and speed, for it relieved the shooter from the necessity of glancing across the sights. Aiming a Colt was akin to pointing a forefinger.

The puncher and the military alone used this type of pistol; but the military, chafing under compulsory target practice and not having to pay for the ammunition it used, was less disposed than the cowboy to consider carefully each shot and to seek diligently for accuracy and speed.

As to practice in actual firing, the puncher necessarily had infinitely more than had the city dweller; but the average puncher, after his first few years, gave himself no undue amount, since he was wont to consider that he had better use for his money than the purchase of ammunition to be fired through a "noise tool" at a tree or can. He, however, kept himself in form, for, when alone, he frequently practised quick withdrawals of his gun and imaginary shots at objects beside the trail.

All these factors produced men who, with the weapon in question, could on but an instant's notice fairly pour six shots into a two-inch circle one hundred feet away. But very far from all punchers could shoot as well as this, though few of them, at a distance of one hundred feet, would under any circumstances miss with any shot a target as large as a standing man.

The average cowboy was a relatively better shot with the pistol than with the rifle. He used the pistol with more frequency, and had greater interest in its potentialities.

The cowboy's gun had plain wood in its stock. The novelist has supplanted it with carved ivory or mother-of-pearl. The metal of the cowboy's gun was colored black or dark blue. The novelist has nickel-plated it.

For the purpose of self-defense the gun was no more potent than often was the unflinching eye of a man with an established reputation for steady nerves and for ability to "draw quick and shoot straight."

Jim Green at Wichita Falls learned, one day, that gathered in a saloon were several armed men who had planned to kill him. He immediately rode to the saloon's door, entered it, said quietly but very firmly to the conspirators: "Gentlemen, I understand you want to see me and drink with me." Not one of the men addressed dared "reach for his gun," for they all knew Jim's possibilities. The round of drinks was accepted, and this made Jim safe. Under the Western code, none of the men who drank with him might thereafter kill him for the original grievance. They, if still courting murder, would have to pick a new quarrel. A violation of this provision of the code would have made the violator an outlaw and a subject for the ministrations of the vigilance committee. Jim's reputation was useful to him, as throughout the entire transaction he was absolutely unarmed.

Vic Smith, idolized in Montana and Wyoming, had no fear of attack by man or devil, for his marvellous accuracy with gun and rifle was known throughout the Cattle Country. There floated from nowhere in particular and into Charley Scott's saloon at Gardiner, Montana, a long-haired and quite drunken stranger, who presently became obnoxious. The instant after the stranger had completed his announcement that, as soon as he had swallowed his liquor, he intended to wipe Gardiner from the map, the door opened and a head stuck in with a cheery "Hulloa, boys. Just struck town." At the cordial answering, "Hulloa, Vic Smith, you old —— — — ——," the stranger fairly howled "Vic Smith. My God! Vic Smith!" and jumped through the window; at which Charley Scott, one of the finest men who ever "tended bar" in all the West, lost a thoroughly worthless customer and a perfectly good window-sash.

While Jim Green, because unarmed, had to force the issue, more than one man of Green's type was, if armed, able to use a wholly passive method in peaceably ridding himself of a threatening enemy. This passive method consisted of seeming to ignore the enemy when met. This ignoring placed the enemy in a ridiculous position, but could safely be attempted by only such men as were so lightning-like in movement as to be able to "draw" and shoot when but a fraction of a second of time was left for them.

From time to time some ill-balanced person, deranged by liquor or in character, would affect a desire to kill some specific man; and, with much advertisement of intent, would go "looking for" him. The self-heralded ostensible murderer usually was seeking notoriety instead of the designated victim, but nevertheless would openly embark on a search for the latter, and sometimes would unexpectedly come face to face with him. Under such circumstances it was a bit wounding to one's pride not to have the fact of one's presence even recognized, not to be able to move one's hands unless one courted instant and certain death, and, at the same time, to remember all the bold and blood-thirsty announcements one had made.

These affairs were, however, pregnant with danger, because at any instant the tense thread might snap, and the provoker of the trouble might begin wildly to shoot.

A melodramatic coloring was given many episodes of this sort, for the reason that the irresponsible trouble-maker was not unwont to make his ostensible search while on the back of a horse, and to ride the brute into saloons.

Tazewell Woody, in a saloon, was standing with left elbow on the bar, right hand hanging by his side, and eyes luckily pointed at the mirror behind the bar. He caught in the mirror the reflection of a head poked momentarily into the saloon's doorway, and belonging to a man who had publicly stated his purpose of killing Woody at sight. This man, having apparently thought the coast to be clear, and that the saloon contained a sufficient audience, turned his horse, rode through the doorway, and boldly said: "Has any gent here seen that feller Woody? I'm huntin' for him." At that instant the man realized, for the first time, that Woody was in the room, and he realized also that, though he himself was facing Woody's back, the mirror negatived this advantage. He saw that right hand hanging idly down. Woody did not move a muscle. The man's jaw dropped. He remained quiescent for a few seconds, then backed out through the doorway, and on his own initiative rode out of the State.

These preannounced attempts on human life were far less bloody than were the onslaughts by the real "killers," the actual "bad men." These latter men did not announce. They merely shot. Billy the Kid, at twenty-three years of age, had committed twenty-three murders, and had made the question of his extermination a political issue in New Mexico. Incidentally, the sheriff, elected to "get" him, loaded a weapon and "got" him.

In the eighties some "rustlers" "holed up" in a cabin at the outlet of Jackson Lake in Wyoming. Range detectives surrounded them. One of the "rustlers," a wondrously accurate shooter, seeking to escape, rushed from the cabin's door, and, without warning, began to fire. At each shot he "crossed" his rifle, that is he fired alternately from his right and left shoulder, thus increasing the width of his zone of fire without making him rotate his body, and thereby unduly affect his running. He hit five men before he dropped dead at the end of his race of but a few feet.

Riding horses into saloons did not always signify "trouble." Frequently it meant either good-natured drunkenness, or else non-alcoholic prankishness. The much-suffering cow-pony has been ridden in places stranger than saloons, for he has been made to climb stairs, traverse railway trestles, and travel other equally distasteful routes.

Pseudo "bad men" of the "I eat humans for breakfast" kind functioned in the presence of tenderfoots by fierce looks and snorts, by savage remarks, and sometimes by the recital of speeches ferocious in phrase and committed to memory. These men would "wild up" whenever they obtained an impressionable audience, and their braggadocio often was picturesque, even though made up at least in part from strings of stereotyped Western anecdotes. Old, harmless Jim ———, when in his cups, would fervently relate: "I'm the toughest, wildest killer in the West. When I'm hungry I bites off the noses of living grizzly bars. I live in a box canyon, where everybody is wild, and shoots so much they fills the ar plumb full of lead, so there ain't no ar to breathe. The further up the canyon you goes, the wilder the people gits, and I live at the very top end. Whoop!" If tenderfoots continued their presence, Jim would persist in this strain; and perhaps, because of him, a diary or two would receive the entry: "Saw to-day a real Western 'bad man.' He carried two large revolvers in holsters which hung, one just above each knee. This marks him as being what is called a 'two-gun man,' and a person who 'totes his weepens low.'" If only Westerners were auditors, Jim soon would quit his oratory, go to sleep, and snore himself to peaceability.

Bill ———, when alcoholically beset, would announce: "I live in Jack County, Texas. Thars whar the human man-eaters come from, and I'm one on 'em. Every pusson they don't take no fancy to is drug out and scalped alive. My hum range is so plumb full of murder and sin that hell won't be no treat to me." He, too, presently would cease his clatter, and would slumber back to sobriety.

This Jim ———, this Bill ———, and the other men of their type had no wish to "try it out" with any "real Westerner," for it was a foregone conclusion as to which side in such a contest would "weaken," "back down," and "pull out."

The actual "bad man" was "short on conversation." He spoke infrequently, and when he opened his mouth what he said was to the point.

He usually talked in quiet tones, for his nerves always were well in hand. His nerves had to be thus in order for him to do the jobs which he essayed.

All actual "bad men" were wholly untrustworthy, were natural killers, moral and mental degenerates, inhuman brutes who would slay for personal gain or merely to gratify a whim. All of them were among the horse thieves and train robbers, the "hold-up men" and "road agents," but far from all the followers of these vocations were low-browed criminals or "bad men." Though most of the persons in these callings might kill when "on duty" and performing the functions of their crafts, many of them when "off duty" were very human, warm-hearted and companionable beings, normal in everything except moral attitude toward horses, cattle, public vehicles, and bank safes.

Wyoming's Hole-in-the-Wall Gang might plunder the Overland Limited, but it more than once succored a solitary traveller who was in trouble upon the trail. It rarely robbed either the men it liked or any one in deep distress. Personal popularity and dire suffering each tended to insure immunity in the Cattle Country: and this not only to spare the innocent from being robbed, but also to keep the guilty out of jail.

The actual "bad man" was a feature of the towns rather than of the Range, for he preyed mostly upon the gold and silver that, starting from the mines, had been intrusted to a lumbering stage, or to an express car upon the railway.

But, all in all, there were very few of the actual "bad men." The West did not like them. They ran counter to the actuating Western motive, which was fair play or justice, as the West conceived it. Consequently, each "bad man" sooner or later would "go out of the territory for his health or to hell on a shutter." If he "passed out," it would be either on the end of a rope or before a bullet. His demise was sometimes referred to as his "snuffing out," "bucking out," "croaking," "cashing in," or "passing in his checks."

One should not include in the class of "bad man" such cowboys as, from time to time, rented out their services to factions that were engaged in local civil wars. In the factional fights which occurred in Texas, New Mexico, and Wyoming, cowboys served for pay upon the side of each belligerent. But these punchers were not "bad men." They were not at war with civilization. They merely were fighting certain people whom for the moment they mistakenly, honestly believed to be real enemies. The spirit of youth, the love of adventure, the trusting adherence to an individual leader blinded such a puncher from realization that he was leasing himself to the mere cause of killing men.

The pistol had one use to which the average cowboy would, from time to time, enthusiastically devote it, and that was the production of noise. When put to this use the weapon was fired either directly upward into the air or slantingly downward at the ground, for the West had no blank cartridges. On such occasions the pistol's efforts would be supplemented by Indianlike screeches and coyote-like howls.

Sometimes liquor would start this pandemonium. Sometimes suddenly received pleasure would do it. Often and particularly when the puncher was in company with others of his kind, the motive was that indefinable, contagious something that runs like wild-fire through any American crowd of men or boys, and makes the gathering give a cheer or whoop.

One autumn morning at the Glendive railway station, seven cowboys were sitting on their sleepy horses and idly watching the passengers alighted from a delayed east-bound train. Among these passengers was a college undergraduate, sunny-faced, attractive-looking, of the type that everywhere makes friends. He inquired unsuccessfully of the telegraph operator as to the result of "the big football game," played the previous day, and then began to pace up and down the platform. Presently the west-bound train arrived, and from it an older man called to the undergraduate: "Hulloa, Jim ———. Congratulations. You beat us yesterday, ten to nothing." The undergraduate emitted an impulsive cry of joy, and danced down the platform. He suddenly stopped, for bedlam had begun. Seven cowboys were yelling and shooting from the backs of horses that, no longer sleepy, were plunging, snorting, and rushing about.

The undergraduate's train started. He climbed aboard it. The punchers and their horses relapsed into quietude. A woman from the still halted west-bound train asked the cowboys what they had been celebrating, and received the respectful and truthful answer: "We don't know, ma'am. A nice-lookin' young feller that was on the other train heard somethin' that pleased him, and took a contract to deliver a lot of noise. He didn't have much time, so us boys tried to help him out."

Of course what actually had happened was that the spirit of unaffected youth had appealed to its twin, and its voice had been recognized.

The rifle never was carried except when there existed one of the serious conditions already mentioned as producing the pistol's appearance, or there was big game to be shot. The rifle, when carried, was conveyed, not by the cowboy himself but by his horse, which bore it in a quiver-shaped, open-mouthed scabbard, into which the rifle went up to its stock. This scabbard sometimes hung from the saddle horn, but more commonly was slung, butt forward, in an approximately horizontal position along the near side of the animal, and passed between the two leaves of the stirrup-leather. The rifle was thus eschewed, because, being heavy, it interfered with ready saddling and unsaddling; and, being bulky, it materially detracted from the rider's comfort.

After the early seventies the rifle, regardless of its make, was usually called a "Winchester," though this particular term, because of its similarity to the name of a well-known condiment, was occasionally paraphrased into "Worcestershire." Failing these titles, the weapon was styled merely "rifle." It, except in the case of the rifles specially designed for bison-shooting and called "buffalo guns," never was termed "gun," that word, save for the single exception noted, being consecrated to the pistol.

"Scatter-guns," otherwise shotguns, were occasionally produced by tenderfoots; but they, unless with "sawed-off" barrels, loaded with nails or buckshot, and in the hands of express messengers, served for the Westerner only as objects of derision.

The rifle, rarely the pistol, was at times discharged at wild horses, at unbroken members of the ranch herd, or at erring, already-gentled steeds, in any case for the purpose of "creasing" them. Such shooting actually did occur, but it was extremely infrequent. Its dramatic phase gave it such publicity as to earn for it what it did not at all deserve, an ostensible place among the customs of the Range.

Creasing, successfully accomplished, meant shooting through the neck of a horse in such a way as to touch but not injure the cartilage above the bones. Thus done, it would temporarily and completely stun the animal, but would do him no serious injury. Creasing, as usually attempted, resulted in entirely missing the animal, or in killing him.

It was legitimately tried and sometimes achieved by men who, dismounted in a waterless country, saw their truant steeds already out of reach, sneakingly abandoning their riders to death from thirst. It was, on occasion, illegitimately attempted by "rough-riding bronco-busters," when cruel bravado had sufficient foundation of either temper or whiskey.

But Westerners in general had no stomach for unnecessary creasing.

The subject of creasing wild horses suggests that of an unique vocation, "walking down" these animals. Although wild horses for many years, and in great numbers, had been caught by the lariat, some of these beasts, through unusual speed or conspicuous cunning, had been able wholly to evade capture.

They eluded even the "mustangers," as the men were called who devoted themselves to the trade of raiding the "wild" bands and selling their captures to the ranchers.

As the wild horses became fewer in number these elusive survivors stood out in bolder contrast with the domestic herd, and more and more awakened human cupidity. An imperious stallion, heading an obeisant harem, outrunning all pursuers, circumventing all cunningly planned fence traps, haughtily would defy capture and proudly would flaunt the ranchers of an entire range. Although, true to the habit of all Range horses and cattle, he would cling to a restricted area, twenty or thirty miles along each boundary, he never could be cornered.

There eventually was developed among the mustangers a class of men who, by native instinct and constant study, understood the thought and habits of the wild horse. These men, usually queer, cantankerous characters, making their pursuit ordinarily on horseback but sometimes on foot, operating from a strategically located camp, and working in successive squads, strung themselves along the course customarily followed by their prey. They endeavored never to scare the quarry into any desire to run long distances; but, hour after hour, whether in daytime or at night, they methodically, unremittingly, pitilessly denied the harried animal a moment's opportunity for rest, and sooner or later it became so desperately tired as to withhold all attempt to avoid a thrown reata. These men actually walked down the horse, an effort usually of hours only, though occasionally of two or three days. Many of the animals thus caught were superb beasts, aristocrats in blood, for all their ancestors had mated wisely and had refused degenerate brutes admission to the family tree.

These elusive wild horses were undesirable neighbors, because they displayed a habit of enticing ranch horses, particularly mares, away from their accustomed range, away from all willingness to be subject to man's dictation, and of "running them off" beyond the edges of the local map.

The wild horses' itinerant drove, their "manada," as the Southwest correctly spelled it, "menatha," as the Southwest incorrectly pronounced it, their "band," as the Northwest termed it, was not a convenient keeper of one's domestic animals.

Although the man on the Range regarded generically the horses of the ranch herd, assigned no names to any of the ordinary steeds, was not particularly interested in his companions' animals, however fine they were, he had a very different attitude toward the highly trained ponies that he personally, habitually rode. He adopted them into his family, and they took him into theirs.

Nevertheless he at times might enthusiastically quirt them, and assuredly they frequently deserved the treatment.

The expressions of his affection might be intermittent and be made in rough words or rude pats, but they were sincere.

The riders, in their solitary excursions, talked continuously to their mounts. When Al Smith, a "top rider" of the M-K Ranch, fell in love with the schoolma'am at Buffalo Fork, he told the whole story to a sympathetic little four-footed buckskin brother, as they came back together across the prairie. However close-mouthed a man might be with all his fellow men, he imparted all his secrets to his horse.

This intimacy, which came from loneliness, showed no sentimental weakness, for one of these very men who prattled into a pointed hairy ear carried in his body eight bullets from three separate fights.

Short names like Jim and Buck, supplanted for such animals the mere descriptions accorded other horses, descriptions such as "Jack Tansy's star-faced buckskin," "that mealy nosed, blue roan from the Star M Outfit," "that wall-eyed, white cayuse with the K Bar brand."

All this almost humanized some of the ponies. Reader, if you love horses, thaw out some old-timer of the Cattle Country, and ask him to tell you of Pete and Imp and Scoot and Prunes, and other horses that he knew. He will begin his narrative. Presently his face will overspread with a reminiscent, loving smile; he will say: "But, of all the horses I ever ran across, I knew one once that was all horse. Make no mistake about that. He was a little 'California sorrel,' and his name was Mike," and then you will hear a story such as, though truthful, no writer dares to put in print, lest the public brand him as a liar. You will be told of a saucy little devil which suppressed its impudence, and grittily struggled on through snow or desert, to kill itself from effort, but to land its wounded rider in safety; or you will learn of a little brute which came galloping to the house with a blood-soaked saddle hanging from its side, which impatiently nipped the shoulders of the ranchmen that they might hurry more in sending out relief, and which, all through the progress of the expedition, led it and urged it on.

All horses were not of this caliber, but some were; and that some were is why, in little corners of the West, under spreading yellow pines, or amid the piñons, or at the points of aspen groves, not with extreme infrequency, appeared boards, or else slabs of slate, either of them rudely inscribed by heated iron or by scratching metal point. Their legends varied with the stories they had to tell, often were illiterately phrased, but occasionally disclosed assistance by some scholar among the regretful cowboy's friends. Three of them read respectively as follows:

JIM
a reel hors
oct 1, 82

HERE LIES
"I'M HERE"

The Very Best of Cow Ponies,
A Gallant, Little Gentleman.
Died on this Spot, Sept. 3, 1890.

HERE LIES
"WHAT NEXT"
Born ——, ——, 1886, at ——,
Died July 16, 1892, near Ft. Washakie, Wyo.
He had the Body of a Horse,
The Spirit of a Knight, and
The Devotion of the Man
who Erected this Stone.

Of the names commonly used, one alone conveyed instant information. That name was Buck, for every buckskin-colored horse throughout the West was christened Buck. The bearing of this appellation did not in any way imply that the animal that bore it had been concerned at any time with the bucking motion. It related wholly to color.

The broncos ran the gamut of the coloration employed by Eastern horses, but in comparison rather stressed certain shades. Bays, browns, sorrels, grays (whether these last were plain, dappled, or "flea-bitten"), whites, blacks, buckskins, roans, and piebalds were the color schemes. The last three were noticeable, because buckskins, roans, and piebalds were more common in the West than in the East. Roans were, in tint, red (called strawberry roan), blue, or occasionally even distinctly purple. The piebald was the same in coloration as is the "calico horse" of the East, and, deriving his name from a Spanish word meaning paint, was termed generally a "pinto," but in parts of Texas was called in good plain English a "paint horse."

Southern California had a local type, the "California sorrel," its body in a lustrous, solid, light sorrel monotone, its mane and tail in lighter sorrel, almost cream-colored, and its feet white-stockinged. It was a beautiful animal, but, being of limited numbers, very few specimens of it came onto the Range. It was a product of local conditions.

When the wild horses started northward from Old Mexico, some of them followed one route, others a second. Most of them travelled on the easterly side of the coastal mountain range, and inhabiting, generation after generation, a sparsely watered country, developed that itinerant, wiry, sinewy, athletic little imp, the bronco of the plains. Others of them moved along the well-watered, seacoast lands westward of that mountain range, and evolved a type which, because less inured to thirst and hunger, eventually became somewhat heavier in build and a bit more muscularly soft. To this latter type belonged the original cayuses of early Oregon. From these Oregon horses men of the far Northwest derived their initial bands; and from Oregon came the horses' name, "cayuse." That State was the home of the Cayuse tribe of Indians, an equestrian people.

These coastal horses often divided themselves into groups which severally clung, for generations, to various well-favored sections of the country; and, by close inbreeding, produced in each group distinguishing peculiarities. Thus may have come the California sorrel.

Universally, when by reason of illness or injury a horse had to be destroyed, it was killed by a shot carefully placed at the base of the ear.

But in the performance of this rough act of mercy to a suffering cow-pony, its rider almost always chokingly begged a companion, if one there were, to pull the trigger.

The rifle had an occasional function dear to the writer of thrillers, the firing of distress signals, three shots evenly spaced as to time. Inviolable custom demanded that whoever heard this signal forthwith hurry to its source. So insistent was this demand that, upon the sound of any shot, all persons within hearing gave most concentrated attention that the later sounds, if any, and the pauses between them might not be unnoticed. Woe betide the careless hunter who, in bringing down a deer, unwittingly gave this alarm. This system of signalling has been called erroneously a Western invention. In reality, it dates in American usage from the early colonial period, and was prescribed by one of the initial laws of the Massachusetts Bay Colony.

Some cowboys, in copy of the Indians, used, in signalling, smoke released in short puffs and long streamers by intermittently raising and lowering the corner of a blanket which had been laid above a smudging fire. This gave in effect the dots and dashes of the telegraph. Few of the men attempted an alphabetical code, and most of the messages were simply prearranged, arbitrary signals.

The last weapons to mention are the knife and the lariat. After the earlier Indian fighting had ceased, long knives never were carried by cowpunchers unless they were hunting big game, or were Mexican in blood or spirit. A stout pocket jack-knife, or clasp-knife, contented the majority of men.

The long knife in the hands of a competent user was, within a range of thirty feet, the deadliest weapon of the West, for pulled and thrown it usually would reach its goal before the opponent's pistol could be drawn and shot, and this though the thrower and shooter simultaneously started to act. In a hand-to-hand fight the knife was driven by an underhand thrust, edge up, into the abdomen, and was terrible in its effect. As was said at Santa Fé by Sam, by just Sam, for so far as appeared he had no more extensive name, "The knife is a plumb ungentlemanly weepen, and it shore leaves a mussy looking corpse."

The lariat, when quiescent, may have appeared like a mere section of every-day rope, but it had latent capability of deadliness. Such persons as do not already know its possibilities may come to an awesome regard for that bit of line when once they see it whirling.

CHAPTER IV

COWBOY CHARACTER

NECESSARY COURAGE—BODILY INJURIES—UNCOMPLAININGNESS—CHEERFULNESS—RESERVE TOWARD STRANGERS—ITS CAUSE—CUSTOMS WHEN MEETING PEOPLE, AND WHEN ENTERING A CAMP—PERSONAL NAMES—ETIQUETTE OF GUN AND HAT—INTRODUCTIONS—CURBING CURIOSITY—ATTITUDE TOWARD WOMEN—ILLNESS AND MEDICAL TREATMENT—SENTENTIOUSNESS—DEFINITIONS—QUIZZICALITY—SLANG—PROFANITY—DEFINITIONS—RELIGIOUS ATTITUDE—POWER OF OBSERVATION—CHARACTERISTIC POSE—USE OF TOBACCO—BOWED LEGS—DEGREE OF HONESTY—ESTIMATE OF EASTERNERS—INTELLECTUAL INTERESTS AND SCOPE—SENSE OF DIGNITY—VANITY.

UNIVERSALITY of courage was an earmark of the cowboys' trade. Bravery was a prerequisite both to entering and to pursuing the vocation.

When a man suddenly "lost his riding nerve," as he occasionally did from his own serious illness or from witnessing distressing accident to a loved companion, an accident such as plastered Bud Thompson's face with his brother's brains, he sometimes lost it forever, and with it his calling. Unless unhorsed by this infrequent cause, he rode until he received injury that promised permanence, or he sooner voluntarily retired.

Physical injury, ordinarily the gift of bucking, and in the form of hernia, allowed to the average man but seven years of active riding. Once dropped from the centaurs, whether through injury or, much rarer, loss of riding nerve, he still lived on horseback, but regretfully, humiliatingly refrained from "hair-pinning" or "forking" at sight "anything on four hoofs," and restricted himself to such animals as supposedly were not vicious.

Courage was needed elsewhere than on the bucker's back or amid the cattle. The cowboy by the nature of his work was required, from time to time, to endure the pitiless Northern blizzard, to traverse the equally pitiless Southern desert, to fight the bandit or the Indian, to go ahorse upon the mountain's cliffs or amid the river's whirlpools, to ride madly over ground pitted by the gopher and the badger, to face death often, and much of the time when alone.

Some wise old Westerner defined a cowboy as "a man with guts and a horse."

The puncher rarely complained. He associated complaints with quitting, and he was no quitter. Custom, however, allowed guarded criticisms of the cook, though these strictures were made with an amusing risk. Whoever ragged the cook was subject to be impressed by him for twenty-four hours as an assistant or a complete substitute.

Out of this grew the story of the cowboy who, by diplomacy, saved his initial blatancy, for he is reported to have said: "This bread is all burned, but gosh! that's the way I like it!"

There often was ground for adverse comments on the cuisine. The average ranch cook well might have been defined as a man who had a fire; and who drew the same wages that he would have earned if he had known how to cook. He ordinarily had been a cowboy, and in many instances his ideas of culinary art had originated, seemingly, from atop a bucking horse. A very few establishments had a Chinaman in the kitchen, but such an attempt at luxurious living was not typical of the Cattle Country.

Maintenance of cheerfulness was part of the philosophy of the Range. The Western lands were not smiling ones. Nature in the West offered great riches to whoever had the courage to come and take them, but she was austere and majestic, rarely gentle. The desert, the mountains, the canyons, the quicksands, and the blizzard asked no favors and gave no quarter. Each Western man was forced to hear so constantly the roars of the nature which he regarded with deep, respectful admiration, that he had no wish to listen to whimpers from mere humans like himself.

Andy Downs, imparting social compass-points to a newly arrived tenderfoot, said: "The West demands you smile and swallow your personal troubles like your food. Nobody wants to hear about other men's half-digested problems any more than he likes to watch a seasick person working."

This carefully nurtured cheerfulness was, not improbably, the mother of that quality sometimes known as "Western breeziness."

Reserve toward strangers, a fourth characteristic of the puncher, was due, in part, to the mental effect from rarely seeing any but extreme intimates, and for days together not even any of them, and in part to the fact that any newcomer might prove to be a horse thief or an intending settler, and thus in either case undesirable upon the Range. The moment the visitor established that he was not such an interloper all reticence vanished, and he automatically became a courteously welcomed and bounteously treated guest.

This not illogical suspicion of strangers evoked two customs pursued in common with all frontiersmen. One of these customs required that a man nearing another, particularly when upon a trail, should come within speaking distance and should "pass a word" before changing his course, unless, for self-evident reason, he were justified in a change. The excuse for this usage was the acknowledged right of every person to have opportunity to ascertain the intent of all other persons about him. Its unwarranted violation was interpretable as a confession of guilt, or as a deliberate and flagrant insult.

The other custom, for a like basis, demanded that whoever approached a person from the rear should halloa before getting within pistol-shot, and that a camp should be entered always upon like signal, and if possible from the direction most easily viewable by the camp's occupants.

There was no prescribed hailing phrase, but there commonly was given at short range to unknown persons, if men, "Hulloa, stranger," or "Howdy, stranger"; if women, "Good day, ma'am"; and at greater distance to anybody the long-drawn, accented "Whoo-up, whoo-up, whoo-pee"; though at this greater distance to persons whose identity was recognized might float instead the password of the ranching fraternity, a password which was a copy of the shrill, insistent cry of the coyote.

When thus ascertaining the purposes of a stranger, or even when dealing with an acquaintance, one had always to accept at face value whatever name the stranger or acquaintance cared to put forth as his own. It was indefensible to dispute it, unless it were patently assumed for purpose of committing some local impropriety. Moreover, extreme tact was necessary to hurry the announcement of even a pseudonym, for its user admittedly was its natural custodian, and possibly had valid and innocent reason for withholding it. Because "none came West save for health, wealth, or a ruined reputation," and because traditionally the sand-bars of the Missouri River were made of discarded results of christenings, and because it was recognized that, on the banks of that river, "many a real name had been bucked out of the saddle," and because many interrogators were themselves on shaky patronymic ground, the West rarely asked one for one's name, and gravely accepted as it anything one cared to volunteer.

Nevertheless, the West reserved the right to say, behind one's back: "You know Bill Adams. That's his name. It's the name he's using now. But what's his real name?" Sometimes the West called the latter his "oncet name."

The West also reserved the right to select a nickname for a man, and to substitute it for the appellation which he himself had proffered, though in so doing there was intended no reflection upon his truthfulness. Hence each section of the Range had its Shorty, Slim, Skinny, Fatty, Squint, or Red as a prefix to Bill or Jack or Brown or Smith; its Texas Joe, Arizona Kid, and Missouri Jim; its Cat Eye, Hair-Lip, Freckles, or whatever as a prefix to Riley, Jones, or White.

Sand-Blast Pete, now dead and gone, the small-pox that pitted your face and gave you your name never pitted your heart. You proved that one night in the desert, when, although almost exhausted, you went forth alone and obtained help for a stranded party of strangers.

Although every "Greaser" (*i. e.*, Mexican) might, in the Southwest, live under his characteristic Spanish prenomen, Juan, Jose, or what not, he automatically became Mexican Joe for the purposes of the Northwest the instant he reached that section.

A curious phase was that many a man passed always by only his given name, and that none of his associates ever stopped to consider that he must have a surname "cached somewhere." The ranch foreman, on welcoming Mr. New Yorker, a visitor, would say something like the following: "Mr. New Yorker, shake hands with Hen. Hen, this is Mr. New Yorker from back East. He's a friend of the boss. Mr. New Yorker, Hen's been with our outfit for six years, and is generally reckoned to be the slickest rider in this half of the county." If, after Hen had passed beyond ear-shot, Mr. New Yorker had asked the foreman for Hen's last name, the questioner would have seen a look of sudden surprise, and would have heard: "Well, I'm damned. I never thought of that. He likely has got one somewhere. I dunno what it is. He's just Hen, and if he thinks that's good enough for him it shore is for us, and that's about the size of it. Say, stranger, let me give you some advice. You're a pilgrim. Excuse me, that there just means you're new to this country. If I was you I wouldn't try to hurry nothin', and I'd travel on the idee that Hen likely gave a first-class funeral to the rest of his names, and I wouldn't ask him for no resurrections."

Onto whatever single names survived the West often tacked descriptive phrases. By this system there was avoided any confusion in identity among the "Johnnie down with the Four Bar K Outfit," the "Johnnie who rides for the Two Bits Ranch," the "Johnnie up on the White River Range," and "that busted-snoot Johnnie."

As an incident of greetings between strangers it was good form for each to bow to the extent of temporarily removing his hat, or at least to raise his right hand to his hat's brim. This took the theoretically dangerous hand away from the gun's position at the belt. Likewise good form required that a man discard his "shooting iron" before entering another person's house. This latter result usually was accomplished by the man's unfastening his belt, and hanging it with its attached holster from the horn of his saddle.

Furthermore, even at one's own table one's gun was no proper attendant at an indoor meal.

Though a man when entering a dwelling-house had thus to dispense with his revolver, he was not required to take his hat from off his head save during the moments of a bow or two. Behatted heads were common within doors, even at the dinner table, though except in the earlier years they were somewhat frowned upon at dances.

In New Mexico the local law recognized the wisdom of the disarming custom, and forbade the carriage of weapons inside the limits of a town. Wherefore the local official charged with the duty of temporarily impounding the weapons of visitors would greet incomers with a statement which, as phrased by one such official, was "Howdy, gents. Sorry, but no guns allowed in town. Get 'em when you leave. So skin yourselves, skin yourselves!" And thereupon the visitors resignedly would "shuck" their weapons.

When a man was introducing to each other two of his acquaintances, the operation was somewhat formal, though of short duration. For the moment every one, according to sex, was referred to as "Mister," "Miss," or "Missus," and there was employed, without any modification of wording, one of the four conventional phrases which, as adapted to men, ran "Mr. ——, shake hands with Mr. ——," "Mr. ——, step up and meet Mr. ——," "Mr. ——, let me make you acquainted with Mr. ——," or "Mr. ——, meet Mr. ——."

In all affairs of ceremony every white male above sixteen years of age was a "gent" unless the matter were one of icy coldness, possibly near to shooting. Then he was a "gentleman," with syllables slowly spoken and widely spaced.

The title of mister as a token of honor was permanently bestowed upon such elderly men as possessed dignity of carriage and had made brave accomplishment.

The respectful word "ma'am" occurred repeatedly in all conversations with women.

Except for an occasional "Adios," the universal parting salutation was "So long."

The cowboy's reserve and even his suspicion had their corollary in the carefully followed precept that it was not good form to exhibit curiosity. A puncher, passing a stranger or entering the latter's camp, would not demean himself by seeming to note the stranger's apparel or equipment. Nor, on leaving, would the cowboy gaze back over his shoulder.

Punctilious as were the ranchmen in compliance with all these customs, their adherence to the code regarding women travelling upon the Range transcended punctiliousness and rested on the plane of highest honor. A woman journeying alone upon the open Range was as safe as though in her own house, excepting only there were danger from Indians or from border Mexicans. Any passing ranchman could be impressed into an escort. Many a schoolma'am has, sometimes alone, sometimes accompanied by a conscripted attendant, ridden from the fringe of the settlements to her little school in some hamlet far out on the plains.

Any violation of this code meant the hang-knot of the vigilance committee, or on occasion the latter's more terrible "staking out," wherein the culprit, minus eyelids, face to the sun, was laid upon an ant-hill of giant size, wrists and ankles tied to pegs in the ground, to lose in a few minutes his mind, and in a few hours the final vestige of his flesh.

There having been no typical cowboys, there were no typical tastes in which they as cowboys shared; but as men they, like almost all other men of parts, had only restricted admiration for the masculine-mannered female. Years since, some Englishwomen, exaggerated types of the hunting set, visited at their brother's ranch in the Far West. Horseshoe jewelry and loudest of mannish raiment were predominant. Upon the visit's close and an hour after the guests, homeward bound, had finally left the ranch, its cook, red-haired, freckle-faced, one-eyed, thus addressed a sympathetic cowpuncher in the hearing of another and unsuspected auditor: "Huh. If ever I have to git married, I'm going to marry a woman what's all over gol-durned fluffs."

One of these same women, riding up to a group of cowboys, made to one of them a remark which contained no impropriety beyond that the speaker placed herself and the men upon a common level. There flashed back to her the answer: "For God's sake, woman, why can't you let us look up to you?"

Whatever might be any puncher's treatment of his own womenfolk, woman in the abstract was an object of respect and obeisance.

No ambulance from a metropolitan hospital could have offered more gentleness in the transport of a female patient than was intended by the group of silent men escorting across the snow a figure huddled on a "travois" and bound for a hospital via the railway over a hundred miles away. More rude nurses, more solicitude accompanied this horse-dragged, bumping stretcher than would have done so had its contents been a man.

Feminine sick-beds as compared with those of the other sex attracted a larger quantity of the medicines which, as the news of serious illness passed up the Range, came in on the gallop, and in a variety which embraced not only most of the then current patent remedies, but also numerous unlabelled and unidentifiable pills and liquids. With the last-mentioned items would be vouchsafed: "I disremember just what they is, but they done me a powerful lot of good oncet. Take 'em and try 'em."

The Range, in medical matters, dosed itself, and took naught but patent medicines; in dental affairs treated itself with blacksmith's pincers; but, in surgical cases of seriousness, conveyed its patients to the settlements, where real doctors might be found.

Its nursing was faithful and untiring, however amateurish, for a dangerous life tends to make men womanly; and the average puncher was womanly, though Heaven knows he was in no wise ladylike.

The Cattle Country's self-administered medicines were limited to Jamaica ginger, cathartic pills, "Cholera Cure," "Pain Killer," "Universal Liver Remedy," "Rheumatism and Kidney Cure," and horse liniment, this last being kept only for human use, and being diluted when administered.

The liniment's action not infrequently was supplemented by a steam bath taken in Indian fashion. For this purpose there was erected a "wickyup," a low, dome-shaped framework of sticks covered with hides. On the ground in the middle of the structure were placed red-hot stones. The patient stripped and nestled near them. A bucket of water was thrown onto the stones, and human parboiling forth-with commenced.

Transport of such surgical patients as could not sit the saddle was effected by wagon or by the travois. This latter appliance was adopted from the Indians, and consisted of two long poles, one attached to each side of a horse, and both dragging behind him, just as would a pair of elongated carriage shafts if disconnected from the vehicle's axle. Behind the horse's heels there was fastened, between the poles, a basket or framework, and into this container went the comfortless invalid.

Sententiousness was another characteristic of the Range. Sententiousness, which among the earliest cowboys may have come wholly from the loneliness of their life, was in their later generations founded not so much on this cause as on mere convention. Ultimately it became more than fashionable, it became socially obligatory, to speak in terse terms, and when framing a sentence to "bobtail her and fill her with meat." So adverse was the man of the Cattle Country to unnecessary words that he often advised a discursive conversationalist to "save part of your breath for breathing." One puncher, when asked for his opinion about his employer, replied: "Can't put it in words. Give me an emetic!"

This does not mean that the average cowboy was not talkative. It means merely that he was epigrammatic. It also indicates that he could make word-pictures. A tramp suddenly appeared in a Montana cowboys' camp. After the manner of tramps he had silently, slinkingly, self-effacingly merely arrived. Bug Eye, whatever his last name, one of the punchers, looked up, and to a companion behind him announced: "One no work, much eat just sifted in." Can there be found a better word than "sift" for the typical, aimless, shifty movement of the tramp?

A man in chaps, taking his first look down into the Grand Canyon of the Yellowstone, remained quiescent for two minutes, then straightened in his saddle and made a soldierly salute to that great abyss and galaxy of color. All that he later said about it was "God dug that there hole in anger, and painted it in joy."

Another man, Tazewell Woody, who, while not a ranchman but instead a scout and hunting guide, yet lived in close relationship with ranchmen, was with a companion searching for mountain-sheep. The men had reached the summit of a peak the moment before the morning sun rose from behind another peak, and shot a golden pathway across the intervening field of snow. Woody's companion, with eyes glued to binoculars which were pointed elsewhere, said at that climactic instant: "There's a big ram," and was answered: "Shut up. God's waking."

The sententiousness, and still more the reserve, led occasional observers to conclude that punchers, as a class, were taciturn, even morose. This conclusion was erroneous. A few punchers, it is true, were morose, but most of the punchers, like all other old-time Westerners, merely withheld their intimacy from every stranger until the latter should fully have disclosed his nature and have established whether he were a "white man" or else what, if in expurgated form (as it rarely was), was termed a "son of a gun," the latter either unqualified or else "plain," "fancy," "natural born," "self made," "pale pink," "net," or, worst of all, "double distilled."

For some inexplicable reason the word "net," when used, always followed the "gun," or the word that it displaced, while all the other qualifying expressions, when they appeared, preceded the "son."

If the Westerner eventually released his intimacy, he took to his heart the stranger and forgot reserve completely, though sententiousness not at all. The stranger by his own worth had, in the language of the Westerner, "gotten under the latter's skin."

The cowboy was quite apt to talk in quizzical terms. Jim Stebbins and Joe —— (?) accompanied a military detachment during the Sioux campaign of 1876. In a skirmish the horse of one of them fell and laid a stunned rider on the ground. There ran toward this man a squaw armed with one of the stone-headed, long-handled hammers known as "skull crackers," and used by Indian women for crushing the heads of wounded enemies. The semi-insensible puncher was recalled to action by his companion's announcement: "Look out, Jim. There's a lady coming."

Dave Rudio, of Oregon and Texas, thus described a Texas ranger's killing of a renegade: "The ranger came up and said quietly: 'You're wanted. You'd better come along peaceable-like.' The outlaw he began to throw talk. The ranger he said: 'Don't act up. Be sensible and come along with me.' The outlaw, still jawing, started to reach. He hadn't a tenderfoot's chance at that game, for the ranger he just whirled out his own gun, and that outlaw stopped plumb short talking to the ranger and began a conversation with Saint Peter."

Digressing for a moment from the cowboys, but still sticking to this quizzical phase and to old-time Westerners, Jake Saunders of Denver was besought by an ex-ranchman for a loan of twenty dollars. Saunders, knowing the man's proclivity for borrowing, and so curbing his own usual generosity, handed over to the borrower but one-half of the sum requested. The borrower said: "I asked for twenty," and received the answer: "That's all right. We're even. You've lost ten, and I've lost ten."

Pop Wyman, deservedly respected in Leadville, Deadwood, and elsewhere for his honesty, was dealing faro. A particularly obnoxious player had been fingering chips, pushing them out on the table and then withdrawing them. Upon the announcement of a winning card, the player claimed that one of his peregrinating stacks of chips was within the lines bounding the paying counterpart of the successful card. He vehemently asked, "Am I on or off?" and was told, "Neither, you're out." He was. He landed on the sidewalk, and deserved it.

Among the punchers many words disclosed their intended meaning only from their context. For instance "jamboree" might indicate, among other things, an innocent dancing party, a drunken debauch, or an active event, whether the last were a pistol fight or a stampede of animals. "Clean straw" either denoted exactly what it said, or else it signified fresh bed-sheets.

A few other words and phrases had arbitrary meanings, akin to those employed in the cant of professional criminals. Thus a "blue whistler," because of the pistol's blued frame, denoted a bullet, while a "can't whistle," for obvious reason, signified a hare-lipped person. A "lead plum" was a bullet, while a "sea plum" was an oyster. Many of these arbitrary expressions had local rather than general usage.

The cowboy's utterances were permeated with slang. Slang, since the foundation of the United States, has been the natural expression of its youths, and the cowboy, whatever his years, was at heart always a youth. To the slang of ordinary young America the cowboy added by picturesque perversions of technical terms of his business, the whole supplemented everywhere by gamblers' expressions; in the Southwest by various Spanish words, and particularly in the Northwest by limited extracts from the local Indians' languages. The Latins' "hombre," "mañana," "pronto," and "quien sabe" were as useful in Arizona and New Mexico as was the Red Men's "teepee" (i. e., "tent") in Oregon.

The farther "quien sabe" drifted northward from the Mexican border, the more damaged became its pronunciation. A few leagues of northing produced "keen savvy," and a few more leagues "no savvy."

On some of the Mexican border's ranches Spanish instead of English was the prevailing language.

Everywhere "waltz" and the French word "chassé" were current as interchangeable synonyms for the English word "go," though none of the three words attempted to substitute itself for the homely term "git." "Git" or "you git" was the most affirmative form of Western command for an undesirable person to begin immediate retreat. No qualifying profanity was attached, because custom had decreed that none was necessary. Everywhere it was recognized that "git" and "you git," if unheeded, were possible curtain-raisers to bullets. Mules might safely disregard "giddap" or "glang," but they knew that "you mules, git" prophesied the hissing of the whip-lash.

"Chasséd into" and "waltzed into" might be equivalent to the phrase "happened upon," so that, when Joe Edwards, to repeat his own words, "chasséd over to Albuquerque and waltzed into my aunt's funeral," it meant merely that he had travelled to the city in question and unexpectedly had come upon his relative's burial.

Pidgin-English contributed its quota of words and phrases. Its "long time no see 'em" conveniently set forth the status of a searcher for some lost object, while its "no can do" definitely expressed personal impotence.

In the extreme Northwest a few words were borrowed from the Chinook jargon of the coastal trappers and traders. The words most commonly taken from this last-mentioned source were "skookum" (great), "siwash" (an Indian; hence, in secondary sense, not up to white man's standard, second-rate), "muckamuck" (food, or to eat or to drink), "hiyu muckamuck" (plenty to eat), "muckamuck chuck" (to drink water), "kaupee" (coffee), "cultus" (despicable, worthless), "cuitan" (a horse), and "heehee" (fun or a joke). A "heehee house" was any place of amusement.

Throughout the West references to Indian customs, beliefs, or terms were used commonly, and in a slangy sense. Thus a puncher was apt to describe as "making medicine" his preparations for a journey, or his planning of an enterprise; to state later that this "medicine" had been "good" or "bad," according as his preparations had proved sufficient or insufficient, or his planning had resulted fortunately or otherwise. His affirmative thwarting of a rival's project was, by like adaptation, termed "breaking the medicine" of the rival.

The puncher frequently would signify his acceptance of an offer of a drink of whiskey by giving an Indian sign, usually that for medicine, or that for good or that for peace.

The punchers in general knew a number of these Indian signs, and often used them in lieu of spoken slang in order to dress up light-hearted conversation. But only such of the cowboys as were brought into intimate contact with the Red Men made any pretense of mastering the rest of the Indian sign-language, that remarkable, voiceless means of conveying information.

Tobacco often was termed "killikinic" or "kinnikinic," names given by the Indians to their smoking mixture of willow bark, whether without or with an admixture of tobacco.

Many gambling terms were used in a figurative way. Dice, faro, poker, casino, seven-up, and keno each contributed. The dicer's "at the very first rattle out of the box" expressed prompt action, while poker's "a busted flush" pictured plans gone awry, and poker's "jack-pot" signified either a general smash-up or else a perplexing situation. Poker gave also, among other terms, "showdown," "freeze-out," "call," "see you," "raise," "bluff," "ante," and "kitty," all with self-evident slangy meanings, unless the uninitiated should fail to appreciate that "ante" might include any payment for any purpose, and that "kitty" might embrace any public or charitable fund. Thus Lafe Brown, in Oregon, receiving from his mother an appeal to contribute toward the rebuilding of the church in his native Eastern town, advised her that he would "ante ten dollars to the church's kitty."

Whatever idea or physical asset was expected when ultimately put in use to bring success was one's "big casino." In the class of big casino were included not only schemes for outwitting rivals, but also powerful weapons presumably intimidating to enemies, attractive presents supposedly irresistible by females, speedy horses assumed to be invincible in racing. If, as often, expectations miscarried, the disappointed person ruefully asserted that his big casino had been "trumped."

Faro's terms permitted one puncher to "keep cases" on another man, rather than prosaically to observe the latter's actions or analyze his plans; and further permitted this puncher, if dissatisfied with these actions or plans, to "copper" them by initiating a diametrically opposite sort of performance or scheme. From this same source came "getting down to cases" as an antonym for "beating about the bush."

Because of seven-up, "It's high, low, jack and the game" became an exclamation announcing successful accomplishment of any task.

Keno, of which the Sacramento Chinaman said: "Fline glame. Velly slimple. Dlealer slay 'Kleno,' and ellybolly ellse slay 'O hlell!'" though played in the early mining-camps, was not played upon the Range. Nevertheless it lent its name to the ranchmen for exclamatory use when heralding the ending of any act. The throwing of an elusive steer, the breaking of a whiskey bottle, the being thrown from a horse's back, each might evoke "Keno!"

The average cowboy was a bit ruthless in his treatment of grammar; this, in some cases, from lack of education, in other cases because not satisfied with the amount of damage done to conventional English by slang alone.

Despite this ruthlessness, and despite the cowboy's generous use of slang, his language was not generally as remote from that of Easterners as many tale-writers have suggested. Except for grammatic lapses the puncher departed from conventional English no more than do the average American newspapers of this year 1922 in such of their articles as describe the game of baseball.

The puncher's conversation customarily was redolent with profanity; but, if profanity be identifiable from the sense and not the spelling of words, many of the puncher's expressions, while sacrilegious on the tongues of others, were but slang when used by him. The common misuse of the name of the Deity signified no purpose to revile God. All through the West the word damn descended from the pinnacle of an oath to the lowly estate of a mere adjective unless the circumstances and manner of delivery evidenced a contrary intent. Words could be, according to the tone of their speaking, an insult or a term of affection. Wherefore men frequently were endearingly addressed with seeming curses and apparently scourging epithets. From this sprang the phrase beloved of tale-writers: "Smile, when you say it next. Smile, damn you, smile!"

Damn as an innocent adjective had various quizzical shades of meaning. It was, among other things, synonymous, or semi-synonymous, with "very" or "exactly." Thus "promptly at one o'clock" and "immediately" might severally come from a puncher's lips as "at damned one" and "damned now."

Damn, however, was not the only oath used by the buckayro. He had an impious repertoire which was of amazing length, and contained appallingly blasphemous phrases. Some men devoted considerable thought to the invention of new and ingenious combinations of sacrilegious expressions.

To specialized phrases of this sort the admiring public accorded a sort of copyright, so that the inventor was allowed to monopolize for a time both the use of his infamous productions and the praise that they evoked. These individual creations were known as "private cuss-words."

Some men held in reserve, as private cuss-words, phrases which sounded as of childlike innocence, but which, having been arbitrarily appointed by their owners as symbols to express the last stages of anger or despair, represented, in fact, the extreme of profanity. To the owner's acquaintances such phrases were danger-signals. Snake Wheeler, Pinto Bill, or Nebrasky —— (?), each could for many consecutive minutes comment upon the topography and temperature of Sheol, upon the probable destination of the souls of the bystanders or of certain cattle or horses, upon alleged irregularities in the descent of various persons, yet the human auditors remained entirely blasé. But when Snake icily said, "My own Aunt Mary!" or Pinto fairly hissed, "My dead sister's doll!" or Nebrasky quietly but firmly remarked, "Little Willie's goat!" some individual either ducked or "dug for his cannon," or else a horse or steer learned how it felt to be martyred.

The ranchmen were so permeated with profanity that, though most of them endeavored to refrain from it when in the presence of decent women, but few of the men were able long "to keep the lid on their can of cuss-words." An Eastern woman, riding on a forest-girt Wyoming road, rounded a corner and trotted into the full blast of blasphemy flowing from the lips of the driver of a bogged mule team. The moment the driver saw the woman, he curbed his tongue, and apologized sincerely and in these very words: "Excuse me, ma'am. I didn't know there was ladies present. If I had, I wouldn't a swore. Hi there, you mule. Hell's roarings be damned, ma'am. How in hell can a man keep from dropping out a cuss-word now and then when a lot of —— —— —— mules jack-knife on him. Excuse me, ma'am. I sure begs your pardon. It just slipped out. Hi, there, you lead mule, you —— —— —— —— —— ——." And the woman fled, pursued by first a plaintive wail of "Excuse me, ma'am," and next by another "Hi there, you mule" and its unprintable codicils.

Nevertheless the puncher's swearing was, to no small extent, a purely conventional exhibition of very human and quite boylike desire to impress bystanders. Humor rather than wickedness was its principal source. Where in the wide world, other than in the West, would grown men have ridden miles to engage in a competitive "cussing match," with a saddle for the prize, or a person been held forth as probably the State champion in blasphemy?

Western tradition was that much the best judges of profanity were mules, and that these animals instantly could detect the difference between the bold, swinging blasphemy of a "regular" and the timorous "parlor swearing" of a "pilgrim."

"Regular," the antonym of "tenderfoot," began early in the decade of the seventies to be wholly supplanted by the terms "Westerner" and "real Westerner." As between these latter terms, a "real Westerner" was merely a "Westerner" who had unusual force of character, and thus, in another phrasing by the Range, was a "he man."

The subject of profanity suggests the subject of religion, as regards which the cowboys as a class were negative. Some of them, either atheistic or merely agnostic, were open scoffers, and with unction displayed to all newcomers a certain vicious, stupid, and hopelessly vulgar printed parody on the Bible. This particular parody was scattered all over the Far West, and was one of its recognized fixtures, along with the lariat, tin can, and sage-brush. But most of the men, whatever their inner feelings may have been, touched lightly, if at all, upon religious matters. "Sunday stopped at the Missouri River," and many of the men never had opportunity either to enter a church or to talk with a clergyman. A fair statement is that, never having been religiously awakened, they were religiously asleep.

Very marked was the power of detailed and accurate observation of such things as were within the realm of the cowboys' interests, and, from the things observed, simple inductions were instantly, if unconsciously, made. Then, too, the puncher by training had the eye of a hawk. He had no need for field-glasses.

Whatever he "raised" upon his solitary rides, he diagnosed at a single glance.

When an object suddenly appeared within an observer's horizon, this observer, if a Westerner, would state that he had "raised" the object; while an Easterner, under like circumstances, would say that the object had risen.

Did the cowboy "raise" a horseman, however far away, an instant's glimpse told whether this horseman were an Indian or a ranchman. The differing poses in the saddle were unmistakable; the Indian always squatting and seated like a sodden bag of meal. Closer inspection would disclose that the Indian's toes were pointed outward, and that his heels drubbed on his horse's sides at every step the poor brute took.

The lope could not carry a rider so rapidly past five or six closely bunched animals that he would not note and remember all the beasts' identifying points.

Were his progress slower, his observation would be much increased. There approached each other upon the trail a man and thirty horses, the latter herded by men behind. The horses, some on the trail, some beside it, here one, there two or three abreast, interrupted their steady walk only by stops for an instant to snatch a grass tuft or to place a kick. These movements of the head and heels momentarily so turned the animals as to show all their markings to a practised human eye. The man swung off the trail, around the band, and to its herders at its rear. Two minutes of conversation and he resumed his way. Then and for days thereafter he could have described with certainty the color, marking, sex, size, and brand of every animal. One brute did not attempt to dodge before receiving a kick upon its left shoulder. The man, of course, noticed that, and it forthwith informed him that the animal was blind on that side.

At the conversation behind the band there doubtless occurred a simple but characteristic act. At least one of the men, to rest himself, would have thrown a leg over his horse's neck and sat in the saddle, either with one knee crooked about the horn, or else squarely sideways, with a stirrup flappingly hanging from one toe. That was a typical Western pose.

Smoking, while universal, was practically restricted to cigarettes, which were pronounced cig-a-reets, and were made by the smoker. Although in fact the great majority of cowboys had to use both hands in the operation of rolling and lighting, consummate elegance dictated that but a single hand should be employed; and that the rolling should be effected by the finger-tips of this single hand, or, better still, through a method which was successfully followed by some of the cowboys and was studiously attempted by all of them.

In this latter method, the paper, laid above the knee, received a charge of tobacco, and then, without change of position, was rolled into shape by a quick sweep of the ball of the thumb. Next, with the finished cigarette held between the fourth and fifth fingers of the rolling hand, the thumb and forefinger of that hand grasped one loop of the tobacco-sack's draw-string, the puncher's teeth seized the other loop, and a whirling of the sack like a windmill closed its aperture. A dab by the tongue along the papered cylinder, a match drawn by that same rolling hand across tightened trousers, and the cigarette was "working." The performance of this feat was one of the conventional ways of exhibiting ostensible nonchalance when on the back of a bucking horse.

"Eating and spitting tobacco" was in common but far from universal use.

Bowed legs were a sign of the puncher's craft. The Westerner, from his earliest boyhood, when not sitting on a chair sat on a horse. With no small number of men, did a pedestrian journey out of doors rarely exceed the ten feet between the house-door and the horse-rack. So habited were these men to riding, that a projected trip to another building, two hundred feet away, would send them into saddle. Nature, as her price, subtracted symmetry from their legs, strength from their ankles, and created a gait akin to that of a sailor ashore. Dear old Wedding Ring Charlie bore a sobriquet descriptive of his nether contour, and, though ever able firmly to sit his saddle through twenty-four consecutive hours, could only with greatest difficulty walk for twenty yards.

The feet at the ends of such curved legs were very apt to toe in, not to "track" as the West, in wagon builders' language, described a deviation from normal pointing.

The ranchmen, whether owners or employees, in common with all other then Westerners, while thoroughly honest in their mutual dealings, had a very easy conscience as regards accepting Eastern, and particularly English, money in return for what was sold. They at times would go so far as ostensibly to convey large rivers and huge tracts of governmentally owned land.

This attitude was not due to affirmatively intended dishonesty for personal gain, but arose from a combination of factors which largely were in the nature of erroneous assumptions.

First of all, the West, as an undeveloped section, was in such dire need of money for the development of natural resources that "bringing money into the country" was regarded as a particularly public-spirited act. Each new fund, when put into circulation, aided so many men that the arrival of any fund obscured the inducement offered for its coming.

A second factor was the Westerner's unflattering opinion of Easterners and Englishmen, this opinion having, as regards Easterners, a not illogical tang of bitterness.

The West, despite its progressiveness in most matters, was thoroughly unregenerate in its clinging to prejudices of the sort by which early Anglo-Saxon America was beset, and consequently affected a contempt for "foreigners," the West including Easterners in that category. From this view-point the Range had toward the financial trimming of some "effete" person the same complacent attitude as the world has ever maintained toward the misfortunes of such people as had forfeited public respect, as for instance toward the excessive gambling losses of gilded youths.

Nor did the West see any ground for pity for the victims. The Westerner, having started life when financially "flat broke," and having lived in a country where lands were given to the asker and natural products belonged to the finder, confidently assumed that the victim's monetary losses could be fully compensated by his "hunting up" a mine or other national largess of value. Thus the West, from personal experience, believed that "going bust" or "being busted" was not a serious state and was terminable at any time by the insolvent's initiative. Incidentally, this was why the West always was ready to do what the East often could not risk, to "take a chance" in a business operation.

Next, each Westerner arrogated, not to himself but to his fellow Westerners, the possession of the major portion of the nation's brains, and took the stand that, if weaklings chose to invade the country of men and to trade with them, the weaklings should look out for themselves. The Range made no allowance for the fact that the settled business customs of England and the East, and the established significance of the trade expressions used there might differ from such as obtained within the Cattle Country. It assumed that its own customs and its own construction of technical terms were exclusively controlling. With this tacit creation of a seemingly fair field for contest, the West viewed a business transaction of intersectional or international application as being to no small extent a competitive trial of intellect, and considerable local pride was aroused among the friends of a ranchman who had "shown some Easterner or Englishman how to think." This ranchman's success was measured, not so much by the amount of his financial profit, as by the extent to which he cleverly had outwitted his "effete" victim; and, if the latter had been made to appear ridiculous, so much the better.

Furthermore, the Westerner, in addition to relegating Easterners to the impersonal status of foreigners, stored up against them three affirmative grievances. The Westerner resented, first, the East's lack of interest in the former's country, resented, second, the East's so largely profiting from a rehandling of the West's productions, and, third, to some extent believed that the latter condition spelled more than unfairness, and that he, the Westerner, ever was being affirmatively defrauded by the East. Thus he countenanced recoupment from individual Easterners.

The puncher's intense admiration for the scenic beauties of his Western country, and the failure of Easterners in general to visit it contributed largely to the creation of the puncher's antipathy toward the East. Every Easterner who went to Europe instead of to Colorado or to California, every Easterner who mentioned the Alps instead of the Rockies fertilized this prejudice. The West's censure of the East in this regard was based, not on the theory that the moneys spent in European travel might otherwise have gone Westward, but on the fact that the Easterner preferred admiration of the sights of Europe to worship of Western landscapes.

The Westerner had never been brought face to face with great buildings, great paintings, great statues, and thus he did not sense their possibilities, did not realize that there could exist objects of this sort worth crossing the Atlantic to see, and that Europe was their storage place. The single beauty field of which he knew was natural scenery, and he sincerely believed that, in this, nature had given her best to America's West, to "God's Country," as all its dwellers termed it.

The salient scenery of the West consisted of mountains, canyons, and waterfalls, punctuated by the geysers of the present Yellowstone National Park.

The puncher confidently matched the Rockies against the only foreign range with the existence of which he was familiar, the Alps, and against the only Eastern range the character of which he kept in mind, the White Mountains of New Hampshire. With his back confidently braced against the Rockies, anchored as they were to the Arctic and Cape Horn, he called the Alpine "Mount Blank" a badger-hole; and, discovering that the bottom of a deep depression in a plain in Colorado had exactly the same altitude above sea-level as had the summit of New England's highest peak, joyfully named the bottom of that hole Mount Washington.

The West was particularly rich in majestic waterfalls, their least one more important than any Europe had. Wherefore the puncher, with indignant partisanship and great enthusiasm, berated Lauterbrunnen and the falls of the Rhine. Even America's Niagara at times was scolded. One night, below the great cataract of the Snake River, one of the tremendous spots of North America, Jim, *i. e.*, Jim whatever his last name may have been, having dismissed the Staubbach Fall of Switzerland as "a mere watering-pot," announced with exultant pride: "European waterfalls. Hell! Bring over the biggest of them, and this here real one will squirt it to a finish."

Did a tenderfoot mention canyons to a Westerner, the latter merely grinned, said, "Yellowstone, Colorado," and, if he chewed tobacco, bit his plug.

As for geysers, the West knew that there were three principal fields: New Zealand ("how did one reach there?"), Iceland ("nobody went there"), and the Yellowstone. Europe and the East had no geysers. From the cowboy's view-point, they did not deserve any.

In the railroad yard at Green River, Wyoming, one hot afternoon, there ran between a complacent native son of Utah and a homesick ex-Bostonian a bitter debate on the comparative scenic beauties of New England and the West, and the relative merits of the inhabitants of those localities. The debate bumped along now in favor of this side, now of the other, until suddenly terminated and conclusively won by this uncontrovertible argument: "By G———, if your Eastern folks ever had guts, why didn't they get their own geezers?"

The cowboy could not understand why the Easterner should prefer to stay on the Atlantic coast or to go to Europe when, as the Cattle Country thought, ordinary common sense should have taken him Westward.

And when the Easterner did go Westward, he could not properly saddle a horse, he could not properly ride the beast, he could not find his way through a trackless wilderness, he could not take care of himself in the open, he expected some non-existent woman to do his cooking and to wash his clothes, he carried a very shiny and very small-bore pistol, and, while tracking big game, he stepped on every dry stick within his reach. He called the corral a barnyard; and, though he had seen the West, he permitted his relatives to remain "back East." The Range, realizing that the Easterner was very bungling in every attempt to do any of the particular, technical things that every Westerner had of necessity mastered, looked, when gauging efficiency, no farther than the boundaries of the Cattle Country, and did not appreciate that beyond those

boundaries might be an important field of activity and thought with
which the West was not conversant, and that the very tenderfoot who
called the corral a barnyard might be a leader in that field.

The Cattle Country complained that the West exerted itself to produce the nation's raw materials in the way of meat, hides, wool, wheat,
and precious metals, that the East was wholly unproductive, but that
nevertheless the East, by ownership of the factories and by control of
the markets, unfairly reaped the major portion of the profits from the
raw products which the Westerners laboriously had originated. The
cowman berated commissions and stock-yard charges upon the sales
of his cattle.

The Westerner, who was accustomed to obtain through federal
gift whatever lands, water, grass, fuel, building wood, and wild meat
he needed, did not pause to consider that in the West alone did the
government make such gifts; and, on reading in his newspaper that
some little parcel of New York City realty had fetched a tremendous
price, he vaguely or more definitely concluded that "Wall Street" was
allowed all the cream of the federal benefactions, and that in some
undisclosed manner the West had been cheated out of its fair share
of the profit. The puncher assumed that, if land at the corner of Wall
Street and Broadway in New York brought fifty dollars per square foot
while productive tracts in the Cattle Country rarely rose above ten
dollars for each acre, there was some dishonesty in the situation, and
he gave the blame for it to the East.

The Cattle Country had for itself the same kind of complacent self-
satisfaction that the then contemporary Atlantic coast had for what
the latter called the United States; the United States, according to the
Atlantic coast's then view-point, consisting of three thousand miles in
width of territory which might or might not contain inhabitants living
westward of Chicago.

The Cattle Country extended, out of its self-complacency, a friendly
interest to so much of the Middle West as did not lie eastward of
Chicago; but, beyond the easterly boundary of that city, the curiosity of
the Cattle Country did not go, save on occasional trips either to gather
diverting bits of information like a jumping from the Brooklyn Bridge
or Captain Webb's attempt to swim through Niagara's whirlpool, or
else to obtain a grievance against the East. A considerable amount of
admiring interest was incited both by the rapid growth of Chicago
and by the heights of its successively erected "skyscrapers," particularly
in so far as they promised an ultimate, hopeless outdistancing of the
City of New York in both population and tall buildings.

A friendly interest was extended also to the Pacific slope.

Very definite acquaintance was had with Mexico, its geography, industries, and political affairs.

The rest of the world did not function on the Cattle Country's map except in so far as, even back in the early eighties, a few prophets said that some day California might have trouble with Japan. The only news the Cattle Country received from Europe was that which, from time to time and in squib-like form appearing in Western newspapers, was largely of the Captain Webb variety, or else related to royal assassinations or the burning of cities.

In all this, the West was relatively not a whit more insular than the rest of the United States. America has ever restricted its intensive interest to itself, and has saved its most burning curiosity until a new family should move into the house next door.

Of its own affairs the Cattle Country had an astonishingly definite and accurate knowledge. The West's own geography down to its minutest details was at the finger-tips of everybody upon the Range. Whatever visitor might wish information as to the crossings of the Rio Grande could obtain reliable information at Sumpter, Oregon, or at Medora in Dakota, information no less specific and trustworthy than he could procure at Laredo upon the stream's very bank. Texas knew as much about the Gallatin River as did Bozeman, Montana, past which it flowed. Even every little creek had Rangewide notoriety. Arizona had no more knowledge about her San Francisco peaks than had Wyoming, while the dwellers by the Bitter Root Mountains of Idaho and the people who lived in the shadow of Colorado's Sangre de Cristo Range knew every principal trail and canyon in both these chains.

This geographical knowledge had causation other than merely abstract interest. The Range dweller was called upon in connection with the business of his live stock to travel often and far. He never knew when and whither he next might journey. Distance never balked him. The school of the Texas Drive taught the meaninglessness of miles. And yet, though he saw many places, he could not visit every place upon the map. His intimate knowledge of these unseen spots he obtained from the descriptions given him by other Westerners, descriptions such as could be given only by frontiersmen and by engineers, descriptions by which his brain received through the medium of his ears a picture and topographical plan as vivid and detailed as his eyes might otherwise have procured.

The Cattle Country kept somewhat close track of all its people. Ranchmen on Montana's Musselshell knew in general as to who was raising cattle in the Texan county of Palo Pinto, while "down in San Antone," one not improbably might learn the names of almost all the outfits along Nebraska's Platte.

Cattlemen on some of Oregon's Grant County ranges, making an onslaught on local sheep, drove hundreds of the "woollies" into the forests of the Blue Mountains, and fire did the rest. Presently the entire Cattle Country knew all the details, just as it promptly knew all the details when "lumpy jaw" appeared in the Neutral Strip, "hoof and mouth disease" crept in at North Park, drought struck Judith Basin, or Green River was "up," *i. e.*, in unusual flood. A ranchman scarcely could move his thousand steers at Laramie without their transit being eventually reported along the Pecos.

A man would alight from a train in Nebraska at Grand Island or in Kansas at Abilene. Some local resident in chaps would give him a second glance, a searching if a hurried one, and would thus address the train's conductor: "Captain, ain't that Angus, the new sheriff over in Johnson County, Wyoming? I ain't never seen him, but a feller down in Texas told me what he looked like." Thus, in another phase, the frontiersman's descriptive power had functioned, and Sheriff Angus's picture had been painted with accuracy as pronounced as had obtained when a mountain range and the trails across it had by word of mouth been set with vivid clarity before some inquirer.

Incidentally the Cattle Country obtained its news not so much through the media of its newspapers and the mails as it did through the spoken words of men who, meeting in the open country, stopped their ponies and "passed a word."

The Cattle Country was interested, of course, in things other than those above enumerated; but, unless these latter matters involved mechanical inventions, or either discoveries or theories in science, or else epoch-making events, they usually, to obtain a hearing, had first to prove that more or less directly they would affect the Range. International relations could find no audience.

The Cattle Country, as regards the intellectual subjects that interested it, had a very lively curiosity, was little disposed to be mentally lazy and to take anything for granted. Nor was it apt, without investigation of its own, to accept as conclusive other people's opinions and to rely upon them. It directed to these subjects painstaking, tireless, and extensive consideration. The loneliness of the life gave ample time for thought, none of which was wasted on neurotic introspection or was subject to interruption.

The constant working of this curiosity, the habitual exercise of the powers of accurate observation and of mental concentration collectively produced, from time to time, data valuable in the field of science. The range and habits of the several species of wild animals, the location and area of the way stations used by the different varieties of migratory birds, the latters' several migration time-tables, the situs of fossil deposits, marked abnormalities in geological formations, peculiarities in the dress and customs of various Indian tribes, and other matters of like character were observed, and frequently were reported to the Smithsonian Institution, to a local university, to some locally operating scientific expedition from an Eastern university, to some field party of the federal government's Geological Survey, or, occasionally and strange to say, to the nearest United States marshal.

Though most of these reports brought no additions or amendments to scientific knowledge as it then existed, some did, and laid real foundation for new theories to be created in scholarly laboratories, or else confirmed theories previously so made but then not as yet conclusively established, or else they caused either a doubting or a complete rejection of theories that had obtained.

It is safe to say that no equal number of amateur investigators in any other section of the United States would have produced anywhere nearly the same quantity of useful data.

The Cattle Country, thus committing its mind actively to concrete, tangible matters, was not prone to interest itself in abstract, intangible, philosophical subjects. It sympathized with the view-point of Steve Hawes, a cook with convictions: "Such things, they don't bring no facts to nobody. The feller that's a-goin' to do the talkin', he just natcherally begins by pickin' out a startin' pint that rully ain't nowhars at all. He brands that startin' pint 'Assoomin' that,' so he can know it if he runs acrost it agin. Then he cuts his thinkin' picket-rope, and drifts all over the hull mental prairie until he gits plumb tuckered out. And when he gits so dog-gone tired that he can't think up no more idees to wave around and look purty in the wind, he just winds up with 'Wherefore, it follows.' Follows. Hell! It don't follow nothin'. It just comes in last."

Then, too, the Cattle Country, with its directness of thinking, was apt to content itself with ascertaining the merely proximate cause of the phenomena that attracted interest, and to consider that attempts to trace further back into the chain not only were futile, but also took one into purely speculative channels and away from "facts."

That same Steve Hawes, after patiently listening to two college graduates academically discuss the cause of Julius Cæsar's death, thus summarized the whole affair: "What did recurrin' desire for constitooshanl guvnment, return of democracy, and them other vague things you've bin talkin' about have to do with it anyhow? All there was to it was that Cæsar, he didn't draw in time, and got in front of that feller Cassius's dofunny, while Brutus he come in with the sweetener. Now it appears to me that them was the facts, leastwise the true facts and all that's wuth considerin'."

The essayist's type of presentation found small favor. For the essays upon light subjects the Range had little sympathy, and for the frothy ones that not only delighted many an Eastern dilettante but also marked the limit of his intellectual research, the Range had an unmitigated and robust contempt.

The West pinned its faith and its interest to "facts." Incidentally, the salient, important, controlling elements in any matter of fact were called the "true facts," or the "real facts," while the occurrence or existence of immaterial elements was acknowledged and dismissed by the statement: "That might be," or "That might be so."

Reddy Rodgers, a Gallatin Valley hunting-guide, having, in company with a tenderfoot sportsman spent an entire day in unsuccessful quest for game, came toward nightfall upon a bear. The tenderfoot became excited, broke a branch lying on the ground, and the bear thus alarmed disappeared forthwith. Upon the men's return to camp the tenderfoot, when giving to one of his fellow sportsmen a recital of the event, described in minutest detail and with strictest accuracy every happening before the bear had been sighted, while it remained in view, and for some time after it had left. There was not a single statement that was not absolutely truthful. When he had finished, Reddy summed up in these words: "All that mought be so. But the true facts was. The bar thar. The dude he stepped on a stick. Skiddoo."

The West desired that persons, when describing "facts," should do so with definiteness and accuracy, but it did not require that any effort be made to dress the presentation in an artistic way. The West contained such endless quantity of beauty in its natural scenery, that, as already stated, whoever upon the Range hungered for the beautiful turned instinctively to nature and not to art. The result was that the Cattle Country tended to ignore most of the human attempts to create beauty, and so brought upon itself the Easterner's averment as to lack of cultivation.

The Westerner, with his methods of thinking and his uninterrupted opportunities for thought, was able in each subject that interested him to arrive ultimately at a clearly cut conclusion, and to hold in definite mental storage all the argument that had led him to that end.

Along would come an Eastern or English tenderfoot, and, in the ordinary course of conversation, one of the Westerner's favorite topics would arise. It very likely would be one to which the tenderfoot had previously given little heed, perhaps none at all. The Westerner under such conditions often had good reason to think that the tenderfoot in his discussion made a sorry presentation as compared with the Westerner's well-ordered offerings. The difference in extent of preparation suggested itself to nobody, and the tenderfoot, himself chagrined, was by the Westerner classed as mentally his inferior and possible as markedly stupid.

On the other hand, was there put forward a topic in which the tenderfoot was well prepared and in which the Westerner took no interest, one of two things would promptly happen. Either the topic would be summarily changed, or the Westerner would rid himself of an unwelcome phase in the conversation by hastily forming an opinion and stating it in very positive terms. He would assume both that the subject was not worth his expenditure of thought and also that nothing that the tenderfoot might say about it would have any value.

The Easterner had his own social customs, and these were largely predicated on urban life. Practically none of them were compatible with, or were adjustable to, the style of living which conditions in the West locally compelled. And yet the fact that Easterners, even when in their Atlantic coast homes, should not attempt to follow Western standards, was a bit complained of by the Cattle Country as against the East.

The Cattle Country did not resent the individual Easterner so long as he stayed in the West and tried to fit into the life. It merely pitied him for his fancied total inefficiency. But the Cattle Country did resent, and deeply resent, the fact that neither the man's relatives, his "folks," as the Range termed them, nor the vast majority of all Easterners either came to the West or showed any interest in that section. The people of the Cattle Country were aggrieved at having their own existence as human beings overlooked and at being abstractly considered as merely so many annual pounds of wheat, silver, gold, leather, wool, and meat. In other words, that which the West really most resented was being ignored, and this resentment was the fundamental motive for the specific and affirmatively made complaints enumerated above.

The Western skin, despite its sunburn, was very thin and very easily hurt.

The resentment was a bit augmented by a secret dread that adverse criticism of Westerners might come from the Atlantic coast when the latter should eventually direct its attention to the Cattle Country. Previously and for years, the East had had the same fear of Europe. In each case, it was the latent anxiety of a virile, youthful civilization lest it be judged severely by an older people; and, in each case, the anxiety came to the surface in the shape of defiant antipathy. The Cattle Country's "tenderfoots" and "effete East" spoke the same language as did the East's prior railings against "effete monarchies" and "worn-out Europe."

But the cowboy, although he did not understand the Easterners, although he branded them as "effete" and "stuck up," and very stupid, although he objected to their governing themselves by their own settled customs, this last despite the fact that he himself unconsciously was ruled by convention as much as consciously were the Easterners, although he ruffled when they ran counter to his code, nevertheless welcomed them to his country; and, if they expressed true admiration for it and fitted into it, he became their undying friend.

The moment an Easterner settled in the West, his sins of birth were forgiven him. He was assumed to have recanted from his iniquity, and to have travelled in search of light. His new companions did not arrogate to themselves any idea that he had sought to be taught by them. Merely he had come to "God's Country," to learn from it and from all that was in it how contemptible his past had been, how great his then present privilege was.

Not even a large minority of Westerners would themselves commit the sharp practices described above, but to such men as were successful in pursuit of them was extended the admiring and well-nigh unanimous sympathy of the Cattle Country. However, these overreachings usually were launched against only such persons as, either not living in the West, were regarded as impersonal and hence as fair targets, or else, residing in the West, were generally disliked and so were considered legitimate victims.

As a whole, the matter represented principally a desire to teach the disliked East and England "another lesson."

The sharp practices rarely were aired in the courts. The denizens of the Cattle Country engaged in formal litigation and entered the courts only under either one of two conditions; *i. e.*, when they were dragged in by some aggrieved tenderfoot victim of an abortive local promotion scheme, or they, with confident reliance on the bias of a jury of friends, served process on an Easterner or Englishman. The tenderfoot victim rarely thus dragged a Westerner into court, because the stanch partisanship of the local juries was well advertised.

Such disputes between Westerners as were not settled by private treaty or on occasion across a gun's sights were quite apt to be submitted for adjustment to the local sheriff. He, jovial but firm, very friendly but sternly just, always courageous and everywhere regarded with esteem, arbitrated many such contests, and his decisions had morally the same effect as they would have had if he had been a circuit judge.

The cowboy had a very clearly defined regard for what he conceived to be the dignity of his calling, and would brook neither disparagement of his trade nor any act or statement which tended materially to belittle himself. He deeply resented seriously offered derision.

Easterners in general, wholly ignorant of the West, thought the cowboy wofully conceited. He was not so.

Many of his statements about projected action may have sounded boastful to such as were unacquainted with his capabilities, but these statements usually were launched as matter-of-fact announcements of readily performable plans. When the puncher said that he was about to ride what seemed to his tenderfoot auditors an unconscionable distance, he not only was going to do so, but doubtless had done so many times before.

Admittedly the cowboy was vain in a feminine way and displayed his vanity with boylike naïveté, but his apparent blatancy was not a direct bragging about himself. It was enthusiastic advocacy of his Cattle Country and of the people whom he loved. That he might be included among those people by his auditors was of course no drawback. But really the country and the people came first; and, when he thought of them, he instinctively gambolled like a lamb.

CHAPTER V

WHAT THE COWBOY WORE

THE clothing worn by members of the trade was distinctive. Although picturesque, it was worn not for the production of this effect, but solely because it was the dress best suited to the work in hand. Inasmuch as it was selected with view only to comfort and convenience, it knew nothing of variable fashion and suffered from no change in style.

It, however, was subject, as were many of the cowboys' customs, to differences in form according as the locality involved was the Northwest or the Southwest. The line of demarcation between these sections, though never very clearly defined, was in effect an imaginary westward extension of Mason and Dixon's Line, this extension zigzagging a bit in some places.

The hat was, in material, of smooth, soft felt; and, in color, dove-gray, less often light brown, occasionally black. It had a cylindrical crown seven inches or more in height, and a flat brim so wide as to overtop its wearer's shoulders. The brim might or might not be edged with braid, which, if it appeared, was silken and was of the same color as the felt. In the Southwest, the crown was left at its full height, but its circumference above the summit of the wearer's head was contracted by three or, more commonly, four, vertical, equidistant dents, the whole resembling a mountain from whose sharp peak descended three or four deep gullies. In the Northwest, the crown was left flat on top, but was so far telescoped by a pleat as to remain but approximately two and a half inches high.

Few men of either section creased their hats in the manner of the other. A denizen of the Northwest appearing in a high-crowned hat was supposed to be putting on airs, and was subject openly to be accused of "chucking the Rio," vernacular for affecting the manners of the Southwesterners, whose dominant river was the Rio Grande. Present-day Northwesterners, faithless to this tradition, have foresworn the low crown and assumed the peak. The United States War Department recently has flown into the face of history by formally designating the dented high peak as the Montana poke.

Around the crown, just above the brim and for the purpose of regulating the fit of the hat, ran a belt, which was adjustable as to length. The belt was made usually of leather, but, particularly in the Southwest, occasionally of woven silver or gold wire. The belt, if of leather, commonly was studded with ornamental nails, or, did the owner's purse permit, with "conchas," which were flat metal plates, usually circular, generally of silver, in rare instances of gold, in much rarer instances set with jewels. Rattlesnake's rattles, gold nuggets, or other showy curiosities not infrequently adorned the leather. For leather, some men substituted the skin of a rattlesnake.

From either side of the brim at its inner edge, depended a buckskin thong; these two thongs, sometimes known as "bonnet strings," being tied together and so forming a guard, which, during rapid riding or in windy weather, was pushed under the base of the skull, but which at other times was thrust inside the hat.

Did the brim sag through age or unduly flop, it could be rectified by cutting, near its outer edge, a row of slits and threading through them a strip of buckskin.

The wide brim of the hat was not for appearance's sake. It was for use. It defended from a burning sun and shaded the eyes under any conditions, particularly when clearness of vision was vital to a man awake or shelter was desirable for one asleep. In rainy weather it served as an umbrella. The brim, when grasped between the thumb and fingers and bent into a trough, was on its upper surface the only drinking-cup of the outdoors; when pulled down and tied over the ears, it gave complete protection from frost-bite. It fanned into activity every camp-fire started in the open, and enlarged the carrying capacity of the hat when used as a pail to transport water for extinguishing embers. The broad hat swung to right or left of the body or overhead provided conspicuous means of signalling; and, when shoved between one's hip or shoulder and the hard ground, it sometimes hastened the arrival of a nap. Folded, it made a comfortable pillow. No narrow-brimmed creation could have had so many functions.

A Philadelphian manufacturer virtually monopolized the making of at least the better grades; and, from his name, every broad-brimmed head covering was apt everywhere slangily to be designated as a "Stetson," instead of by either one of its two legitimate and interchangeable titles of "hat" and "sombrero." While these two legitimate titles were interchangeable throughout the West, the Northwest leaned toward "hat," the Southwest toward "sombrero."

There were slang names other than the one just mentioned, but none that had more than infrequent usage. These other names included "lid," "war-bonnet," "conk cover," "hair case," and a host of like inventions.

Southwesterners often wore, in lieu of the hat already described, the real sombrero of Mexico, with its high crown either conical or cylindrical, its brim saucer-shaped, and its shaggy surface of plush, frequently embroidered with gold or silver thread. No Northwesterner ventured, while in his home country, to "chuck the Rio" to the extent of such a head-gear.

Most of these sombreros, though reaching the American wearer by the route of importation from Mexico, had been made in Philadelphia by the very manufacturer who is mentioned above.

Along the Mexican border, some men, principally "Greasers," wore the huge straw hats of Mexico; but these head coverings were not often assumed by Americans, for there was a suggestion of peonage in the straw.

Many punchers had such vanity as to their hats that the makers gave, in the so-called "feather-weight" quality, a felt far better than that used in the shapes offered to city folk, and so fine as to roll up almost as would a handkerchief, a felt so costly that only ranchmen would pay its price, and thus they alone made use of it. Not infre-quently a puncher spent from two to six months' wages for his hat or sombrero and its ornamental belt.

Those hats and sombreros, while by Western classification "soft hats," should not be confused with the unstiffened, cheap felt hats worn by city-dwellers; for these latter head coverings, though admit-tedly "soft," were subject to the contemptuous accusation of being mere "wool hats." Furthermore the Range knew that the city-dwellers wore also "hard" or "hard-boiled" hats, subdivided into the two classes of, first, "derby" or "pot" and, second, "plug" or "stovepipe"; but no "hard hat" attempted, unless accompanied by a tenderfoot, to appear within the Cattle Country.

The handkerchief which encircled every cowboy's neck was intended as a mask for occasional use, and not as an article of dress.

This handkerchief, diagonally folded and with its two thus most widely separated corners fastened together by a square knot, ordi-narily hung loosely about the base of the wearer's neck; but, as the wearer rode in behind a bunch of moving live stock, the still knotted handkerchief's broadest part was pulled up over the wearer's mouth and nose. The mask thus formed eliminated the otherwise suffocating dust and made breathing possible. It offered relatively like protection against stinging sleet and freezing wind.

The cowboy did not dare risk being without this vitally necessary mask when need for it should come, and so he ever kept it on the safest peg he knew; under his chin.

In color and material the handkerchief, though sometimes of silk, usually was of red bandanna cotton; of red, not because the puncher affirmatively demanded it, but because ordinarily that was the only color other than white obtainable from the local shopkeepers. The shopping cowboy was very tolerant save in his selection of hats, chaps, spurs, guns, ropes, and saddles.

The handkerchief-selling shopkeeper in his own turn had followed the line of least resistance; and, being subject to no special demand for green, blue, or whatever, had forborne to make among the manufacturers a hunt for varied colors, and had stocked himself with an article which he readily could obtain, the red bandanna.

Thanks to the requirements of the Southern negro, this article constantly was manufactured. Thus the "Aunt Dinahs" of the Southern kitchens unwittingly dictated as to what the cowboy of the West should hang about his neck.

A relatively similar reason foisted the Texan heraldic star upon the saddles, bridles, chaps, and boots of many of the Northwesterners. The Texans, with their intense State pride, asked for this adornment, and the manufacturers, putting it on the Texans' accoutrements, standardized output, and starred the equipment of almost everybody who did not object.

White handkerchiefs were eschewed by many punchers, because these handkerchiefs, when clean, reflected light; and thus sometimes, upon the Range, called attention to their wearers when the latter wished to avoid notice by other people or by animals. Moreover white soon so suffered from dust as to appear unpleasantly soiled.

There was nothing peculiar about the shirt beyond that it was always of cotton or wool, always was collarless and starchless (not "boiled," "biled," or "bald-faced"); and, though of any checked or striped design or solid color, almost never was red. That latter tone was reputed to go badly among the cattle, and, in any event, belonged to the miners. Furthermore, the puncher's taste in colors was in the main quite subdued.

Collars were unknown. A white one starched would have wrecked its wearer's social position. This denying the ranchman a white collar did not withhold it from such of the professional gamblers as cared to wear it. A "turndown" collar of celluloid (of paper in the early years), provided the wearer's handkerchief and salivary glands occasionally functioned in unison, would make the gambler showily immaculate, and so would advertise apparent prosperity.

Each of the cowboy's shirt-sleeves customarily was drawn in above the elbow by a garter, which was of either twisted wire or of elastic webbing, and frequently, and as an exception to the general demureness of sartorial tone, was brightly colored, crude shades of pink or blue being much in favor.

Nor was there anything distinctive about the coat and trousers, which were woollen and, in cut, of the sack-suit variety; then, as now, the usual garb of American men, unless one regards as distinctive the fact that almost universally these garments were sombre in hue.

Possibly this predilection for black and darkest shades found its source in Texas and Missouri, where the frock coat, string tie, and slouch hat of the Southern "colonel" had ever been of black.

However, the cowboy sometimes substituted for his woollen coat one of similar cut, but made of either brown canvas or black or brown leather.

Denim overalls were considered beneath the dignity of riders, and were left to wearing by the farmers, the townsfolk, and the subordinate employees of the ranches.

The puncher's trousers, universally called "pants," stayed in place largely through luck, because the puncher both avoided "galluses," the suspenders of the tenderfoot, as tending to bind the shoulders, and also was wary of supporting belts, as the latter, if drawn at all tightly, were conducive to hernia when one's horse was pitching. However, if the puncher were of Mexican blood, he would gird himself with a sash of red or green silk.

In the mending of rents the safety-pin often functioned in lieu of thread and needle.

The pistol's belt, wide and looped for extra cartridges, ever loosely sagged, and so threw the weapon's weight upon the thigh instead of placing strain upon the abdomen.

When possible the cowboy went coatless, but he always wore a vest. The coat was arrestive to ease of motion. Also it somewhat invited perspiration, and perspiration for a man condemned to remain out of doors day and night in a country of cold winds was uncomfortable, if not dangerous.

In every-day life the vest was of ordinary, civilian type, and usually was left unbuttoned. It was worn, not as a piece of clothing, but solely because its outside pockets gave handy storage not only to matches but also to "makings," which last-mentioned articles were cigarette papers and a bag of "Bull Durham" tobacco.

Mixed in with these necessaries were, in all probability, a gold nugget, an Indian arrow-head, or an "elk tush" or two. These "tushes," the canine teeth from the wapiti's upper jaw, now widely known as insignia of a great secret order, were in the West of years ago equally well known as the most treasured jewels of the Indian squaw. Every cowboy acquired all the "tushes" he conveniently could, doing so usually with no purpose of ultimate trade with the Indians, but only because of a vague, boylike idea that somehow, some day, they might be useful. In reality, as he got them he gave them to Eastern souvenir hunters, as he also gave the nuggets and the arrow-heads.

This naïve predilection for so-called "natural curiosities" went hand in hand with desire to benefit either science or the federal government; was shared, in this public-spirited form, with the scouts and hunters, and worked for the inconvenience of the receiving clerks at the Smithsonian Institution. There flowed, for years, to the door of the latter's museum and from out of the West a steady stream of useless bones, horns, skins, crystals, pieces of wood, and other things, all enthusiastically started on their journeys and most of them ultimately and properly landing on the scrap-heap at Washington.

Men would undergo great personal risks to obtain "fine specimens."

The prevalent desire to patronize "The Smithsonian" was exemplified in the experience of two Northwestern scouts who had the same beneficent attitude toward science as had the punchers.

The Crow Indians had "jumped" their reservation and were on the war-path. They were being trailed by Taze-well Woody and James Dewing, Woody riding a horse, Dewing a mule.

These scouts discovered an enormous bald eagle, which, feeding at a carcass, was so gorged as to be helpless. The tremendous size of the bird suggested immediately that Washington was in great need of this fine specimen, so a heavy stick was brought down on the national emblem's neck, and the latter's immediate owner was then pronounced to be dead. The eagle's legs were lashed to the back of Dewing's saddle, while a thong held in place the folded wings of the hanging bird.

The men mounted, and forthwith a war party broke from cover and attacked them. The scouts spurred their mounts into a retreat, but were rapidly being overhauled by the Indians, whose ponies were fleeter than Dewing's mule. Meanwhile shots were flying.

Just as it began to look hopeless for the two whites, there happened simultaneously three things: First, a bullet struck the ground in front of the galloping mule, raised a flurry of dust, and caused the brute to spin around and to hurry toward the foe. Second, a bullet cut the thong which had bound the eagle's wings. Third, the eagle came to life, and, though with legs still fastened to the saddle, stood erect.

Then the charge completely reversed its direction and appearance. It had been to both whites and Reds a hundred armed warriors chasing two helpless victims. Now it seemed to the Reds a pursuing demon hastening to destroy a fleeing Indian tribe. What Woody witnessed was a screaming eagle with talons imbedded in the rump of a crazed mule, with wings outspread and beating the air, and with beak digging, amid the screams, into uncomfortable Dewing's back, while the mule rushed after the Indians, intermittently pausing to buck and bray, Dewing himself meanwhile shouting, cursing, and shooting.

The matches in the cowboy's pocket, like all matches on the Range, were in thin sheets like coarsely toothed combs. They had small brown or blue heads that were slow to start a blaze, and, for some time after striking, merely bubbled and emitted strong fumes of sulphur. To obtain a light, the West tightened its trousers by raising its right knee, and then drew the match across the trouser's seat.

There has been described the vest of every day, but there were occasional days which were not like every day, the occasional days when the puncher went in state either to town or to call upon his lady-love. On these infrequent and important errands, he was fain to put on a waistcoat which was specially manufactured for the Western trade, and which, though normal in size and shape, was monumental in appearance. Plush or shaggy woollen material was prey to the dyer's brutality, and on the cowboy's manly but innocent front the Aurora Borealis, and the artist's paint-box met their chromatic rival. A man of modest taste, and such were the majority of the punchers, was content with brown plush edged with wide, black braid. But what was such passive pleasure as compared with the bouncing gladness which another and more primitive being derived from a still well-remembered vest of brilliant purple checker-boarded in pink and green?

The overcoat was of canvas, light brown in color, with skirts to the knee, was blanket-lined, and, to make it wholly wind-proof, commonly received an exterior coat of paint; which latter process often successfully invited the sketching of the owner's brand upon the freshly covered surface.

All men donned gloves in cold weather; this, of course, to keep the hands warm. In warm weather most men wore gloves when roping, this to prevent burns or blisters from the hurrying lariat, and wore them also when riding bucking horses, this to avoid manual injury. But some men, regardless of temperature or the nature of their work, wore gloves all the waking hours. This latter habit, while an affectation, did not necessarily indicate effeminacy. It rather was an expression of vanity, and permitted the wearer tacitly but conspicuously to advertise that his riding and roping were so excellent as to excuse him from all other tasks. The hands of such men frequently were as white and soft as those of a young girl.

The ungloved fraternity, being without excuse for absence from the wood-pile, resented the fragile hands, though not their owners, and to visitors gruntingly descanted on the theme that it was "cheaper to grow skin than to buy it."

The gloves were sometimes of horse-hide or smooth-surfaced leather, but usually were of buckskin of the best quality. Whatever the material, they customarily were in color yellow, gray, or a greenish or creamy white, though brown was not infrequent.

They had to be of good quality, lest they stiffen after a wetting; for an unduly stiff glove well might misdirect a lariat throw, or even cause a man to miss his hold upon the saddle horn when he essayed to mount a plunging horse.

Practically all gloves had flaring gantlets of generous size, five inches or so in both depth and maximum width, the gantlets commonly being embroidered with silken thread or with thin wire of silver or brass, and being edged with a deep leathern or buckskin fringe along the little-finger side. The designs for such embroidery followed principally geo-metrical forms, and very often included a spread eagle or the Texan heraldic star.

Conchas not infrequently augmented the decoration.

When the thermometer was very low, either gloves or mittens of knitted wool or of fur made their appearance.

Almost always in the absence of gloves, and frequently when gloves were present, men wore tightly fitting brown or black, stiff, leathern cuffs, which extended backward for four or five inches from the wearer's wrist joint, were adjustable by buckled straps, protected the wrists, and held the sleeves in pound.

Although upon the Range any one not professing to be a puncher incased his feet in whatever form of leather covering he preferred, all cowboys wore the black, high-topped, high-heeled boots typical of the craft.

These boots had vamps of the best quality of pliable, thin leather, and legs of either like material or finest kid. The vamps fitted tightly around the instep, and thus gave to the boot its principal hold, for there were no lacings, and the legs were quite loose about the wearer's entrousered calf. The boots' legs, coming well up toward the wearer's knees, usually ended in a horizontal line, but sometimes were so cut as to rise an inch or so higher at the front than at the back. The legs were prone to show much fancy stitching. This was of the quilting pattern, when, as was often the case, thin padding was inserted for protective purposes.

A concha or an inlay of a bit of colored leather might appear at the front of each boot-leg at its top.

These tall legs shielded against rain, and supplemented the protection which was furnished by the leathern overalls or "chaparejos."

The boots' heels, two inches in height, were vertical at the front, and were in length and breadth much smaller at the bottom than at the top.

The tall heel, highly arching the wearer's instep, insured, as did the elimination of all projections, outstanding nails, and square corners from the sole, against the wearer's foot slipping through the stirrup or being entangled in it. The tall heel also so moulded the shod foot that the latter automatically took in the stirrup such position as brought the leg above it into proper fitting with the saddle's numerous curves. The heel's height and peg-like shape together gave effective anchorage to the wearer when he threw his lariat afoot, instead of from his horse's back.

The sole usually was quite thin, this to grant to the wearer a semi-prehensile "feel of the stirrup." To these necessary attributes, the vanity of many a rider added another and uncomfortable one, tight fit; and throughout the Range unduly cramped toes appeared in conjunction with the enforced, highly arched insteps.

The conventions of Range society permitted to the buckaroo at any formal function no foot-gear other than this riding-boot. It was as obligatory for him at a dance as it was useful to him when ahorse.

The puncher with vanity for his tight, thin boots, and with contempt for the heavily soled foot coverings of Easterners, "put his feet into decent boots, and not into entire cows."

In very cold weather, this boot sometimes gave way to one of felt or to the ordinary Eastern "arctic" overshoe worn over a "German sock," this last a knee-high stocking of thick shoddy. Save under such frigid conditions and save also when the puncher was in bed, his feet were ever in his leathern boots.

Spurs were a necessary implement when upon the horse, and a social requirement when off its back. One, when in public, would as readily omit his trousers as his spurs.

The spurs were of a build far heavier than those of more effete sections of the country. Their rowels were very blunt, since they were intended as much for a means of clinging to a bucking horse as for an instrument of punishment. This assistance to clinging was augmented in many spurs by adding, to the frame of the spur, a blunt-nosed, up-curved piece, the "buck hook," which rose behind the rider's heel, and which it was reassuring to engage or "lock" in the cinch or in the side of a plunging horse. A rider, intending to lock his spurs, usually first wired or jammed their wheels so as to prevent their revolving. Ordinarily, the rowels were half an inch in length, the wheel of which they formed the spokes being slightly larger in diameter than an American, present-day, twenty-five-cent piece; but spurs imported from Mexico, and having two-and-a-half-inch wheels with rowels of corresponding length, frequently were used in the Southwest as a matter of course, in the Northwest as an advertisement of distant travel.

Each spur, or "grappling-iron," as slang often dubbed it, was kept in place both by two chains passing under the wearer's instep and also by a "spur-leather," which last-mentioned object was a broad, crescentic shield of leather laid over the instep. This spur-leather tended as well to protect the ankle from chafing, and incidentally was usually decorated by a concha and stamped with intricate designs.

The shank of almost every spur turned downward, thus allowing the buck hook, if there were one, to catch without interference by the rowels, and also permitting the wheel, when the rider was afoot, to roll noisily along the ground. This noise frequently was increased by disconnecting from the spur one of the two chains at one of its ends and allowing it to drag, and also by the addition of "danglers." Danglers were inch-long, pear-shaped pendants loosely hanging from the end of the wheel's axle.

A cowboy moving across a board floor suggested the transit of a knight in armor. This purposely created jangle fought loneliness when one was completely isolated, and was not abhorrent in public, even though it might announce the presence of a noted man.

Not more specialized than the spurs but more conspicuous were the "chaparejos," universally called "chaps." They were skeleton overalls worn primarily as armor to protect a rider's legs from injury when he was thrown or when his horse fell upon him, carried him through sage-brush, cactus, or chaparral, pushed him against either a fence or another animal, or attempted to bite; but also they were proof against both rain and cold wind.

Take a pair of long trousers of the city, cut away the seat, sever the seam between the legs, and fasten to a broad belt buckled at the wearer's back as much of the two legs as is thus left. Then you have a pattern for a pair of chaps. Reproduce your pattern in either dehaired, heavy leather, preferably brown, but black if you must, or else in a shaggy skin of a bear, wolf, dog, goat, or sheep, and you have the real article. You must, of course, make your pattern very loosely fitting, have on the length of each leg but a single seam, and that at the rear, and do a bit of shaping at the knee. Should you employ dehaired leather, so cut it that long fringe will hang from the leg seam, and you might well cover this seam with a wide strip of white buckskin. You will hurt nobody's feelings should you stamp the leather here and there with frontier animals or with women's heads, or all over in tiny checkerboard, or should you stud the belt with conchas. In so doing you will be no inventor, but merely a follower of custom.

The long hair or wool upon a pair of shaggy chaps represented not so much artistic preference as it did judgment that thereby protection would be increased. Naked leather was not oversoft under a prone horse, and could not be relied upon to withstand the stab of either the yucca's pointed leaves or the spines of the tall cacti.

The cowboy wore chaps when riding and also when either within the confines of a settlement or in the presence of womankind. Chaps and his fancy vest, if he had the latter, were, in combination with his gun and spurs, his "best Sunday-go-to-meeting clothes," or what he called his "full warpaint." When there was no riding to be done, no social convention to fulfil, or there were neither jealousies to excite nor hearts to conquer, the chaps, unless their owner was either a slave to habit or very vain, often hung from a nail. They were heavy and, for a pedestrian, quite uncomfortable.

"Hung from a nail," to be truthful, is poetic license for "thrown on the floor." The Cattle Country, thoroughly masculine, "hung its clothes on the floor, so they couldn't fall down and get lost." Only saddles, bridles, lariats, and firearms received considerate care.

Fur coat and cap for winter use, of buffalo skin in earlier days or wolf pelt in later times, were regularly worn in cold climates, but were distinguishing not of the vocation but of the temperature. Generally they were not owned by the cowboy, but were loaned to him by his employer.

The conditions which called forth the furs often compelled a cowboy, as a preventative of snow blindness, to "wear war-paint on his face," that is, to daub below his eyes and upon his cheek bones a mixture of soot and grease. This made him look, as Ed Johnson said, like a "grief-stricken Venus."

Lastly and affectionately is recalled the horsehair chain, which was laboriously and often most excellently woven from the hairs of horses' tails. These chains usually were of length sufficient to surround the neck and to reach to the bottom pocket of the vest, and, at the lower end, had a small loop and a "crown knot" wherewith to engage the watch. They were a factor in the courting on the Range, for among cowboys it was as axiomatic that the female doted on horsehair chains as it now is among the cowboys' descendants that she has no aversion to pearl necklaces. The puncher, disdaining to shoot Cupid's arrows at his inamorata, essayed to lasso her with a tiny lariat made from the discards of his favorite pony's tail.

Ranch owners and such of their employees as were not cowboys dressed as did the cowboy; save that, having no dignity of position to maintain, they felt less compelled to wear fine quality of raiment and, as already stated, reserved the right to use foot-gear other than the conventional, high-topped boot.

A few of the ranch owners, either Englishmen or such Easterners as had been much in Europe, laid aside from time to time long trousers and appeared in shorts. These latter abbreviated garments, then still a novelty upon the Atlantic coast, were to the cowboy an enigma, a cause of irritation and an object of surprise and contempt. In the words of Kansas Evans, "Bill, what' je think? Yesterday, up to that English outfit's ranch, I seen a grown man walkin' around in boy's knee pants. And they say he's second cousin to a dook. Gosh! Wonder what the dook wears." "Knee pants" were resented as being un-American, and they cost their wearers no small loss of caste upon the Range. None save a ranch owner would dare appear in them.

CHAPTER VI

SADDLES

RIDING SADDLE, ITS NAMES, SHAPE, COMPONENT PARTS AND VARIOUS ATTACHMENTS—LATTER'S NAMES AND USES—MERITS OF SINGLE RIG AND DOUBLE RIG COMPARED—FURTHER SADDLE ATTACHMENTS, THEIR NAMES AND USES—CAMPING AND CAMP-COOKING—STILL FURTHER SADDLE ATTACHMENTS—FONDNESS FOR SADDLE—SADDLING—ADVANTAGES AND DISADVANTAGES OF STOCK-SADDLE—WESTERN RIDING RECORDS.

THE riding saddle of the cowboy merits description, not only because it was the cowboy's work-bench or his throne, according as one cares to picture it, but also because one cannot understand the puncher's ability to ride the bronco except one understands the saddle.

Unless there had existed that particular form of saddle, no man could have ridden the Western horse in the Western country under the conditions that obtained long years ago. There would have been no cowboys and no ranches. The plains would have been forced to wait for their empeopling until the unadventurous farmer slowly had pushed Westward. The course of Western history was determined by that saddle.

The riding saddle universally used upon the Range was of the type which, throughout the West, was known as "cow saddle," "Range saddle," or, more commonly, as "stock-saddle," and in the East was called "Mexican saddle," "Western saddle," or "cowboy saddle." It perhaps should have been termed Moorish rather than Mexican, for, in almost its present basic form, the Moors carried it from Africa to Spain over a thousand years ago.

The flat English saddle the cowboy termed a "human saddle," "kidney pad," or "postage stamp." He regarded it as a token of effeteness, not as an accoutrement for a horse.

All stock-saddles were alike in fundamentals, though they varied in incidental details.

The height and angles of the horn and cantle, and whether the seat were short or long, wide or narrow, whether it were of approximately uniform width or more or less triangular, whether it were level or sloped upward toward either the horn or the cantle or toward both, whether the horn were vertical or inclined forward, and whether its top were horizontal or were higher at its front edge than at its rear were all matters purely of the rider's choice; save that the cantle had to be high enough to prevent the lariat-thrower from slipping backward when his cow-horse after the throw squatted on its haunches and braced itself. Also followers of the Texan custom of fastening the lariat's home end to the horn before the lariat was thrown required at least a fairly high horn. Such men had to have not only the space thus occupied but also additional room for "snubbing," because, the instant the lariat caught its prey, the lariat had to be wound for a few turns around the horn; i. e., to be snubbed.

The several slight variations in shape created special names; and a saddle was designated, according to the form of its tree, as California, Brazos, White River, Nelson, Oregon, Cheyenne, etc.

The American ranchmen's saddles were built by professional manufacturers and not, as commonly in Mexico, by the cowboys themselves.

Extremely stout construction was required to withstand successfully the terrific strains from roping.

Upon the front end of a strongly built hardwood "tree," comprised of longitudinal "fork" and transverse "cantle," was bolted a metal horn; and the whole, covered with rawhide, was fastened down onto a broad, curved, leathern plate which rested on the horse's back. This plate in its entirety was called the "skirt," unless one preferred to differentiate and to refer to the half of the plate on the horse's left side as one skirt, the "near" or "left" skirt, and to the half on the horse's right side as another skirt, the "off" or "right" skirt, and thus, when mentioning the two halves collectively, to term them as "skirts" instead of as a skirt.

Synonyms for skirt and skirts were respectively "basto" and "bastos" (from Spanish "basto," a pad or a pack-saddle), though some men restricted these latter terms to the leathern lining of the skirt, a lining known also as the "sudadero."

On each side of the horse there lay on top of the skirt a leathern piece which was shorter and narrower than the skirt, fitted closely around the base of the horn and cantle, and had its outer edges parallel with, but well inside of, the borders of the bottom and rear edges of the skirt. This leathern piece was the so-called "jockey." It usually was in two sections, its portion forward of the stirrup-leather being termed the "front jockey," while so much as was aft of the stirrup-leather was styled the "rear jockey."

The composite structure fitted onto the horse's back in the same way as would have done a headless barrel if halved lengthwise, and to the entire barrel-like portion of the saddle was colloquially applied the term bastos, although that term had technically the more restricted meaning stated above.

In infrequent instances the skirt and the rear jockey extended backward no farther than to the cantle, and then there was sewn to the latter's base an "anquera," a broad plate of leather which covered the

TOP LEFT: SPADE BIT. TOP RIGHT: "SINGLE RIG" STOCK SADDLE,
NELSON TREE. BOTTOM: SPUR WITH BUCK HOOK.

otherwise exposed portion of the horse's hips, and protected the clothing of the rider from his animal's sweat.

The skirt of usual size stretched from the horse's withers to his rump, and well-nigh half-way down both his flanks. It had so much bearing surface that the saddle tended to remain in position even without the aid of a "cinch." A large skirt was necessary when riding buckers or when roping; but for ordinary pottering about a few ranch owners used a saddle the skirt of which was much curtailed.

Whether the saddle should contain a "roll" was a matter of the rider's individual choice. Some men used the attachment, others did not. A roll was a long welt which stuck out for a third of an inch or more from the front face of the cantle just under its top rim. This cornice-like addition tended to keep the rider from sliding backward out of the saddle during roping and from moving skyward when his pony was bucking.

The saddle was attached to the horse either by one "cinch" passing under the animal at a point approximately even with the stirrups, or by two "cinches," respectively designated as the "front" and the "hind" or "rear cinch," and passing one just behind the animal's front legs and one some twelve inches further to the rear. The saddle of two cinches was designated technically as "double-rigged" or "double rig"; popularly and in pistol-maker's phrases as "double fire," "rim fire," or "double-barrelled"; while the saddle of one cinch had, as its corresponding terms, "single-rigged," "single rig," "single fire," "centre fire," and "single-barrelled," and often was also called "California rig," this last because Californians commonly used but one cinch.

However if a person, while using colloquial language, wished to make technical subdivisions among single-cinched saddles, he would limit "centre fire" to the saddle in which the cinch was either slightly behind the stirrups or, at most, even with them, and would specify as "three-quarters" rig the saddle in which the cinch was in a slightly more advanced position.

Some Texans called the cinches "girths," and the rearward of them the "flank girth."

Whether a saddle should be single or double rigged was a matter of its owner's preference. The single as compared with the double was more easily put on and taken off, was a bit more flexible in riding motion, but it was more apt to shift position during roping and bucking and upon steep trails.

Riders differed greatly in the direction and force of the thrusts which they imposed upon their saddles. With creating this result, the men's weights in actual pounds had but little to do. The controlling factor was the method of sitting the saddle. Some riders of however much or little poundage ever kept themselves not only in balance upon the horse, but also in balance with it. Such riders made no pulls or pushes that by antagonizing the horse's movements subjected the saddle to twisting or dislodging strain. Horsemen of this type could go for miles without retightening cinches, rarely galled their horses' backs, always could ride their steeds long distances without an undue tiring of the brutes, and, save in roping or bucking or when upon steep "side hills," little needed to care whether their cinches were loose or taut. Such men were called "light riders." They each might weigh two hundred pounds and yet "ride light." Of such men, some used a saddle with single rig; others preferred the riding motion of the double rig, or thought the latter a more prudent risk and so employed two cinches.

Still other riders were by the nature of their saddle-sitting forced to employ the double rig, and thus to "carry their pony in a shawl strap." These latter riders would on occasion get out of balance, and would rectify themselves by impulsive twists and yanks. They would sway a bit across and not in strict accord with the line of the horse's motions. All this would tend to divert the saddle from its normal position. Such riders "rode heavy," had frequent cause to taughten latigos, and caused many a saddle sore upon their ponies' backs. These men could cling to the bucker and throw the rope as successfully as could their "lighter-riding" brothers, but they "gimletted" or "beefsteaked" far more horses' backs and tired far more ponies.

Finally, in certain regions, the prevailing type of local horse had a chest so short and sloping as to give insufficient anchorage to but a single cinch; while, in other regions, the shortness of the corresponding horses' "barrels" gave little room for the double rig.

Users of double rig were careful to obey a regulation prescribed by horses and requiring that the front cinch be tightened before the rear one be pulled upon. This rule was strictly enforced by the animals, which, upon its infraction, waited only till the offender had mounted before they went into executive session. Many a tenderfoot, unmindful of this order of procedure, has "hit the ground," "sunned his moccasins," or "landed," which is to say, in other forms of Range English, has been "spilled," "chucked," or "dumped," in any case to hear that conventional, derisive call: "Hi there! You've dropped something." Many a competent rider has been furnished with conclusive if circumstantial evidence that, during his absence, cinches had been tampered with.

Sometimes with a double rig the cinches, to avoid a sore, or more firmly to grip a sloping chest, were crossed below the horse, making a letter X.

Galled backs and cinch cuts were common, but usually were ignored by the riders, who credited the ponies with having iron constitutions. Certainly the animals seemed to suffer little pain from their skin abrasions.

Usually the under surface of the bastos was smooth. If so, there was put between it and the horse's back some form of padding, either a shaped pad called a "corona" or else, more commonly, a folded blanket; and under the corona, or blanket, for ventilating purposes was placed a gunny-sack. In some saddles the bastos was lined with woolly sheepskin, and in such case the padding was omitted.

The "cincha" or, as usually termed, the cinch was a broad, short band made of coarsely woven horsehair or sometimes of canvas or cordage, and terminating at either end in a metal ring. On each side of the saddle-tree was attached, for each cinch, a second metal ring called the "rigging ring," "tree ring," or "saddle-ring," and from which hung a long leathern strap called a "latigo." This strap, after being passed successively and usually twice through both the cinch ring and the corresponding tree-ring, was fastened below the latter by much the same method as that in which the present-day masculine "four-in-hand" necktie is knotted. The latigo on the saddle's off side was permanently left thus fastened, and, in saddling and unsaddling, operations were restricted to the strap upon the near side.

A variation from this method of fastening the latigo was often used on the near side during the breaking of a horse. A wide, metal buckle offered a speedier means of attachment, and haste was desirable when the steed was plunging.

While camped within a forest, punchers had carefully to guard their latigos, because, for some inscrutable reason, the latter bore to porcupines the same relation that candy does to children. It was no uncommon thing to see a dismounted puncher, when not using his saddle as a pillow, hang it from a limb or place it on a pole fastened horizontally and high above the ground.

The rough cinch adhered well to the horse's body and offered a good hold to the rowels and hooks of the spurs. While the cinch was, strictly speaking, merely the broad band, the term customarily was applied to the combination of both this band and its own two latigos.

Despite the stout material of the cinch and latigos, one of them occasionally would break under the strain of bucking, whereat both saddle and rider would disappear from the horse's back. Out of this not infrequent occurrence arose the myth of the prudent cowboy who, in his cinch, substituted lead pipe for woven hair.

From each side of the saddle hung vertically, in unequal lengths, the two leaves of the "stirrup-leather," which was a broad strap looped through the saddle's tree. The end of the longer leaf was passed through the stirrup's top, and then was made fast to the bottom of the shorter leaf. A buckskin thong, threading a series of holes in the two leaves, provided means of fastening and ability to adjust length; a thong, instead of a buckle, because so far as possible metal was excluded from the saddle. The cowboy not only wished his outfit to be susceptible of immediate repair, but he had faith in the durability of leather and none in that of metal. He might countenance the use of buckles upon saddles used for breaking horses in the corrals near the ranch-house, but he wished no buckles under him when he was riding far afield.

It was this reliance upon simplicity as conducive to sureness that made him prefer his pistol to be of single, rather than of the slightly more complex double action.

Each stirrup-leather hung, as already stated, from the saddle's tree. These two leathers at their starting-point almost met behind the horn, and, severally leaving, one to the saddle's right, the other to the saddle's left, rested in shallow grooves cut in the wood of the tree. In some saddles, the seat's leathern covering, starting forward from the cantle, went only to this groove's rear edge. In other saddles, this covering extended over the entire seat and completely hid the upper portion of the stirrup-leathers. Technical names were given to these two forms of seat covering. They were respectively "three-quarter seat" and "full seat."

Where each stirrup-leather emitted from the saddle's side, was overlaid a flat leathern plate. This plate, known indiscriminately as the "seat jockey" or "leg jockey," shielded the rider's leg from chafing.

Sewn to the back of each stirrup-leather was a vertical, wide leathern shield, the "rosadero"; sometimes, though incorrectly, called the "sudadero." It protected from the horse's sweat and offered stout defense to the rider's leg.

At the bottom of each stirrup-leather, was a stirrup made of a wide piece of tough wood bent into shape, bolted together at the top, and so sturdy as to defy crushing by a falling horse. Into the stirrup went the rider's foot clear to the latter's heel, his toe pointing inward and either horizontally or downward. The sides and front of the stirrup were ordinarily enclosed by a wedge-shaped, leathern cover open toward the rear. The technical name of this cover was "tapadero," though colloquially this almost always was shortened into "tap."

Commonly each side of each of the "taps" was in the form of a triangle with apex pointing downward, and was so long that this apex barely escaped the ground; but some men used "taps" which, following the historic Spanish model, were shaped somewhat like horizontally laid coal-scuttles. The "taps" prevented the rider's feet from passing completely through the stirrups, being snagged by brush, or being bitten by a savage horse. When long and flapped under a ridden steed, they were of no small use as a whip.

"Open" stirrups, *i. e.,* "tapless" ones, were rarely seen upon the Range.

From each side of every saddle hung four sets of thongs, two thongs in each set. One of these sets was at the saddle's front, one near its rear, while the other two were spaced so that the rider's leg just passed between them. The two sets of rear thongs embraced whatever might be laid across the saddle behind the cantle, almost invariably the "slicker," which was a long rain-coat of yellow oilskin such as coastal fishermen wear; though in the Southwest the thongs instead of this sometimes confined a Mexican "serape." The front and side thongs held any package of the moment.

If a cowboy were starting on a trip which, while forcing him to camp overnight, did not call for many supplies and a consequent pack-horse, he would, nevertheless, not limit himself to the traditional Hudson Bay Company's ration of a rabbit track and a cartridge, but would insert within the folds of the "slicker" tied at his saddle's rear the journey's necessaries. These were a frying-pan, some flour, bacon, coffee, salt, and, as a substitute for yeast, either a bottle of sour dough or a can of baking-powder.

When halting time arrived, the camp was pitched wherever both forage for the horse and drinkable water met. The water, though drinkable, was not always pleasing, for it might taste somewhat of sheep, contain the carcass of a steer, or be girt by banks marked with the telltale white of alkali. It might be so full of sand as to demand admixture of juice from a cactus leaf before showing clearness. It might be so warm as to suggest the betterment of cooling in a porous earthern jar clad in a wet blanket and hung aloft for evaporation's chilling aid. Will power, hard boiling, and a cactus leaf were available to do away with unpleasant thoughts, with ptomaine dangers, and with floating sand, but the earthern jar would be at the distant ranch and unattainable. Thus the uncomplaining cowboy sometimes, as he said, "drank his cold water hot." Fortunately most of the Western waters were not of this unpleasant sort.

Occasionally, in the desert, water was either non-existent or else so alkalinely saturated as hopelessly to "rust the boilers" of whoever drank it. In the latter case, although the horses were left grimacingly to gulp the biting fluid and run the risk of being "alkalied," the men might have recourse to canned tomatoes. The liquid portion of the can's contents assuaged thirst and counteracted the effect of the already swallowed alkali dust, while the solid vegetable wiped across one's face would heal the bleeding cuts which that cannibalistic dust had made. A tomato might occasionally be pressed against a pony's lips for their comforting.

The can-opener was irresistible, since it was a pistol fired horizontally at the can's top edge.

The pitching of camp was a simple process. It consisted of stripping the saddle and bridle from the horse, of turning the latter loose to graze either at the end of a picket rope or within the grip of hobbles, and finally of building a fire. Lighting the fire was not always an easy matter, for matches might be wet or lost. Then it would call for powder from a dissected cartridge, and the igniting of it by a pistol-shot. Careless aiming might "hang the kindlings on the scenery."

If, as was usually the case, the camp's coffee were unground, its beans were mashed on a rock with the butt of a pistol. The resultant mixture of vegetable and mineral substances was set aside until the frying-pan should have cooked, first, bread and, next, bacon.

The bread was quite eatable. With a thick batter spread thinly over the bottom of the pan, the latter was laid upon hot coals for a moment and until a lower crust had commenced to form. Then, tipped on edge, it was held far enough from the fire for a little heat to reach it and to raise the loaf. This achieved, the pan, still on edge, was pushed to within baking distance of the coals, and was left there until the pan's contents were done.

The thus baked bread, the historic "frying-pan bread" of the West, vacated the pan, and into the latter went strips of bacon. When these had been fried, the pan was rapped against a rock or tree, to expel such of the grease as readily would leave, and then received a charge of water and the coffee-gravel mixture. When the boiling fluid was fairly well covered with fat melted from the utensil's sides, the dose-like beverage was ready for consumption.

There might be a slice or two of jerked meat from either beef or elk, or else, long years ago, from buffalo.

All this crudity was due not to epicurean depravity, but entirely to the restricted transportation facilities which beset the cowboy as well as the scout, the trapper, the prospector, and the explorer.

The menu of the puncher upon his travels rarely became more extensive than the one described above. A pack-horse, when there was one, indicated quantity rather than variety of food. But it did insure the presence of a coffee-pot.

The lee side of a rock or bush, the saddle for a pillow, the slicker and horse blanket for a covering, a pile of wood for replenishing the fire, collectively made the bedroom and its furnishings.

> "The moon now cleared the world's end, and the owl
> Gave voice unto the wizardry of light;
> While in some dim-lit chancel of the night,
> Snouts to the goddess, wolfish corybants
> Intoned their wild antiphonary chants—
> The oldest, saddest worship in the world."*

Tents and extra bedding, because of their troublesome carriage, were almost unknown even in winter. In the latter season, burrowing under the snow protected the sleeper from the wind, while logs placed side by side atop the snow made a platform for the fire.

In cold weather the puncher, when thus afield, customarily took to bed with him his horse's bridle, that the bit might be kept warm and the horse be spared the pain which mouthing frigid metal would have caused.

Camping in the colder climates was often a trying process marked by nocturnal contests between soporific desire and rheumatic pains, a contest which vacillated according as a sleepy hand dropped fuel upon the fire or the embers chilled.

However, the topic under consideration is the cowboy's saddle and not his troubles.

There might be at the base of the saddle's horn a "buck strap," which was a loop that offered a convenient hand-hold during pitching. Its owner never bragged about its presence. Top riders scorned it, and excluded it from their saddles.

Not infrequently a pair of leathern pockets bestrode the saddle, sometimes behind the cantle, more rarely at the horn. These receptacles were called either "cantineses" or saddle pockets.

The word "cantineses" was used also figuratively, and in colloquial usage was extended to include any heterogeneous medley of small

*From "The Song of Hugh Glass," by John G. Neihardt.

objects. In this latter sense and particularly when qualified, as often it was, by the word "little," the expression was equivalent to the homely New England phrase, "small contraptions."

If the saddle were being used in desert country, then from the horn might hang a pair of felt-covered, metallic canteens, or two water-bottles of leather or of coated canvas.

The leather of the entire saddle, inclusive of taps and stirrup-leathers, usually was covered with handsomely impressed designs of leaves and flowers. A saddle, if so decorated, would cost, in the decades of the seventies and eighties, some fifty dollars. In the Southwest, occasionally not only was silver laid into the groundwork of the impressed designs, but both the horn and cantle were subject to be ornamented with precious metal. Then the cost assuredly mounted. Ten months' wages often went into decoration. At least one ranch owner had a horn and cantle each of solid gold.

Often on the cowboys' saddles there was applied a homemade ornamentation consisting of brass nails or, again, of rattlesnake skins plastered flat and permanently stuck fast by their own glue.

The saddle's coloring was usually light brown; but sometimes, and especially in the less expensive saddles, it was cherry-red.

Each saddle best fitted its special owner, for it gradually acquired tiny humps and hollows that registered with his anatomy, and induced both comfort and security of seat. These little mouldings, which suited well the owner, would often fight the contour of a stranger's legs. Wherefore each man swore by his own saddle and at all others. Texas Ike, in good faith and with generous impulse, said: "Jim, don't bother to get your saddle. Ride mine. It's the best that ever came out of Cheyenne. It's as comfortable as a trundle-bed." Jim mounted, squirmed, grunted, and in equally good faith remarked: "Tex, where in hell did you ever find this Spanish Inquisition chamber anyhow? You must be using it like the priests wore hair shirts."

A cowboy so valued his saddle, particularly after it had been broken in, that he almost never would part with it. He has gone so far as, in a poker game, to lose his money, gun, chaps, horse, and even shirt, and then, with saddle on his back, to "strike out" for the ranch still thoroughly cheerful and with "his tail up." Even such punchers as upon completion of the Texas Drive returned to Texas by rail instead of on horseback carried their saddles with them.

Moreover, it was a bit disgraceful to sell one's saddle. It was akin to disposing of the ancestral plate and family jewels. The phrase "He's sold his saddle," became of general usage, and was employed in a figurative way to denote that anybody in any calling had become financially or morally insolvent. Years ago in a little school at Gardiner, Montana, a small, tow-headed youth, when asked by the teacher as to who Benedict Arnold was and what he had done, replied: "He was one of our generals and he sold his saddle."

Because the saddle from its shape and large bearing surface had so good a hold on the horse's back, riders usually, except when on fractious animals or in a mountainous country, let the cinches sag loosely. This gave comfort to the lungs within the confining straps. The horses aided in procuring this sag, for Western steeds, when being saddled, puffed themselves like adders at the first pull on the latigo. They might be momentarily thrown off their guard by a kick behind the ribs, but the beasts reconcentrated their attention upon inhaling before the strap could be pulled again.

To "cinch up" any bronco (he was "cinched up," not merely "cinched"), one had to place one's foot against the brute's ribs and, in the case of the front cinch, to pull with almost all one's strength upon the latigo, meanwhile standing ready to dodge precipitate bites from the indignant head-tossing bronco. Pulling upon the rear cinch exacted much less muscular effort, but much greater circumspection; for bites were apt to be more frequent, and good measure might throw in a kick or two.

The cowboy's saddle was not suitable for racing. It was too heavy, thirty pounds at the very least and usually forty pounds or over. But the usual and useful gaits of the Range were not of racing speed. They were the running walk, the jiggling trot, the lope, with now and then a short dash after errant live stock.

The cowboy's saddle well-nigh inhibited jumping of hurdles. Its occupant, the instant he assumed the posture necessary to encourage his horse to "take off," lost his balanced seat, and was, from the saddle's shape, unable to cling, as on the English tree, by constrictive force. But there were few hurdles upon the Range.

Nor could a rider, when in this saddle, rise to the trot. But the cowboy did not wish to rise. In his own language, he "postage-stamped" the horse.

Nevertheless the saddle was ideal for the service in which it was used.

It made wholesale roping possible. It made possible riding the American bucker. It made possible long and compulsory rides on animals so indifferently broken as to have been unserviceable under a seat less secure. It made possible the "night herd," because it permitted the tired cowboy to sleep while still ahorse. Repeatedly men on herding

"CINCHING UP"

From a photograph by L. A. Huffman

duty were, through storm or other circumstance, kept upon their task for forty-eight consecutive hours. In the wild nights of winter, the most courageous puncher did not dare to permit his pony chance of escape, so there were cat-naps in the saddle, rather than more restful sleeps beside a picket pin.

The saddle offered its occupant opportunity to sit in perfect balance, and such a seat was the one best suited to the type of horses and to the character of riding which were involved. The saddle's occupant, because with body entirely relaxed and legs at full length and hanging flexed below him, was shifted from and had instantly to regain his equilibrium at every movement of his steed. The rider thus reverted to the primitive and subconscious balancing practised by the walker, the skater, and the bicycler, each of whom is ever righting a wrong position. The horseman with subconsciousness thus alert sensed through the stiffening muscles of his animal plan for untoward action, and thereby was forewarned of intended whirls, balks, or jumps.

At first sight, the horseman when at high speed appeared perhaps a bit grotesque, for his elbows were extended to either side, were held even with his shoulders and bobbed up and down, his hands were close together and before his chin, his legs hung loosely and straight downward, and his relaxed body, never rising from the saddle, swayed in seeming semidrunkenness. At second sight, the observer realized that all this mutualized the rider and his pony into rhythmic motion, and that the rider's security of seat came from the synchronizing of man and beast.

This attention to the time beat was what insured the seat even during bucking, the spurs and buck hooks giving but incidental aid. It was what enabled the buckaroos in graceful swoops to lean from galloping horses and pick up objects from the ground. It was what permitted the acrobatic puncher to drop from a moving animal and mount another plunging past.

Finally, the stock-saddle was the almost universal pillow of the sleeping cowboy whether in the bunk house or afield.

It was on such a saddle that Leon, a Mexican, changing horses, traversed in 1876 one hundred miles in four hours, fifty-seven minutes; in 1877, five hundred and five miles in forty-nine hours, fifty-one and one-half minutes. It was on such a saddle, though one of light weight, that, in a still earlier year, F. X. Aubrey of the Pony Express rode across-country eight hundred miles in five days, thirteen hours.

Those homely-looking leathern structures helped to make the West, and should be regarded with affectionate respect.

CHAPTER VII

BRIDLE, LARIAT, AND QUIRT

FROM the saddle's horn usually hung the so-called "quirt" (from Mexican "cuarta," a whip; and this, in turn, from Spanish "cuerda," a cord), a flexible, woven leather whip, which, exclusive of its lashes, was some twelve inches in length. Its upper end ordinarily was filled with lead, this "loading" providing means to strike down a rearing horse which threatened to fall backward. To its lower end were attached two long thongs as lashes. A loop extending from the upper end, or head, provided means of attachment to either the rider's wrist or the saddle's horn.

In some sections of the country the whip consisted of a short wooden or iron stock carrying a lash a yard in length.

The quirt, occasionally in slang termed the "quisto," was all-important to the man who, as a "rough-riding bronco-buster," or, as sometimes called, a "flash rider," broke his horses, not by patiently weaning them from their desires, but by "busting their spirit."

Another intimate with the saddle was the reata.

"La reata" of the Mexicans became on the Range the "reata" (Spanish for rope), "lariat" (contraction of Spanish "la reata"), "lasso" (from Spanish "lazo" meaning a snare or slip-knot), or "rope," though the word lasso very rarely was used and then only by visitors from California, and when employed served only as a verb. Rope was the usual term, with reata, particularly in Wyoming, as a close second. Lariat and rope, like lasso, might be used as verbs; reata might not.

So much for the dignified synonyms. "Clothes-line," "lass rope," and "string" were occasional alternates.

The rope, when not in use, was gathered into a coil some eighteen inches in diameter and hung from a spot which, below the base of the horn, was on whichever side of the saddle its owner preferred. Some men used the near side, other men the off, according as to which side was found the more convenient for rapidly moving hands. The thus stored rope was held in position by passing through the hole in the centre of the coil either a looped thong, the two ends of which were permanently attached to the saddle, or else a strap, one end of which was similarly attached; and then either dropping the loop over the horn, or else fastening the strap's outer end to a metal buckle planted at the horn's base.

In the earlier days of the Range the rope was made usually of buffalo-hide, but the later cowboys threw ropes of rawhide or, particularly in Texas, of fine hemp.

If of hide, they commonly were a half inch in diameter and were braided from four strands, sometimes from as many as eight. If of hemp, their diameter ordinarily was three-quarters of an inch. They varied in length from a minimum of forty to a maximum of seventy feet.

The loop was formed by passing one end of the rope through the "hondo" at the rope's other end. This hondo, or, as often called, "honda," was sometimes a cunningly devised, knotted or spliced eyelet, each in the rope itself and lined with smooth leather; sometimes a metal ring; but more commonly was a stout rawhide or brass object, shaped like an inverted letter "U," with a bar across its opening and firmly attached, at the middle of the bar, to the rope.

Lariats varied in length, not only because of the differing capabilities or preferences of their wielders, but also because of differences in the methods of using them. Although the manner of enlarging the noose and throwing it was universally the same, the home end of a Texan's rope very commonly, before the throw, was tied by a half hitch to the saddle horn. No such fastening was attempted in the far Southwest or in the Northwest, except by occasional men, and by them only when roping animals of light weight.

Because the last few feet at the home end of a thus "tied" lariat were necessarily passive, the user of that style needed more length in his rope than did the man who threw a "free" reata and thus, in other technical, interchangeable terms for this form of throw, "dallied," "daled," "vuelted," "felted," or "dale vuelted," his rope. Each of these five interchangeable terms was derived, seemingly, from the Spanish phrase "dar la vuelta," which means to give a turn to a rope or to belay it.

Practically speaking, the Texan used a long lariat, but actively employed only a part of it.

Conscience compels the reluctant admission that the average Southwesterner, and particularly the Texan, not only outthrew but also outrode his more northerly average brother, and that the Mexicans were the most expert of all. The Mexicans outrode as regards ability to stick to the horse's back, but they were a failure as producers of well-broken steeds. Their cruelty begat equine cussedness that never was outgrown.

The Mexicans, however, did not reach that limit attained by the Apache Indian when the latter not infrequently rode his horse to exhaustion and then dismounted and ate the beast.

Sometimes the puncher, for the fastening of his horse when afield, carried on his saddle a hempen stake-rope or picket-rope, or else bore there a line of woven horsehair.

This horsehair line was useful for picketing, and laid about one's bed was supposed to keep rattlesnakes away. Tradition had it that certainly no snake, and probably no centipede, scorpion, or tarantula, would cross its scratchy surface.

The wooden stake, which was driven into the ground and to which one end of the picket-rope was attached, was called by many Texans a "putto," a word derived from the French "poteau," meaning a post.

A lariat was hesitatingly used for picketing last it be cut by dragging over rocks; although when new it would be trailed from a saddle's horn, and thus, under human oversight, would be pulled along the ground in order to induce suppleness.

The Western world divided on the subject of picketing into two camps; of which one stoutly maintained that a horse's neck was the only place proper for fastening the rope, the other sect equally holding out for a front leg. Many an hour in many a place was spent in supporting or attacking the alleged merits of each system. The mere fact that by no possibility could there be involved any question beyond whether it were his animal's neck or its leg that the rider preferred to jeopardize never curtailed debate.

This subject for argument was the one best liked, because custom permitted that, when it was under discussion, close holding to the title was not compulsory. Invariably sooner or later somebody interjected the collateral title: "What makes a pinto the hardest bucker of all, and a walleyed white horse the next hardest?" The propositions involved in this quoted collateral title were traditional and untrue, but were powerful producers of logic.

At times the debaters would stray off to the topics as to what hole rent, if any, the owl and rattlesnake paid the prairie-dog, as to the comparative merits of single- and double-rigged saddles, and as to why all Easterners and Englishmen were so "plumb wuthless and ornery"; but sooner or later picketing and the wall-eyed white horse would come triumphantly to the fore.

Although any cowboy gladly would drop at any time into a picketing debate, he ordinarily did not picket his horse at all, but instead "hobbled" it. A few men used the United States Government's form of "hobble," a leathern cuff buckled about each of the fore legs above the pastern joint, the two cuffs being connected by a short, swivelled chain. The great majority of men produced the same result through a wide band of cowskin or buckskin, or, more commonly, through the diagonally cut half of a gunny grain sack, either of them so applied that there was reproduced by knots the effect of the cuffs, and by twists a rope which took the place of the chain. With the cowskin or buckskin, a buttonhole and wooden button, or cross-stick, sometimes, were substituted for the final knot.

The purpose of the picket-rope and of the hobble was self-evidently to hold the fettered animal at its rider's camp. Hobbles did not always achieve this result, for many horses became proficient in a ludicrous but effective gait, wherein the hind legs walked while the front legs coincidentally made short jumps forward. An adept would thus hop several miles in a night. Mares were the worst offenders in this hoppity-skip method of flight. To forestall this retreat, some brutes were hobbled by connecting a front and a rear leg instead of the two front legs. This fore-and-aft hobbling was designated as "side-lining," unless the legs involved were on opposite sides of the horse, in which case some men called it "cross-hobbling."

Picketing and hobbling were employed only about a camp. At the ranch, a horse, if not placed in a corral, was turned loose, to be rounded up when needed. He and his fellows were usually content to stay within hearing of the bell, which ever hung from the neck of some eminently respectable old horse that long since had proved its unwillingness to stray far from home.

The bridle and bit deserve mention; the bridle because of the specialized form of its reins; the bit because, to speak enigmatically, it either was specialized to a high degree or did not exist at all.

The bridle, "head stall," or, as the West often termed it, "bridle head" most commonly employed was in form like the ordinary equestrian bridles of world-wide use; and like them comprised, when complete, a "crown piece," "brow-band," "throat latch," and, on either side, a "cheek-piece," and had no special characteristic beyond that frequently the brow-band was omitted, and not uncommonly hooks, instead of buckles, were used for attaching the bit. These hooks, one on each side, were shaped like a letter "J," the shorter stem being sewn to the bottom of the cheek-piece, while the longer stem rose vertically above the horse's mouth.

Another and common form of bridle was highly specialized. It consisted of a single strap, which terminated at each end either in a buckle or in such a hook as is above described, and thus was fastened to the bit. The strap was passed above the horse's head and was held in place by the simple expedient of longitudinally slitting the strap far enough to permit the horse's ears, or at least his left ear, to project through the slitted opening. The strap, in order that its length might be adjustable, usually was in two pieces, which were connected by a buckle.

The bridle, whatever its form, was made ordinarily of straps; but sometimes for some or all of the straps were substituted finely plaited leathern strips or else cords of braided horsehair. The bridle was subject to be ornamented at the horse's ears by conchas, and throughout by tassels and pendants of horsehair or leather. A few men possessed bridles made wholly of woven silver wire, but these ornate constructions were used only in affairs of state such as love-making and holiday trips to rival ranches or to town.

The reins, but one on each side of the horse, were, at the saddle end, either "tied," i. e., fastened together (if so, not uncommonly continuing into a flexible whip which thus attached was called a "romal"), or else they were left "untied." Most men preferred this latter form, as with untied reins a rider, when thrown, was spared the danger of being entangled; and furthermore, a bridled horse turned loose was little apt to be ensnared in brush.

Rarely was a Western horse made fast to anything after his rider had dismounted. Usually the reins were merely thrown directly forward over the horse's head and allowed to hang downward from the bit and to the ground. The animal was then at liberty to wander about and graze, and would make the most of this opportunity unless the reins, when thus thrown, had fallen across a tree limb or the bar of a hitching rack. In this latter contingency the horse almost never questioned appearances; and, convinced that he was firmly fastened, fearful lest he make a pull upon his cruel bit, was wont to stand patiently with sagging head for hours at a time before a horizontal branch or spar, and to attempt no more activity than an occasional nibble at his fancied cross.

Presently out came his rider, who, picking up the reins, was careful not to replace them over the horse's head until ready to mount, for reins over the head was the equine starting gong.

The nag was led away from the rack. The rider, standing in front of the near shoulder of the animal and facing toward its tail, seized with his right hand the near stirrup, twisted it half-way around, and held it in that position. The left hand threw the reins over the horse's head and simultaneously caught the horn. That same moment the left foot went into the stirrup. Instantly thereafter the right hand either also clutched the horn or else swung at the end of a fully extended arm, four hoofs moved, and the rider was fairly snapped into the saddle.

Sometimes, and particularly with a horse prone to lunge to the rear, this method of mounting was varied to the extent of seizing, with the left hand, either the horse's left withers, or the bridle's left cheek-piece, while the right hand grabbed the horn.

Some athletic men, scorning the stirrup, trusted wholly to their grip upon the horn, leaped from ground to saddle, and thus made a so-called "flying" or "running" mount; what the programmes at modern Wild West shows term a Pony Express mount.

In any of these forms the animal's quick start was for a competent rider an aid to mounting, because the jerk it created tended to throw the rider upward.

Swift movement by the mounter was necessary, for otherwise his horse might innocently move from under him, and furthermore so thoroughly might resent slow motion as to begin to buck.

The reason for this particular resentment was that Range horses as a class were creatures of habit, and, however docile when meeting accustomed conditions, nevertheless were apt to object to any happening that was unusual. They had been broken at high speed, and expected its continuance. Objection ordinarily was expressed in terms of pitching.

All ranchmen while breaking a horse stood at the latter's left when placing the saddle on the brute's back, and made the mount not only with swiftness but also, and unlike Indians, always on the animal's near side.

Ever afterward, it was on its near side that the thus semi-broken Range horse expected human beings to effect their initial close approach. As a result, if a prudent ranchman had occasion before mounting to make a saddle adjustment on his steed's off side, he would open negotiations from the beast's opposite flank, and then half circumnavigate the brute, preferably by the head rather than the heels route. Under the latter circumstances the horse, suspicious, would preserve an armed neutrality, but would stand ready to repel boarders from the right.

Usually before mounting, the right rein was held in shorter grip than was the left, this tending not only to prevent bites but also to swing the starting horse under the ascending rider. Neglect of this precaution has laid prostrate more than one tyro, whose horse, with no motive save impatience, has "whirled" and thus, like a compass needle, changed its direction but not its locality.

The reins always at the mount were kept fairly taut. A horse was more apt to buck at the moment of mounting than at any other time, and he could not buck with satisfaction to himself unless allowed to put his head between his front legs, to "stick his bill in the ground." The top of his horse's head was a pleasing sight to the man halfway into saddle, and few in this defenseless position resented the absence of that taunting warning: "Good-night, Ears."

All this relates to the mounting of already "gentled" animals, or of animals which, although never previously ridden, tacitly promised reasonably decent behavior.

Brutes suggesting "trouble," supposed to be "mean horses," were saddled, bridled, and mounted while impotent under the imprisonment of the reata, and frequently while "blinded" by a cloth tied over the eyes. Either a lariat about each foot pulled the latter to either side, with also the front feet well forward, the hind feet equally far to the rear, thus reducing a virile entity to the plane of a flare-legged, sway-backed table; or else a lariat about both front legs, a second reata about both hind legs, drawing them to front and rear, threw the animal prostrate on his flank. The rider climbed into the saddle upon the momentary table, or stood astride over the prostrate if latent earthquake, and called "shoot," "turn lose," "ease up," "throw off," or "let her go." In any case, "she went wide, high, and pretty," and "rollicked all over the lot," while from the side-lines came much unwelcome advice to "stay with it," to "cinch her when she bucks," to "rise to the trot," to "tickle her feet," to "waltz with the lady," to "throw in your hooks"; comments such as "frolicsome little beast," "real hunk o' death," and "cutey, little grave-digger"; and came also perhaps the babyhood message of "upadaisa."

Upon the signal the human ends of the holding-ropes had "eased up," the "blind," if any, had been snatched off, and the theretofore leashed beast slowly kicking free from its bonds suddenly had realized its freedom and had acted accordingly.

It is stated above that a horse, to buck with satisfaction to himself, should insert his head between his knees. Upon mounting an animal that was standing and was free from the grip of any lariat, the rider, if attentive to drawing in the reins, could hold up the beast's head and so discount a plan to pitch; but human ingenuity never evolved a scheme for controlling a fettered horse's neck and divorcing the brute from his wish to bathe his rider in the stars. A horse, if held by lariats and standing with legs pulled to front and rear, was compelled, for keeping his balance, to stretch his neck forward and downward. This gave him a gambling chance, which he almost invariably won as against his rider; for the horse could move his head still a few more inches downward before the rider could drag it rearward. The head once getting low enough, pulling on the reins made matters worse, for this tended not to raise the head but to haul it directly toward the horse's knees. A horse, if held by lariats and if prone, had to be given free rein that he might rise, and this free rein rarely could be drawn in before the brute's head started toward the danger point.

Often a careless rider already safely mounted, having thus far held his animal's head above what physicists well might term the centre of deviltry, let loose the reins, to see an equine head go down and feel a human form go up.

Westerners usually dismounted as rapidly as they mounted, employing for the purpose either a single stirrup or none at all. The rider, whether using or scorning a stirrup, might with one or both hands grasp the saddle horn, and, during the descent, swing his body so violently that as his leading foot struck the earth he would spin part of the way around and face almost with the horse. He also, if acrobatic, might make a running dismount by throwing a leg over the horn and sliding diagonally forward and to the ground. At high speed, this exit from the saddle required skill. With the horse walking, it was a common route, but then it lost its title of "running dismount."

Dismounts were made ordinarily on the horse's near side. However, if the rider were quick in his motions, his animal, without undue opposition, would allow him to use the off-side route. This equine tolerance arose from the fact that, though the horse might make violent objection to being mounted on the off side and so receiving its load by an unconventional avenue, it did not deem to be equally important the direction by which the load left, provided it surely and speedily departed.

This off-side egress nevertheless might have human objectors, for, in some parts of the Range, notably in Texas, it was an insult to a man for a rider to go near him and without apparent excuse to dismount to the rider's right. It suggested that the rider intended to employ the body of his horse as a protective breastwork, to "roll his gun," which is to say, "to set his gun agoing," and thereby to "put windows in the skull" of the citizen thus rudely approached. The affronted citizen would be justified, if he "dug for" his own "blue lightning," "talking iron," "lead-pusher," or "flame-thrower," and "unravelled some cartridges."

Even when about to dismount on the near side, a rider, if in the presence of strangers, usually saw to it that he on alighting should not have his horse between himself and the strangers. Courtesy forbade the seeming barricade. So, before dismounting, he ordinarily took pains either to halt to the right of the strangers or else to turn his horse into proper position.

A very few ranchmen, principally Englishmen, used ordinary bits of snaffle or straight bar form, but such men were negligible in number.

The bit regularly employed was often a thing of beauty, and always an instrument of latent torture. Artisans were wont to fashion into intricate designs the cheek-pieces and the bar or chain connecting them at their bottom ends, to garnish them with gold and silver inlay, and to apply conchas wherever there was room. Derived by the Range directly from Mexico, the bit was of the Spanish and earlier Moorish type, either in pure form or modified, as its owner saw fit, and according to the absence or extent of these modifications it was classified as "ring bit," "spade bit," or "half-breed bit."

If the bar in the horse's mouth humped up in the middle like a narrow croquet wicket for two or two and a half inches in height, and within this hump, or port, were a "roller," that is a vertical wheel with broad and corrugated rim, and there were added no other attachment save possibly a curb chain, the bit was "half-breed."

If, for the hump, there were substituted a "spade," a piece shaped like a broad screw-driver three to four inches in length and bent backward at its top, there was thereby created a "spade bit." This was the bit most commonly used. Not content with attacking merely the roof of the mouth, the severity of the latter bit ordinarily was augmented by inserting in the spade, at its bottom or at both its top and bottom, a "roller," and by adding two wires for which there was no particular name and which, closely strung with short metal tubes, extended from the sides of the spade to the inner sides of the cheek-pieces. The wires and spade punished respectively the cheeks and the roof of the mouth. In rare instances the top of the spade was sharply notched.

More than merely an occasional man employed a metal ring which, fastened at the top of the port or near the summit of the spade, according as to which was present, and passing through the horse's mouth, surrounded the lower jaw. This ring, more common in the Southwest than in the Northwest, gradually tended to disappear from both these sections, but remained in general use in Mexico. The presence of this ring gave to the bit, despite any other attachment the latter might have, the generic name of "ring bit."

Fiends at times added to all these things barbed wire, and exulted in the "tool-chest" thus produced; but fiends were frowned upon.

The reins were fastened, usually, not to the bit itself but to chains six inches or so in length and depending from it. The pony could not chew the chains asunder, and furthermore they gave forth a pleasant, clanking noise.

The function of the bit was to suggest physical suffering rather than to cause it. During an animal's good behavior, his reins sagged in his rider's hand, since every broken horse was bridlewise, and turned to right or left at the slightest pressure of the appropriate rein upon his neck. A strand of yarn would have sufficed to guide the beast. He was thus tractable because he ever kept in mind the latent possibilities of the contents of his mouth. Incidentally, though he instantly would have turned to the right if the left rein were pressed against his neck's left side, he would not have comprehended the meaning of a pull upon the right rein alone.

Even stopping a horse produced almost no strain upon the reins. The stop usually was brought about not so much through the rider's pulling with his left hand, however feebly, upon the reins, as it was through his coincidently raising his right hand to the lariat-throwing position, and perhaps, at the same time, prosaically saying "whoa."

All broken horses were thus "bridlewise," and most of them would respond also to guiding signals given by the rider's legs or hands. A push on, say, the right side, if made near the animal's hind leg, would turn him to the right, while, if made on the shoulder or neck, it would turn him to the left.

In times of equine peacefulness, the bridled pony steadily champed the roller of his bit, which, until the reins were tightly pulled, was a pleasant thing upon which to work the tongue and emitted an amusing, rattling noise. In caterance to this desire of the Western horse for constant, familiar and pleasant sound to break the otherwise awesome silence, there was devised the "cricket," a little "roller" which was inserted in a colt's bit and produced small result beyond a chirping noise.

The highly trained horses ridden when stock was being tended and the lariat was swinging, called "cow-ponies" by the Northwesterner, "cow-horses" by the Texan, were accustomed to stop short as the reata left the thrower's hand, and fairly to snap themselves into a posture akin to that of a sitting bear. A horse of this ilk mentally associated the lariat with all movements of the rider, so that either quickly extending an arm from the side, or else a sudden raising of the reins, was apt to shoot the animal into a burst of speed, while he was as prone to stop, almost in his tracks, upon the vertical raising of a hand. Often has a friendly wave by the empty hand of an equestrian novice sent him "grass-hunting" through the sudden jump, or equally sudden stop, which was ordered but not expected.

The antithesis of the severe bit was the "hackamore" (from Spanish "jáquima," a halter). This was sometimes an ordinary halter which carried reins instead of a leading rope, and which offered to the rider no more control over his horse than mere pressure on the beast's neck could effect. More commonly it was a bridle which had, in lieu of a bit, a so-called "bosal," a leathern, rawhide, or metal ring around the horse's head immediately above the mouth. The reins were attached to the bosal, and their pulling operated to shut off the horse's wind. English ranchmen occasionally called the bosal a "cavezon."

The bosal stayed in position through being attached both to the bridle's two cheek-pieces and also to a looped cord commonly made of braided horsehair, and passing from the bosal's front upward and over the top of the horse's head. This cord was termed the "fiador," or sometimes, in corrupted form, the "theodore."

The hackamore, even when rigged to its limit of efficiency, did not possess the bit's cruel possibilities, but commonly was used on the initial ridings of a horse which was in the process of being broken. Some riders continued its use on their broken animals, ruling their horses more through exercise of human personality than through mechanical means.

Mere leading halters, whether in the form of the Eastern stable halter with a short rope attached or else evolved out of various turns and knots in a longer and continuous piece of line, often were, in the loose language of the Range, termed hackamores.

The hackamore, whether used for riding or for leading, might, like the bit, have allied with it an illicit companion, the "ghost cord," a thin string tied about the tongue and gums, and thence passed below the lower jaw and up to the rider's hand. This string with its ingeniously devised ties was, in competent hands, an instrument of either mental diversion or extreme cruelty. Specially effective forms of it known to some men were jealously guarded by the latter as secrets of value.

This ghost cord should not be confused with the "twitch" or "twister," although the latter abomination sometimes used by "rough-riders" was on occasion called a ghost cord. The twitch was a small loop of cord with a stick through it, and was employed to punish a held horse. The loop was placed vertically around the animal's upper lip, and then was tightened by twisting the stick. Often the horse would fairly scream from pain.

There thus have been inspected almost all of the cowboy's paraphernalia, and it is time to meet him face to face and to see him in action.

CHAPTER VIII

EQUIPMENT AND FURNISHINGS

A COWBOY was hired to work at a ranch. He arrived there, wearing clothes such as have been described, and mounted on a horse with accoutrements such as have been outlined. If he had further personal belongings—and these the West called his "plunder," as the East termed them "dunnage" or "duffle," he would be accompanied by a second horse bearing on a pack-saddle parcels of modest size.

The cowboy's extra belongings would be scant in number, would include few, if any, luxuries and certainly few useless objects beyond possibly some ore specimens.

Each of such useless objects and of such luxuries, particularly if it were small in size or novel in construction, was apt to be called a "dofunny." This word in its plural form of "dofunnies" might be given a wider significance, and denote also the entire personal belongings regardless of their character. When used in this sense, it was synonymous with "plunder."

The West employed two types of pack-saddle, respectively designated as the "cross-buck saddle" (usually contracted into "cross-buck") and the "aparéjo."

The cross-buck was named from its similarity to the frame known as cross-buck or sawhorse and used by wood-cutters, and was the usual civilian pack-saddle. The aparéjo rarely appeared save in the Southwest or upon the federal government's animals.

The cross-buck consisted of two short, parallel planks connected together at each of their two ends by a stubby, wooden, Saint Andrew's cross, which rose vertically and fronted at a right-angle to the saddle's length. To these two crosses were fastened the ropes that held the pack in position during the time that its principal fastening, the so-called "lash rope," was being applied. The saddle laid upon padding and lengthwise of the horse's back, one plank on either side of the animal's spine, was fastened to the brute by two cinches. The saddle was always double-rigged.

The aparéjo was a stuffed, leathern pad which covered the back of the horse and both his sides.

Whichever form of saddle was employed, its load was made secure by a lash rope, which was a continuous line some thirty feet in length, was cunningly interlaced about the load, and was connected with each end of a special cinch that rested below the horse's chest. One species of this interlacing, if made in strict accord with established formula, produced on top of the pack the figure of a diamond, and thus gave to this species its name of "diamond hitch." It would be so called regardless of whether it were either a "one-man diamond," or else took the slightly different weavings of a "two-man" or "government" "diamond." The hitch, when correctly thrown, was remarkable for its ability to absorb the slackness generated at any particular point, and firmly to imprison the held packages within its grasp.

It was regarded with considerable respect because it had been so great a factor in Western transportation. Consequently, the Cattle Country resented the sight of a sloppily thrown diamond, just as it resented the sight of an untidily rigged saddle, just as every one everywhere resents the appearance of a military uniform worn awry. As soon as a tenderfoot succeeded in throwing a diamond hitch upon a pack, he thereby ceased to be a tenderfoot. Every Westerner shot a glance at the lashing on every laden pack-animal he passed, and, when he spied the hammock-like, rope-consuming weavings by a pilgrim, he grinned.

No self-respecting man would speak of tying a diamond. It always was described as "thrown," though the so-called "squaw hitch," another rope-weaving for attaching a pack, might be "thrown," or "tied," or made fast by any word the speaker selected.

The arriving cowboy's parcels with their "plunder" contents doubtless consisted of commercial gunny-sacks which had been promoted from their original function of holding grain to that of serving as travelling-bags; and which, when in the latter rôle, commonly were termed "war sacks," though they sometimes, in the Northwest, were called "pokes," or else "porfleshes," or "parfleshes," this last term, whichever way spelled, being a corruption of the dictionary's word, "parfleche."

Incidentally, throughout the West, the word "sack" almost wholly displaced the word "bag," and this latter word was used rarely save as a verb and in the sense of "to capture."

The war sacks were laid directly upon the pack-saddle, one on each of its sides and one atop it, unless the cowboy happened to be in the Southwest. In which latter event, all or a part of the parcels might have been stuffed into "alforjas," which were wide, leathern or canvas bags, one on either side of the animal and hanging from the crosses on the saddle's top.

That Spanish word alforja suffered much from American spelling, for it was forced to appear also as "alforge," "all-forche," "alforki," "alforka," and in divers other forms.

If our cowboy owned the horses with which he arrived, he turned them into a corral, that they might accustom themselves to the neighborhood and cease desire to "strike out" for their former home. But probably the horses as well as the pack-saddle had been borrowed either from our friend's last employer, or from some more neighboring ranchman who had provided substitutions for what the more distant, late employer originally had loaned.

While a cowboy invariably furnished his lariat, bridle, riding saddle, and his clothing other than possibly cap and overcoat of fur, he rarely owned the horses on which he rode. He was hired to ride other people's animals, and seldom was the proprietor of any live stock. This infrequency of proprietorship prevented him from more often than very occasionally setting to profitable use the combination of his knowledge of horse-flesh and his gambling proclivity. Then, too, only village-dwellers, farmers, and passing Indians offered a trading field. Otherwise, the classic, horse-swapping deacon of the bucolic novels would have had a rival.

Bud Jackson, at daybreak, left a New Mexican ranch and returned to it soon after nightfall. He departed and returned upon the same gaunt, buckskin horse, Old Buck; but, in the interim of mere hours, Bud had made eleven horse trades, in each of them obtaining a little cash. In the first trade he had exchanged Old Buck for a bay pony and five dollars. Then Bud, in rapid succession and for short terms, owned pintos, roans, and brutes of other colors. Finally, just after dark when close scrutiny was difficult, he swapped to an unsuspecting Englishman a sleek but useless animal in return for good Old Buck and a bit of money. Thirty-seven dollars represented the earnings of the day.

Horses and never cattle were the subjects of such trades. The puncher, like the Eastern deacon, could see no sporting element in swapping cows, and thus never attempted it.

But we must return to our friend, the newly hired cowboy, who, despite our loquaciousness, is endeavoring for our benefit to arrive with his saddle-horse and pack-animal.

If our friend had borrowed his horses, both of the latter would be stripped of all their trappings and turned loose, to make inquisitive approach to other horses grazing within sight, indignantly to be rebuffed, and then with injured mien to begin in single file their homeward trip. The pack-saddle would be returned to its owner at the first convenient opportunity and without fail.

The term "borrowed," as employed a few lines since, was not intended to convey any sinister suggestion. While horses willingly were lent, nobody but a thief would take one however temporarily or however far out on the Range, unless with the owner's clear permission or unless the taker were in real distress, a distress so real that he dared risk that its patency later could exculpate him. Robbing a rider of his horse easily might effect in a sparsely watered country the most cruel form of destroying human life. The West in self-defense refused to permit a thief to plead that his stealing had been done under humane conditions, that the crime had not put any one afoot, and with common voice prescribed the punishment.

Wherefore horse-stealing earned either death by hanging, or, if the vigilance committee were tolerant, life banishment from "these parts," preceded often in the latter case by loss of the upper half of an ear, a mark which was distinguishing and lasted to the grave.

Long hair could overhang the scar, but long hair in itself was regarded as suggesting this purpose of screening or else as indicating a desire to be in appearance though not in fact quite "tough and wild." Consequently long hair did not meet with public approval. A man with a "load of hay on his skull" might be an actual "bad man," but usually he was diagnosed as being either weak-minded or a mere "bluffer." Long hair was of course permissible to any one who wished to grow it, but the extravagantly hirsute failed materially in personal popularity.

The punishment for horse-stealing, once established, was promptly and arbitrarily extended to include the taking of cattle; though cattle thieves ordinarily were rather leniently dealt with, and when raiding for political reasons, as in Wyoming's "Rustler War," were condoned by the public.

The vigilance committee of years ago was no hot-headed lynching party bound to claim a victim. It was the people acting directly instead of through their formally elected or appointed representatives. It gave due process of law commensurate with frontier conditions, and aimed to support, not to subvert, justice.

That soberness of thought underlay the whole matter appears from the fact that the vigilance committees accorded their prisoners actual, if informal, trials, often acquitted, and, when convicting, frequently prescribed as the penalty banishment and not death. Then, too, when death was prescribed, the committees, with respect for law's long-established usages, subjected the prisoner to hanging done with orderliness and decency. The single difference between executions by one of these popular tribunals and those by sheriffs in Eastern States was the Westerners' enforced substitution of a moving horse, box, barrel, or wagon-tail in place of the sheriffs' falling drop.

It is true that the vigilance committee sometimes killed with bullets, but it was only when the accused, resisting arrest, "put up a fight."

The committee held in reserve as a punishment for attacks upon women the awesome "staking out" upon an ant-hill, a punishment almost never called into play. The few cases of its alleged infliction were recorded by tradition rather than by history, though its possibility of infliction was a forceful affirmative deterrent to the evil-minded.

Tradition relates that on rare occasions men were lynched because they erroneously had been supposed to have been the perpetrators of a particular crime with which in fact they had had no connection, but tradition adds that each such victim was known to have performed at least one other act which by itself would have warranted the rope. Thus, while there may have occurred an error in judicial process, there had been none in moral result, even though some low-browed individual might seem merely to have been "hung on his merits."

The vigilance committee never advertised what it had done, or where or how "the event" had occurred, and ever sacredly guarded death-bed confessions of guilt. No non-attendant at the final scene would, if wise, question upon the subject any man who had been present there. This meant on the part of the committee's members no cowardly screening of themselves from the officers of statutory law. Merely, the West considered lynching, however necessary, to be a nasty job, and did not like to talk about it.

However, despite the ban of secrecy, history by chance has recorded the last words of a few lynched men. Some of these ante-mortem statements were picturesque and rather inducive to goose-flesh.

Boone Helm, about to be hung at Virginia City, Montana, and standing beside the gallows from which writhed the body of one of Boone's gang, made this peroration: "Kick away, old fellow. I'll be in hell with you in a minute. Every man for his principles. Hurrah for Jeff Davis. Let her rip." At another time, George Shears more plaintively said: "Gentlemen, I am not used to this business, never having been hung before. Shall I jump off or slide off?"

But the "strangulation jig" is not a pleasant subject. Let us once more rejoin the arriving puncher.

His journey had represented for him a slow, steady grind of several days, and would have been hopelessly monotonous except for various little happenings, for the bigness of the sweeping views, and for the bubbling joy of living which nature saw fit to give through Western air.

Upon the trail there were always happening little things which gently amused the plodding traveller's mind, but did not rob him of the purring, sensuous pleasure that comes from staying half asleep.

The marks upon the trail contained mile after mile a definite, accurate log of the doings by every recent user of the way.

On either hand between the path's edge and the horizon was space where from time to time occurred something to arrest the eye.

A hundred yards away, two sharply pointed ears warily rose above a bush. Presently under them appeared the inquisitive, impudent, disreputable face of a coyote. He gazed inquiringly a moment, and then commenced a retreat, at first made with studied slowness and frequent stops for rearward observation, but finally changing in a second and after a derisive, laughing howl, into a distance-consuming lope.

A mile or so further along the trail and squarely in it, a flat-domed disk of blotchy brown heaved, ran out at one side into a waving stream that led at once into a coil. Then came a shrill, vibrant whir. Our traveller's horse, with a tiny bit of fear, with unlimited abhorrence, and with a prudently cocked eye, deflected three feet or so to the side; and having gingerly rounded the snake, dropped back into the trail and ambled onward.

Some moments later, up popped a jack-rabbit, one ear erect, the other hanging limply. He gave a preliminary hop or two, a shake of his stubby tail, a few, bewildering, zigzag jumps, shot forward, and was gone.

From time to time, antelope rose from their beds, and like undulating, white-feathered arrows skimmed over the sage-brush.

Small isolated lots of cattle here and there in the distance ate their way along in restless feeding, or, strung out behind a leader, were travelling at interchanging walk and trot from the spot they had just deserted to nowhere in particular.

Far overhead was an eagle which, for many minutes and with stiff-set, wide-spread wings, had been cutting circles of a mile's diameter; but he suddenly dropped like a stone to within two fathoms of the ground, landed fluttering on the plain, melted into the verdure, and passed out of sight.

All the way, our traveller's pack-horse, true to type, had, when not towed by a lead rope, been seized periodically by violent thirst or equally insistent hunger. This desire for water always had manifested itself when the trail was far above the stream, while all desirable food had seemed to lie near the summits of steeply sloping hillsides. Wherefore some of the progress of our cowboy had been varied by détours and showered with swear-words.

He will swear at us unless we quit our own détours, so let us from now on stick by his side.

There was nothing unusual in the structures of the ranch to excite his curiosity: merely the typical layout, namely a main building, a cowboys' bunk house, a barn with open shed attached, a hitching-bar, two or more corrals, and, for purpose of obtaining water, whatever appliances local conditions demanded.

Had not surface water abounded at the ranch, there would have been near the barn a windmill on tall metal stilts, and adjacent to its base a series of watering-troughs; or, had there been no sufficient water-supply, either subterranean or on the surface, there would have appeared a "tank," a hollow in the ground with its bottom and its sloping sides lined with hard-packed clay and designed to collect whatever rain might fall. In quite arid countries, these tanks were scattered about the Range, and thus opened to the live stock many miles of otherwise unusable grass-lands.

But in fact the ranch was beside a creek. While, had the latter's banks been low, there would have been a convenient water system consisting of a series of ditches, the banks inconveniently were high. Wherefore there was a road pitching down to the creek's edge and used by a horse-drawn pair of wheels bearing a trunnioned barrel, and was also a "go devil," this last a taut wire which stretched from the bank's top to an anchorage in mid-stream and carried a travelling bucket.

The corrals, called in parts of Texas "round pens," were all circular in form and built of stout, horizontal, wooden rails which were supported by posts set firmly in the ground. The corrals were circular, that there might be no corner into which a pursued animal might dodge, or into which an entering herd might crowd a beast to its physical injury. Always the rails were lashed to the posts by strips of green rawhide, which contracted as they dried and made the entire structure as rigid and as strong as though it were of iron. The structure had to be unyielding, for it received tremendous shocks.

Connecting two of the pens was very likely a narrow fenced lane, which, without regard to orthography, the West termed a "shoot," and which was used in the branding of the maturer cattle. Fifteen or twenty beasts at a time would be crowded into it, to prevent struggles while the branding-iron was doing its searing work.

The West ran true to form when it changed "chute" to "shoot," for previously its Riviere Purgatoire had been mispronounced into Picketwire River.

The barn held the oats and baled hay which, bought at considerable expense and hauled from the railroad, were to supplement bunch-grass or buffalo-grass as food for such horses as drew the wagons. They were called "work horses." They needed strong diet and to be sure of not missing meals.

The operation of placing harness upon a horse as well as that of attaching the beast to a wagon was styled "hooking up." The verb "harness" was rarely used in the Cattle Country.

The barn possibly contained also stalls for sheltering, during hard winter storms, the little group of "kept-up" saddle-ponies. In the better weather, however cold, such live storage was effected in the corral. Always a few horses were thus "kept up" near the ranch-house in order that, under any circumstances and at any instant, a saddled animal surely could be obtained. Not uncommonly they were termed "night horses."

Save for the hitching-bar, the corrals, and the "shoot," there was no fencing, for there was no field of grain or hay, no patch of vegetables, no garden of flowers.

Range animals were required to procure their own food; and this they found in the wonderfully nutritious if apparently wilted grasses that, in little, widely separated tufts, were scattered over the plains, and, according to their several varieties, went by the respective names of "bunch-grass," "grama," or "gramma," "grass," and "buffalo" or "mesquite" "grass." Of all the grasses, it was only these so sun-dried as to be half hay that were of interest to the live stock. Occasional beds of vivid green might to human eyes appear to offer a luscious meal, but the beasts knew that they either harbored viciously stinging flies or would yield merely unappetizing reeds.

Not until the later days of the ranching industry and then only upon the smaller establishments, was any attempt made to grow food for the animals. This effort was limited to the raising of a small lot of hay or alfalfa, which in severe winter weather was dispensed to the weaker cows which had been "brought up" for feeding purposes to the vicinity of the supply.

Except on little establishments near the towns, no vegetables were grown. Such "greens" as the country at large ate "grew in cans," as did also all the milk and cream. He who would have attempted to milk a Range cow would have dared pluck lightning from the skies.

Eggs, too, were imported, for hens were absent from the Range almost as completely as were cathedrals. The imported eggs, coming as they did from commercial raisers in the East, were termed "States' eggs," while the output of the few hens that pecked about the "cow towns," virtually the only hens within the Cattle Country, were known merely as "eggs." These latter objects, whether because lacking the glamour of importation or because of the usually bedraggled appearance of their parents, if parents be the correct word, were not regarded as highly as were the crated "States' eggs." Eggs were the only subject in which the West conceded that the East was its superior. The West, dazzled by the Eastern quantity and thus blinded to the West's greater freshness, agreed with Sad Hooper's dictum at Laramie: "I dunno why it is, but them Eastern men lays eggs betteren we do."

Even near the settlements, gardens were rare and betokened the presence or imminence of womenfolk. When an unmarried man, a "batch" or "bach," planted a few irregular rows of onions, it plainly evidenced that Cupid had been in action.

Flowers were restricted to the bloom of the wild seedlings scattered on the roofs of the ranch buildings and amid the sage-brush, and to the geraniums, begonias, and fuchsias that in such houses as sheltered women rose from tin receptacles which in early life had been tomato cans.

There appeared no wagon ruts, because the vehicles went forth but thrice annually, to the round-ups of spring and fall, these up the Range, and once in the autumn to town for a year's supply of food.

Our friend, having rid himself of his horses, turned toward the main building or "shack," the "ranch-house," and joined the group which was waiting for cookie to blow upon his horn or more aristocratic conch shell, and thereafter announce either "Grub pi-i-ile" or "Come and get it."

The ranch at which our friend arrived was one of size sufficient to employ numerous men. There was the foreman, who sometimes was referred to as the "cock-a-doodle-do," the cook who, if, as commonly, white, was to his face called "cookie" and behind his back was spoken of as the "old woman" or "old lady." But if, as in rare instances, the cook were a Chinaman, these entitlements of cookie and old lady severally were supplanted by "John" and "that damned chink."

As further employees, there were several riders and also two or three ex-punchers, who, efficient in their halcyon days and later victims of physical injury, were virtually as pensioners now on both the constant pay-roll for wages and the somewhat intermittent record for work.

These pensioners "helped up," and thus did all the odd jobs upon which the cook and cowboys welched—teaming, cutting wood, drawing water, "wrangling" the saddle-horses, and making repairs to buildings, harnesses, and wagons.

Thus there were on the scene at least ten or twelve men all ready, able, and willing to argue.

Possibly there was an additional man in the form of a passer-by who had imposed himself upon the hospitality of the ranch. Every traveller had vested right to enter any ranch-house at any hour of the day or night on any day of the year, whether the regular inmates were present or absent, and to expect food and shelter for so long as both his necessities demanded and he did not abuse his privilege. There was not a lock on any door in the Cattle Country.

Such a visitor, if forced by his own necessities to travel on, and if in actual distress, might, in the inmates' absence, help himself to food requisite for the journey to his next prospective shelter and leave a written memorandum in which he stated his name and what and why he had taken. This writing, though strictly demanded by the Western code, was not exacted with any idea of assuring a refund to the particular ranchers who unwittingly had furnished the supplies; it was to impress upon the public that it should borrow only what it needed, and that, whenever once more affluent, it should repay, not to the original lenders, if at all inconvenient so to do, but to some unfortunate vagrant who was in the same predicament the visitor once had been. The West, thus generous to the needy, was severe to the wanton thief who selfishly robbed the larder. He faced the possibility of a pistol-shot, or else of a hempen noose with the two folds and thirteen wraps which formed the hondo everywhere restricted to the hangman's use.

No pay was expected from any guest or borrower. For one of them to offer it was very close to an insult.

But, though every passer-by had vested right to enter the house, it was his bounden duty first to ascertain whether any of the inmates were at home, and, if so, to await their welcome before attempting to pass through the door. Were the visitor mounted and a follower of convention, he would remain ahorse until requested to dismount. In Texas, it was dangerous presumption for him to leave the saddle, did the house have inmates present, until some one of them had said "Light" (alight), "Stranger, light." In the Northwest, it was extremely discourteous to quit one's mount before receiving an invitation such as "Climb down and eat a bean with us," or "Fall off and stay a while."

Convention intended to give the host an opportunity to inspect his prospective guest and to decide whether the latter were a peaceful citizen or needed watching. Despite the novelists' statement to the contrary, violators of customs like these were rarely shot, but they did create distrust, and distrust was always more or less dangerous in a country where each person was largely dependent upon himself for defense against criminals.

The principle of open house made many a strange combination of persons, for the horse thief, the gambler, the murderer had as good a claim to hospitality as had the owner's friends, the passing ranchmen, the guests from England or the East, the "Bishops and other Clergy."

The men awaiting cookie's summons devoted themselves to conversation, including perhaps a resumption of the picketing argument at the point where weeks before it had been discontinued when the homefolk were down country at the newcomer's former ranch. For a while the conversation held the debating group balanced on its toes and sitting on its spurs, a squatting posture which the cowpuncher habitually affected and which he alone could find comfortable. About the time that all blades of grass within convenient reach had one by one been plucked, thoughtfully chewed and spat out, some one announced that there was an animal in a corral. Thereupon all adjourned to the corral's top rail, ten feet above the ground, and gazed interestedly at some commonplace old horse or cow which for years had been a familiar object. Under circumstances like those described, time and little way to spend it, any beast in a corral offered to the rail-birds possibilities as great as does the bottom of any hole to every passer-by.

That top rail was the point from which gratuitous and unwelcome advice was hurled at round-up time to the cowboys toiling and sweating amid the milling animals within the corral. In some localities it bore the name of "opera-house." The untidied ground under the bottom rail was a favorite resort for rattlesnakes.

Pending cookie's summons, there was time also to inspect the local pets, a bear cub waddling about whither it would, a "bear-dog," a cat, and perhaps a cougar in a cage, an elk, antelope, or mountain-sheep within a special corral, these inmates of the cage and corral sooner or later to be intentionally released.

In a country where man laid in a year's food-supply in advance, and had wood-mice and pack-rats as neighbors, pussy became almost a personage. It was no rare thing to see a man riding across-country and solemnly holding on his saddle horn a cat bound ranchward to guard filled flour sacks.

A curious phase of this feline situation during the decade of the eighties was the fixedness of pussy's money value. This always was ten dollars. Whoever wished to buy a mouser never bid a lower price. Whoever had a cat for sale never named a higher value. Of course, the vagaries of birth easily might overstock a ranch, and one large litter could glut the market of an entire Range. Nevertheless, no threatened shortage of supply, no undue excess in reserves made any difference. The catless man had to pay ten dollars in order to change his state.

As for the other pets, ranchmen, from their virile life, liked virile playthings. This quality, as exhibited in another phase, particularly among the cowboys, found vent in the playtime harnessing together of two entirely unbroken animals, either two broncos, or two renegade steers, or a bronco and a maddened cow, fastening the insane team to a wagon and climbing aboard it.

John H. Dewing, now of Livingston, Montana, and a nephew of the James Dewing already mentioned, may still remember the fifty-five-mile drive that, some thirty years ago, he and another man took from Gardiner into Livingston. Of their two horses, neither had ever before been in harness; and one of them, Slim Jim, had "two notches in his tail," having on two occasions when under saddle killed his rider. But, as Dewing said: "Both the brutes will be quick learners." All that saved the expedition was that Slim Jim, with his sixteen hands of height, had in his short-legged team-mate a pony that, despite its otherwise complete indecency, retained the instincts of its roping days, and would, in answer to wild waves from the driver's seat, squat on its haunches. This would throw Slim Jim off his feet, whereupon the pony, on its own account, would twist about and kick the prostrate Jim into once more standing up, and also kick him out of desire for the moment to run away. Late in the afternoon of the second day, the expedition reached the front of Livingston's Albemarle Hotel, to be accosted by a livery-stable's runner with the question: "Howdy, Gents; shall I put your hosses in the stable overnight?" Dewing said: "No, stick the hyenas in the county jail for six months."

Our cowboy friend and his associates before the ranch-house presently heard cookie's summons. The men trooped into the building to receive cookie's final and conventional order: "Fly at it."

At the great majority of ranches, owners and employees ate at the same table, and in seating themselves made no distinction between wage-earner and wage-payer beyond that the seat at the table's head commonly and by tacit consent was ceded to whichever of the owners was regarded as the leader among themselves. A few establishments, particularly those of English cult, set a separate table for employees, and so created some little resentment in a region where democracy was very potent.

Meals usually were of short duration, for the Westerner made no formality of his eating, and but little interrupted it with conversation. In addition, the cook was impatient to begin the dish-washing; and, privileged by his position to speak his mind, he customarily exhorted dawdlers to "swallow and git out." Meals ordinarily were promptly attended, as tardy inmates of most of the ranches received from the cook only a grin, an airy pointing at the bean-pot, and the words: "Beans, help yourselves."

The meal over, a return to work, if it were midday; or, if it were evening, more conversation; or else either an incursion into the ranch library or singing.

The orthodox ranch library was composed of a patent-medicine almanac, a well-thumbed catalogue of a mail-order house, several catalogues of saddle makers, and, finally, fragments of newspapers from widely scattered localities and of vintage dates. That mail-order house's book with its innumerable illustrations was as fascinating as everywhere used to be the final, pictured pages in the early American dictionaries.

The absolute dependence of much of the Cattle Country upon the mail-order system was confessed in the remarks which accompanied almost every announcement of the marriage of an acquaintance, remarks such as: "Say, boys, Bill Smith that used to be down at the Two Star Ranch has roped a heifer for life. He corralled her back East in Omaha. Don't know her name. Don't know nothing about her. Bill must a got her from Montgomery Ward."

With no intended reflection upon the great commercial house which, by the manner of its sales and the excellence of its wares, did much to make the West a habitable place, the entire Range dubbed any homely female a "Montgomery Ward woman sent West on approval."

Nor should the patent-medicine almanac be belittled. It contained the signs of the zodiac, a fruitful field for discussion as to their meanings and "the use of the durned things anyhow." It contained also other matter which, while of no use to the ranchmen, was vital to the Western army posts; this was a schedule showing for each day in the year the times of sunrise and sunset at various places in the United States. Military regulations required at each army post a cannon-shot at both reveille and retreat. The practical, Indian fighting captain in command of a one or two company post did not bother with voluminous, laboriously prepared, governmentally issued tables of sunrise and sunset times; but, referring to the little green-covered almanac, picked out in the schedule the name of the town nearest his post, calculated the difference in time between the two places, delivered the almanac and the calculation's result to the sergeant of the guard, and from then onward the gun boomed according to "Hostetter's Bitters," as amended for difference in longitude.

At this particular ranch, because its owners were college-bred, were additional books, novels of the day and a battered set of Shakespeare. Only the owners and visiting womenfolk found anything of interest in the novels; but, to the shame of owners and guests, cowboys alone attacked the Shakespeare. True, not even half of them did so. True, none of them made more than occasional and limited incursions, but these literary expeditions were apt every month or so to be repeated to the extent of "taking a whirl out of" one of the more dramatic episodes in an historical or tragic play, and later to cause the reader, with no small enthusiasm and in complete oblivion as to the murderous effect of slangy paraphrase, to attempt transmitting to some less-read companion the great author's message. The vast intellectual vitality that came out of Avon arrested attention. It wrung from a top rider, first face to face with the play of Julius Cæsar and its "Dogs of war": "Gosh! That fellow Shakespeare could sure spill the real stuff. He's the only poet I ever seen what was fed on raw meat."

As for singing, the cowboy was fond of music or rather of that kind of humanly created noise which on the Range arbitrarily represented melody. Musical gatherings, so-called "sings," were very popular. Except for banjos, except for infirm violins, each of these instruments with usually an illicit number of surviving strings, except for mouth-organs, jews'-harps, and an occasional accordion, there was little besides the human voice to awake dulcet sounds.

In this singing, nasal tones predominated, and the songs were rendered usually with very considerable seriousness both of sound and of facial expression. Variations in high notes were affectionately regarded, and notes long drawn out were deeply loved.

The favorite songs had numerous stanzas, and in lugubrious terms referred to home or dying mothers. Wording might vary with geography, but loneliness rarely failed to be a theme. "The home I ne'er will live to see" and "I'm a poor, lonesome cowboy" vied in popularity with other dirges such as "The night my mother passed away." It required some ten minutes for that classic, "The Dying Cowboy," to recite his pathetic history and arrive at the point where, with every note held so long as breath endured, he, according to Northwesterners, "laid himself down beside the trail and died," or, in the Texan version, appealed: "Oh, bury me not on the lone prai-rie."

At times mournfulness was laid aside, and great pleasure was derived from ditties of the class to which belonged "I've found a horseshoe. It is rusty and full of nails."

Again sentimentality would prevail, and there would be catarrhally produced "Rosalie the Prairie Flower" in its entirety or so much of "Annie Laurie" and of its kindred ballads as the choristers could remember.

Among the few cheerful bits of music were "Roll on, roll on, roll on, Little Dogies, roll on, roll on," the rollicking lay of the cattle, "Roll your tail, and roll her high; we'll all be angels by and by," and that semichant, "The little, old, gray horse came tearing out of the wilderness."

In this last-mentioned song, the animal never arrived at his destination, for, whenever the choristers thus brought him to the edge of the wilderness, a long-drawn, unctuous "and" whirled the singers back to the song's initial word, and automatically replaced the little, old, gray horse at his original starting-point, whence presently, repeatedly, but unavailingly he came tearing out until Euterpe quit for the night.

She retired soon; for so hard was the day's work, and so early in the morning did it commence, that ranch evenings were very short. Bedtime followed closely on the heels of supper.

There was small incentive to combat drowsiness, for there was scant light in which to stay awake. Kerosene marked the attainable limit of illumination, and ill-kept lamps withindoors and smoky lanterns withoutdoors created little that suggested brilliancy. For these means of lighting, candles, and even torches of fat pine, were substituted in simple establishments far from the railway. The inhabitants of such primitive places ordinarily retired before darkness set in.

CHAPTER IX

DIVERSIONS AND RECREATIONS

MUSIC was not the only recreation.

Not infrequent diversions in such sections of the country as offered the raw materials were mortal combats fought by two or more tarantulas, or waged between a king-snake and a rattler.

The first was the more sporting proposition, as any contestant might win. Each of the huge, repulsive spiders which hopped about the bottom of a cracked soup-tureen, carefully preserved for arena purposes, had financial backers amid the owners of the overhanging human faces. Occasionally a hairy gladiator ceased its cheery occupation of amputating its opponent's legs, jumped from the pit in which it belonged, and bit a spectator.

Each enterer of one of the horrid bugs endeavored that it should be a female, and not from the same colony as that of any of the other belligerents. Males would not bite females or relatives; but the females, while sometimes sparing loved relations, had no pity for the males as such.

The conduct and result of the other duel was foreordained, a terrified rattlesnake making successive efforts to crawl to safety and each time headed off by a moving streak upon the floor, a coil, a rattle, spiral progress which made around the coil was seemingly lazy but was assuredly provocative of hate, another rattle, an angry, aimless strike, a flash through the air, a blur, teeth sunk in just below the rattler's open jaw, a vine-like embrace, a badly squeezed rattlesnake dead from a broken neck, and an immediate gliding away by a slender, graceful whip-lash, by three feet of lithest sinuosity particolored with black and brilliant yellow or orange, radiantly glistening as with a fresh coat of varnish.

King-snakes, which were entirely harmless to man, commonly were intentionally imprisoned by him in houses located in rattler-infested localities, and were permitted to go whither they wished withindoors. Otherwise there always would be the chance of a cucumber-like odor and of a sharp, whirring sound beside the fireplace or in some dark corner. The king-snake would not eat his victim, but would kill it at sight.

To procure with certainty such a snake fight within one's cabin, all one had to do was to go out of doors, capture the nearest rattler by aid of a forked stick or an open gunnysack, and throw him through the cabin door and onto the floor. The king-snake would do the rest.

Occasionally one saw such a combat self-arranged and on the open prairie.

In Texas a black snake would be substituted for our friend the king-snake, but the result of the duel would be the same.

On the range one might see a rattlesnake being done to death in either of two other and equally dramatic ways. A snake would sound its rattle, and anywhere the antelope or deer, or in the Far Southwest the chaparral-cock sometimes would heed the call.

A female antelope and her tiny fawn were quietly nosing their way through the scattered bunch-grass. The mother's head shot up and twisted to one side. She was both listening and scenting to the limit of her tense ability. Suddenly she started, ran, say, a hundred yards, jumped six feet into the air, and, with four hoofs held close together, landed upon the rattler. Up and down she bucked with rapidity suggesting an electric vibrator, with all the effect of the sharpest knife. Her little feet had cruel edges. A moment later she trotted quietly back to her baby, and left behind her reptilian hash.

Or the chaparral-cock might stop its hunt for bugs, seize in its bill a group of cactus thorns, spread its wings wide and low, and, running more speedily than could any racehorse, dodging as elusively as does heat-lightning, drive those thorns squarely into the snake's open mouth, peck out both the beady eyes, and then resume the hunt for bugs.

At the extreme southerly portion of the Range the rattler had another enemy, the peccary. Nevertheless, watching a pig step on a snake, bite into it, pull it apart, and then eat it did not stir one's imagination.

The rattlesnakes, though considered, except for certain ones in Texas, to be much overadvertised as to dangerousness and to be trading on the well-deserved reputation of their Floridan brothers, nevertheless were regarded as being distinctly unpleasant. Yet nobody ordinarily paid much attention to them or had their subject in mind unless they were in one's path or in or near one's house, or unless a man were about to sit on the ground or to sleep upon it.

The average inhabitant of the Cattle Country acquired a habit of circumspection before taking a seat. This desire for a quick, snappy view became almost an instinct. Colonel Pickett said: "You tell a good horse by his configuration, manners, and action. You tell a Westerner by the way he sits down."

When a man was about to sleep on the ground, hard pounding was done upon the earth to scare up from their holes any lurking reptiles. Similar exploratory precaution was taken against scorpions, centipedes, and tarantulas within their domain.

Not infrequently, despite such a preliminary search and despite the cocoon-like way in which every sleeping Westerner tightly rolled his blankets about him, a man on waking in the morning would find that his bed had gathered in various nocturnal wanderers, assorted according to the latitude, a rattlesnake or two or perhaps only a single tarantula, scorpion, centipede, horned toad, small lizard, or disgusting Gila monster.

There was little actual hazard in conducting such a lodging-house; because its human proprietor always quit it before the sun had warmed the guests into activity, and quit it in a manner which, keeping the blankets still atop the lodgers, deterred them from moving to attack.

Safety required that this exit be not made in any violent manner, but rather be circumspectly accomplished by gently uncovering the shoulders, by strategically anchoring the hands into the ground behind the head, and by their rapidly pulling out the body, which was kept as still as though it were paralyzed from the waist down. Once freed from the bed, its real owner always curiously investigated, to see what prizes, if any, he had drawn.

There was very little risk of being bitten by any of these unpleasant creatures at any time. Seemingly they had no desire to attack a man who was sleeping or otherwise quiescent, and, save in infrequent instances, they fled from any one who moved.

The only type of rattlesnake upon the major portion of the Range either stayed on the ground or climbed no higher than the bottom branches of low bushes, almost invariably coiled and rattled before it struck was, when striking, rarely disposed to lunge a distance exceeding one-third of the reptile's length, very rarely was able to lunge further than one-half of its length, and never more than two-thirds of it. As this rattlesnake's length but seldom exceeded three feet and almost never four feet, the striking radius was comparatively short.

Moreover, the snake was easily killed. While a pistol-shot or a "mashing with a rock" were thoroughly effective, there were other no less definitive methods. A slight blow from a quirt or switch insured a fatal break in the spine, a result obtained for the neck by many a cowboy through his

seizing the tail of a gliding serpent and snapping the brute like a whip.
A coiled rattler patently could not at the moment be accorded this latter debonair treatment, so either he was kicked out of his coil and then
seized and snapped, or, having been allowed to strike the sole of a boot,
his head, before it could be retracted, was prosaically stepped on.

Although the Western rattlesnake was known to be death-dealing
in only rare instances, its bite ordinarily provoked heroic remedy. The
historic antidote of whiskey was rarely available, and also was recognized as being a dangerous ally of the serpent's poison. Snake venom
from the outset and whiskey from the commencement of its reactive
effect were each heart constringents. The wound, enlarged by a knife-
slash, and imprisoned by a tourniquetted thong, might be plugged
with either a searing coal or else a pinch of gunpowder and a lighted
match. One chap, bitten on the tip of his finger, drew his gun, and
blew off that finger at its second joint.

The alleged deadliness of the scorpion, tarantula, centipede, and
repulsive-looking Gila monster belonged so far as appeared, in the category with the traditional venomousness of the mythical hoop-snake.

If the ranchman ran but little peril from the snakes and bugs, he ran
no danger at all from any of the wild animals except possibly one, the
"hydrophobia skunk," with its traditionally venomous bite. All the rest
of the wild beasts, bears included, avoided man unless he overtly asked
for war. And, if he did, the grizzly bear alone was dangerous, least of
all that terror in the novels, that spitting, snarling, harmless, cowardly,
overgrown tabby-cat, the mountain-lion.

Occasionally the open prairie or the forest's edge offered entertain-
ment of absorbing interest and of Homeric grandeur. Either two huge
bulls or two great wapiti, crashing head on, charge after charge, struggled for the acknowledged leadership of an onlooking and admiring
harem. Or else in springtime, the grizzly bear, hungry from its winter-
ing, sallied forth for food and fancied veal. Though the great brute
knew its discount through its still soft and tender footpads, it failed to
make allowance for the spirit that was latent in every ox or cow upon
the Range. On the bear's approach, a bunch of cattle nervously threw
up their heads, snorted, and galloped off. Soon a stubby-legged calf
was overtaken and struck down. Upon its squeal, the herd wheeled,
and out of it shot, head down, the bereaved cow or more probably a
berserk steer, at times to hilt its horn in Bruin's chest and simultaneously to receive a neck-dislocating smash from a long-nailed paw.

In early years one might have seen a buffalo make the same assault
upon a bear.

In the springtime, also, there might suddenly appear above the sage-brush the blood-stained visage of a great, gray wolf, interrupted at its meal upon the body of its kill, a little calf which its mother had "cached." With the cattle as with the antelope, when a mother had occasion to travel far for water, she did not take her baby with her, but instead hid it in the brush. The youngster, as though hypnotized, would lie for hours, glued to the ground, absolutely motionless, and would make no effort to escape from any intruder. He might elude the eye of man, but rarely the notice of any passing horse, and never the scent of whatever coyote or timber-wolf might wander near.

In winter there were the footprints of wild life upon the tracking snow, and, from time to time, one might also watch the bear as he, having interrupted his hibernation, intermittently came forth at noon-time on pleasant days, and either stretched and yawned on his seat in the sunshine, or else, with rheumatic motion and crabbed temper, stubbed through an exercising walk.

To whatever observant man loved the out-of-doors, nature was lav-ish in her joyous gifts.

Another means of relaxation was the horse-race, not the formal Sunday one run upon the track at the distant town, not a competi-tion between ponies of the local ranch, for the latter contest made no opportunity for bitter human partisanship, but a race between a pony of the ranch, and some other steed which had come in either under the saddle of a visiting puncher or under the lead of a smooth-tongued individual unrecognized as being a professional horse-racer. This oily man, ostensibly interested only in cattle, presently and with appar-ent reluctance rode to the starting line. Twenty-seven seconds after his reaching there, the race was over and the hosts were in pecuniary distress. An experience of this sort taught nothing to the cowboy, and thus a considerable portion of his loose change periodically passed to fleet-footed vagrants and their hatchet-faced gentlemen escorts.

Perhaps mounted Indians appeared, and then, the competing ponies having been selected, the punchers bet all their surplus possessions against the generous hazards of the Red Skins. Ethnic pride goaded both the white man and the Indian, and the passing of the stakes often left either the punchers insolvent or the Indians afoot.

Such part of the cowboys' winnings as were in the form of blan-kets or fur robes were necessarily and forthwith deposited by their new owners upon ant-hills, to rest there several days in order that the industrious, ever hungry, black ants might delouse completely the wool or fur.

Indians' visits were not welcomed by the cook, as the latter not only had to produce food, but also was held by the ranchers somewhat responsible for the condition of the interior of the house. The visiting Indians had three salient qualities, one of which, great sense of dignity, did not appease the cook's irritation from the other two, possession of an insatiate appetite which was of appalling capacity and possession also of a superabundance of readily emigrating insect companions.

The horse-race over, a foot-race naturally followed. Of all occurrences upon the Range, the most frequent was undoubtedly movement by live stock, but in close succession came human argument and foot-races. It was almost as easy to launch a foot-race as it was to start a debate.

Such a race was a contest more in strategy than in mere speed. It occurred anywhere that there could be found two men not hopelessly bow-legged, and also reasonably flat ground which was sufficiently extensive to permit the contestants without leaving the starting point to determine with their eyes a goal "exactly one hundred yards away to an inch." Coats, if any, and vests came off, but boots and spurs stayed on. The contestants agreed as to which of them should give the starting-signal, and then began edging up the course. When the man intrusted with the word "go" either considered himself in an advantageous position, or by his sense of shame was prevented from "scrouging" farther, he shouted the unleashing word. Although this cost him a little breath, the disadvantage might immediately be more than offset by his opponent's finding himself stepping on a discarded can, confronted by a set of rabbit-holes, rushing up a blind alley in waist-high, sturdy sage-brush, or dragging on his spurs long strands of rusty baling wire.

Because of one's opportunity to chart the location of all bunkers, pits, ditches, cans, and animal's skeletons about one's home, prudence should have withheld all visitors from competing near any ranch-house. But she was disregarded. The home talent always won, for they knew when to tack.

The timing of the race was done by the contestants' guessing, and in perfectly good faith the time was fixed either at ten seconds or at a very slightly higher figure.

The cowboy did not realize the actuating motive for his picking out this time. Fundamentally it was resentment against the East. The Atlantic coast then contained practically all of the good running tracks, and so held all of the records. The cowboys, learning that the official American record for one hundred yards was ten seconds and had been made in the East, not discovering that but two men had been recorded as being so speedy, and reasoning that effete Easterners should run no better than they rode, calmly and with no conscious attempt at deceit or braggadocio labelled themselves as peers of Mercury.

"Pitching horseshoes," a game identical with that of quoits except that horseshoes were used instead of disks, had here and there spasmodic popularity.

Boxing and wrestling nowhere appeared upon the Range. They were incompatible with the cowboy's temperament, and were ill-suited to his distorted legs and enfeebled ankles. Nevertheless, he would now and then in play fling his arms around the neck of some corralled, wabbly-legged, week-old calf or colt and attempt to "wrastle it down," thereupon to be jerked off his feet and thrown into a heap.

Incidentally the puncher almost never engaged in a fist fight. He used his gun instead of his knuckles.

Baseball was never played.

A pleasing sport was riding madly after jack-rabbits. Sometimes it was done in a prearranged way and with the accompaniment of coursing dogs. English ranchmen much affected this. But usually the affair meant no more than an impromptu, harum-scarum dash by a solitary horseman who had been bedevilled into speed by a tantalizing bunny with a sense of humor.

History records comparatively few cases in which the shrewd, fleet-footed, quickly dodging rabbit was overtaken by either dog or horse.

Coursing the prong-horned antelope with hounds, and either with or without the strategy of "flagging," was attempted occasionally, this by Englishmen more often than by Americans. Ordinarily it gave to each rider and his horse considerable exercise, and to but few of the antelope any valid cause for worry.

Horses, men, and dogs would creep forward under cover to within two hundred yards of the quarry, and, firmly confident of success, would burst into the open. The antelope would give one startled look, wheel, hoist their triangular, white-lined tails, their little, full-speed-ahead signals, and, save in rare instances, promptly would change that two hundred yards of intervening space into a mile or two.

"Now, Jack, it was all your fault. If you had used sense, and not gone at it bald-headed, hadn't chasséd out there ahead of the rest of us, we'd have gotten them this time sure, and the worst of it is that that old buck had the all-firedest finest ivory tips I ever seen on any horns. Now, remember next time." The next time doubtless would be like this and almost every other time, save that Joe or Mike or Bill might be the scolded one in place of Jack.

Occasionally, and particularly when the pursuit could be made by successive relays of huntsmen and hounds, the quarry was overtaken.

With these same dogs, sometimes the great, gray timber-wolf was followed to the rock or clump of brush against which he, snarling, was "stood up" and "given his medicine" of lead.

From time to time, a puncher, coming unexpectedly upon some wild beast, impulsively would rope it before it could start its flight. Even the grizzly bear, and in early days the buffalo, occasionally received the noose. In these latter instances a repentant cowboy well might have lost his breath if not his rope. The West would lariat anything that suddenly bobbed up in front and looked saucy. If certain records be accurate, more than one white man and many an Indian quickly passed to the Happy Hunting-Ground, jerked thither by a reata caught about the smokestack of a moving locomotive.

A still further amusement was the hazing of tenderfoot guests. This hazing was never more violent than the visitor merited, and for manly, well-liked innocents was usually restricted to solemn warnings against the vicious bucking alleged to be latent within the visitor's very peaceful nag, to nocturnal expeditions for the tyro's snaring of imaginary birds, to long-winded tales that ingeniously held the listener's interest, but eventually disclosed that they had no point, making this disclosure sometimes by reverting to the starting-place and reiterating word for word, to exaggerated stories of wild animals, and to enticing the gullible man, by a weird howl raised just without the house, to rush out of doors at night, and fire at a can punched with two holes and containing a lighted candle.

The conventional wild-animal stories were all of the sort intended to carry fear to the innocent and to make him a bit ridiculous to his sophisticated fellow auditors. Ferocious attacks by wolverines and huggings by grizzly bears were favorite subjects, the latent points being that, though the wolverine had great fierceness, he was probably the most elusive animal in all North America, and that neither the grizzly nor any other bear, so far as appeared, had ever hugged anybody. The bear's terrible right paw and his teeth were his means of attack. A mythical animal known to cowboy raconteurs as the "wouser" sometimes was descanted upon. The wouser was accorded any physical appearance and predatory habits which the course of the earlier conversation had seemed to warrant. He usually, however, was permitted to have hydrophobia, and was made a subspecies of either the bear or the mountain-lion.

Probably also advantage was taken of the combination of the newcomer's credulity and of the wonderful clearness of Western air, on the joint basis of which he would be sent afoot to reach a hill which seemed to him a league away, but which in reality was three times that distance. His credulity might be victimized in another way, for in good faith he might ride miles to a ranch in a rocky, roadless country, and there ask to borrow what that ranch patently did not possess, a horse-drawn buggy.

A somewhat brutal trick was procuring a pilgrim to pinch the tail of a freshly decapitated rattlesnake. If the expected result occurred, the snake's body through reflex action of the muscles would snap into a circle, the bleeding neck's stump would strike the pilgrim's hand or wrist, and the pilgrim would give a single scream, the audience a series of guffaws.

Another form of amusement which might from time to time be conducted for a few minutes at table or about a camp-fire was a competitive reciting of the inscriptions upon the labels of the cans of condensed milk and other foodstuffs habitually used at the ranch. Partly for recreative nonsense and partly out of loneliness when solitary in camp, every ranchman sooner or later committed to memory the entire texts upon these labels and could repeat them verbatim. With a penalty of five cents for each mistake in punctuation, of ten cents for each error in a word, the competitive recitals offered a sporting possibility.

They were most apt to occur when a tenderfoot was present, not so much because of the opportunity of winning his money (no tenderfoot "knew his cans") as because the incongruity of the matter was apt to disconcert him, and a conventional pleasure upon the Range was to "keep a pilgrim guessing." A tenderfoot making his initial Western trip would, his first night at a ranch, be sitting at the supper table listening with spellbound attention to the conversation of men who had seen things and done things. This tenderfoot would be trying to lose no detail from the talk across the table about the best way in which to ride certain bucking horses, from the talk at the table's end as to just how one of the men in the room had succeeded in escaping from the Nez Percé Indians during the fight on the Gibbon River, when suddenly some one would notice the tenderfoot's rapt expression, would pound on the table, and would begin "——— Brand." Instantly mention of bucking and of Indians would cease, and twelve or fourteen men, being all the persons present save only the astonished tenderfoot, would gaze at the ceiling and swing into a full-throated chorus beginning with "Condensed milk is prepared from," and continuing for some minutes. Or else, the precentor having launched the opening words of a different canticle, the crowd would take over its continuation, and stentoriously would intone, "Of peaches. This can contains," etc.

With the last word of the vociferous recitative, whatever its subject, the whole insane revel would stop short; and with no explanations or apologies, the former conversations would be resumed at the points where they had been interrupted. But the tenderfoot would be "guessing." That was what the Range desired.

The cowboys might play a game of cards, seven-up or poker; but, if so, the stake was as apt to be relief from an unpleasant chore like cutting wood or going for water as to be monetary. However, when "stacked up" against punchers from rival ranches or against the public gaming-table, cowboys were prone to gamble recklessly; because, once saddle, bridle, rope, quirt, chaps, hat, and gun were paid for, there was little to purchase except tobacco and liquor. Risking six months' wages upon the turn of a single card was no uncommon bet, though its making would arouse temporary interest among the men about the table.

There was little or no alcoholic drinking at the ranch, for it harbored very little alcohol to drink, usually none at all beyond a small lot jealously preserved for prospective medicinal use. The one source of supply was the town, and very few cowboys on visiting a settlement were after the first hours of their stay financially able to endow a wine cellar. The only opportunities for inebriety were the visits to town, made as a matter of course immediately after the fall round-up and occurring at rare intervals at other times, the semiannual visits to other ranges to assist in their round-ups and be requited by wholesale, honest thanks, good food, and possibly a little whiskey, and also the very occasional holiday celebrations at the ranch where one was employed or at another ranch within reasonable distance.

Punchers were probably no more given to drunkenness than were the contemporary American men of any other non-religious calling in any part of the United States. The punchers assuredly were apt to drink to excess when they first "struck town" after six months of enforced and continuous abstention from all liquids except water, tea, and coffee; but such of the cowboys as for business reasons had occasion to remain in town for any considerable length of time subsided after the initial exuberance had spent itself, and thereafter imbibed no more than did the town's permanent inhabitants. The cowboy had to earn his living, and he knew that in the long run wages and alcohol were inconsistent.

When the cowboy got drunk he did not do it in any highly specialized way, or signify his inebriety by any technical methods. He merely got drunk. On this point the dramatist has attempted to make a false differentiation, and, after filling his puncher with liquor, invariably has caused him to shoot.

The drunken cowboy was like the drunken Easterner, except in the subjects which he chose for maudlin discussion. One told of the magnificence of the saddle he owned or was about to acquire; the other told of the millions of dollars he had amassed or was about to amass, or else described the *Mayflower*'s voyage from start to finish and filled the ship with his ancestors. Surliness brought up the Easterner's fists and out the Westerner's gun. But that gun rarely went off, for a friendly bystander usually seized it.

Drunken cowboys often made picturesque statements. Charlie (no last name, please, for he has grandchildren now) would offer to go into a biting contest with any grizzly bear, and to "give that thar bar a handicap. He can have first bite."

When the puncher drank, he generally demanded liquor of good quality. Bourbon whiskey was his mainstay, though in the Southwest he at times toyed with mescal. Whiskey was taken "straight." Mixed drinks were so entirely unknown that there was opportunity for some one to invent the story of the Easterner who, in a frontier barroom, said: "I guess I'll take a cocktail," and was told: "You don't guess, you drink, and you gets it straight and in a tin cup."

Courtesy required that the puncher, when he drank, fill his glass to the brim, and, in carrying it to his lips, use his right, his gun hand. He so filled his glass not because he wished to drink that much, not that he might impose upon the purveyor, but solely because a filled glass both showed to the giver that the recipient highly valued the quality of the gift, and also established that the donor was not dispensing goods unpalatable to himself.

The Western barmen eventually offset the draining effect of thorough urbanity by investing in glasses with inordinately thick bottoms.

The cowboy avoided so far as possible sharing as giver or recipient any drinks with soldiers. This antipathy to the military was not founded on any lack of patriotism, but it did have two clearly defined bases. The puncher, whether mistakenly or not, confidently blamed the private soldier for the physical contamination of a certain class of women in the frontier towns. Then, too, the army had been the only policer of the West, and thus the cowboy had acquired toward the army as a whole the same quasi-resentment that has ever marked the attitude of the college undergraduate toward the faculty above him.

As a further source of recreation there was an occasional dance usually on the eve of a public feast-day, the roundup's close, Thanksgiving, Christmas, or New Year's. Although at these functions female partners were at a premium, the men attended with alacrity.

Two hundred miles was not too far to go. The dearth of femininity was partly made good by such men as, unselfishly volunteering to "dance lady fashion," were "heifer-branded" by a handkerchief tied on the arm, and all swept the floor with considerable enthusiasm. The dancing, while not graceful, was assuredly vigorous.

The truth was that, with ranches at least fifteen, thirty, fifty miles apart, and hard work to be done, there were neither means nor leisure for much recreation. Argument and repeated surveys of the mail-order catalogue were the principal sources of relaxation. These surveys released imagination's bonds, and let reason weigh the comparative merits of various pictured grand pianos, wedding-dresses, rowboats, seashore parasols, "nobby clothing for city use," and "best grade gilt frames" containing "genuine oil-paintings."

CHAPTER X

THE DAY'S WORK

THE next morning's "sun up" brought every one, newcomer included, down to every-day work. This was usually of merely routine nature, but from time to time it swung suddenly into exciting channels.

The day's business started early. With the first break of dawn, the crusty, ever-growling cook was out of his kitchen bunk, lit his fire, gave to the "horse wrangler" the unwelcome, conventional, morning saluta-tion of "roll out," and then set about preparing breakfast.

All during the night the riding ponies had grazed in close proxim-ity to the house, had stamped about it, and occasionally had put their noses to its cracks, sniffingly to satisfy either curiosity or a desire for human companionship. Although the wrangler rose the moment he was called and limited his toilet to putting on his hat, the first wreath of blue smoke from the chimney already had warned the horses of impending work; and, by the time the wrangler got out of doors, not within half a mile was there a single steed save only the few dejected "night horses" inside of the corral. One of the latter was saddled, and the much scattered band of ponies was rounded-up, to trot with passive indignation into the fenced enclosure.

Breakfast did not long delay the men. In quick succession, the lesser eaters first in order, they carried their saddles and bridles to the corral, and in a trice had the animals equipped for service.

On cold days the more kindly riders held their bits a moment before the fire, and shielded them by a glove or a coat flap during the transit between the inner house and the horse's mouth. They did this despite foreknowledge of their broncos' prospective seeming lack of gratitude. Each of those exasperating little brutes would stand, head hanging meekly downward, and would resignedly permit the bridle to be put atop his crown, but the instant the bit approached his mouth this latter part of his anatomy in some mysterious way would be pointed almost directly upward and be projected from a semivertical neck.

After withstanding a slap or two and receiving many profane requests, the pony would lower his head to an easily reachable position;

143

would release the vise-like set in which his closed jaw had been; would accept the bit and busily embark upon the champing of its roller; would fairly shove his forehead against his master's hands that crumpled ears might be made more comfortable; would take the saddle; would gaze reproachfully at his tormenter; and then apparently would doze off.

Whoever was outside of the corral could by his hearing alone accurately follow the events within. Seeing was unnecessary.

At the house door a rider had paused and said: "I've warmed up this bit, acause I'm riding the finest little cow horse this State has ever seen. It sure has earned the right to decent treatment."

Then the man had disappeared into the corral. There wafted out of it statements which, if carefully censored, would read as follows: "Good morning, Pete. Hope you're well. Got a little piece of iron candy for you. Stop fooling, Pete. Stop your kidding. Stop that, I tell you. Pete, stop that. Stop it, I say. Look here, you dodgasted, pale pink, wall-eyed, glandered, spavined cayuse, pull down that injur rubber-neck of yourn, or I'll skin you alive, and mash in your sides to hell and gone. Hold still, pony, and I'll fix your ear. Is that comfortable? Now, Pete, here comes the saddle. Whoa, pony, stop twitching your fool back. Now, Pete, the front cinch's fixed. All we've got left is the hind one. Pete, you dog-goned, inflated, lost soul, let out that wind and do it quick, or I'll bust you wide open. Quit that, Pete. Quit it, I say. Good, old Pete, you sure are some horse."

During warm weather life was comparatively easy. There were, of course, the spring and fall round-ups. The resultant "drives" to the "shipping point" at the railroad were made in autumn only, if the ranch were one for raising beef, or more frequently, possibly, than in both spring and autumn, if horses were the product.

There was the "gentling" of these horses. If the ranch were in a section that necessitated use of a different feeding-ground in winter from that of summer, the live stock would be shifted semiannually from one of these ranges to the other, the "winter range" being in the "low country," while the "summer range" would be either upon the higher "benches," or on the upper levels of the hills.

There were inspection trips about the Range, so-called "outridings," to discover the location and physical state of the scattered groups of stock, to ascertain the condition of the water-supply and grass, to move the stock to fresh grounds if food or drink were found to be insufficient, to fend the animals away from known patches of loco-weed, to discover by "riding sign" whether any beasts were straying too far afield and if so to turn them homeward, to rescue through a tightly drawn lariat and straining pony some bogged or mired steer or horse and possibly receive reward in a charge by muddy, irate horns, to watch for signs of thieves, settlers, and predatory animals, and, if necessary, to lay traps or poisoned baits for wolves, and finally, on such ranches as "blabbed" their calves, to put "blabs" on the noses of whatever baby cattle deserved the unsightly little board.

Here and there about the Range would appear a lusty calf with an emaciated mother. If the calf were old enough, a thin board, six inches by eight in size, was, at the centre of one of its longer edges, clipped onto the infant's nose. Thereafter he could perfectly well graze, but he assuredly was weaned. Blabbing was not always easy of accomplishment. The calf and his mater had to be chased so far apart as to permit the cowboy to rope and throw the calf, attach the blab, and remount his horse before there should arrive, head down and on the gallop, an irate and sharp-horned cow.

Diseased or injured animals were inspected, and, according to the nature of the disease or injury, were treated or destroyed. If disease required the animals' isolation, the latter was effected through herding the animals by themselves under charge of a detachment of punchers; for, in the absence of gathered hay, imprisonment in foodless corrals was impracticable. No oversight was given to maternity cases, and births occurred wherever upon the Range the mother happened to be.

The Northwest harbored one particular ailment concerning which many tenderfoots, and even many of the ignorant farmers, had extraordinary misinformation. In terrifically cold weather, cattle's hoofs and horns sometimes would freeze, and thereafter the horns, on thawing, would in some instances fall off. The discarded horns, of course, were hollow, as were the horns of all cattle; but ignorant finders of the castaways created in good faith the disease of "Hollow Horn," and deluged governmental officers with requests for curative prescriptions.

In addition to all these incidents of "outriding," there might be the work of salvage at some cloudburst's scene, a prairie-fire to suppress, an urgent call for aid against marauding Indians, or the start for a drive either on the Texas Trail or from, say, Oregon to Wyoming.

Perhaps, also, there arrived a puncher testy from the import of his message: "A couple of you come up with me to Indian Creek. The porcupines have gotten in there, and ten of our best mares have kicked themselves plumb full of quills." This meant for the unfortunate horses no danger, but considerable discomfort. One by one they would be thrown and triced fore and aft by lariats, while a very irate gentleman squatted at their heels, plied pincers on the offending quills and volubly cursed all the members of the Rodent family from the original immigrants down to the then present generation.

Zoologists possibly know whether or not the porcupine had functions in addition to the three he exhibited to the cowboy. These were eating latigos and saddles, decorating horses' hock joints, and using Towser's inquisitive nose for a pincushion.

Mail had to be carried to and from the post-office, perhaps a hundred miles or more away; and yearly the wagons had to make a long trip for supplies.

These wagons, stout, springless, creaking things, traversing unconscionable roads and country devoid of road, taking to the boulder-strewn beds of streams when the map turned on edge, were dragged on their bumping, noisy way by two or more spans, all driven by a man seated upon the wagon's front and handling ordinary reins.

Or else the wagons were drawn by a "jerk-line string," a string of horses or mules harnessed either in single file or in a series of spans, and, in either case, following a highly trained leader controlled by a "jerk line." This jerk line, a single, continuous rein, starting from its fastening at the top of the brake handle, extended to and through the hand of the driver, who either was astride the wheel horse (the near one, if two) or was seated on the wagon's front. The line continued thence along the long file of horses' backs and to the left side of the "lead animal's" bit, this without touching the bit of any intermediate brute. A single, steady pull on the line guided this lead animal to the left. Two or more short jerks turned it to the right. Constant and loudly voiced reiterations of the old, oxen-driving commands of "gee" and "haw" directed the intervening beasts; and also, with the leading one, supplemented the effect of the jerk line.

Profanity and a whip did the rest; did it easily unless the wagon outran its brake, and sliding onto the heels of its motive beasts caused them to "jack-knife," which is to say, to turn backward at an acute angle. In such event, profanity outdid itself.

Commonly, with animals in a series of spans, the left-hand beast in the front span was the only "lead" animal, and thus alone had the honor of holding the jerk line. In such case, he and his span-mate would have their bits connected by a short strap, thus causing the span-mate to be towed to the left when he was not either walking peacefully forward or, by his companion, being violently pushed to the right. But, if this span-mate were qualified to share in the leadership, the jerk line, toward its far, outer end, would, for a way, be split lengthwise, one branch so produced being attached to the bit of the left-hand lead beast, the other branch being fastened to the bit of the span-mate, in each case to the bit's left side.

The driver of any "string team," whether it were single or double, might operate it unassisted, or there might be upon the wagon an aide who was termed a "lasher," and whose task was to swing the whip, to push upon the brake-handle as the driver, with his jerk line, pulled it forward, and finally to co-operate in the swearing.

The whip mentioned above either was a wooden stock four feet or so in length and with a long, slender lash attached, or else was in the form of the now historic "bull whip." This latter instrument was a short stock which carried fifteen to twenty-five feet of plaited, rawhide lash. This lash was quite thick near the stock and, weighted there with lead, tapered to a point, and so continued into a buckskin "popper" three feet long. It could, at the wielder's choice, land anywhere, silently or with a pistol crack, and this with either the gentleness of a falling leaf or force sufficient to remove four square inches of equine skin.

Often on steep "side hills," cowboys, riding above the wagon, fastening their lariats to the top of its load, and having their ponies pull back with all their might were all that prevented an overturn or a slip to the bottom of the declivity. Upgrades frequently were negotiable only because these cowboys, with lariats taut between wagon and saddle horns, rode beside the vehicle, their ponies "scratching gravel," hauling with prodigious enthusiasm, and giving welcome aid to the "work horses" straining in the harness.

The tractive power in the combination of a man, a horse, a lariat, and a stock-saddle was at first sight astonishing. The logs for many a ranch building thus were "snaked" from the forest to the house site. It was the ordinary way of transporting wood to the camp-fire.

Frequently, when descending a sharp declivity, the wagon was held in check by ropes tied to the rear axle, twined about convenient trees, rocks, or saddle horns, and slowly paid out.

The wagons were driven by "teamsters," not by cowboys. The latter essayed few tasks that could not be accomplished from a bronco's back. The punchers described themselves as being "too proud to cut hay and not wild enough to eat it." The puncher was so wedded to horseback that, when he took to a wheeled vehicle, if only as an extra passenger, he, as he said, "rode the wagon," and did not ride "on" or "in" it. Of course, a teamster might once have been a cowboy, but no one "teamed" or "threw the bull" so long as he still could sit the buck.

Did the teamster quit his ranching life and drive a freight-wagon on some regular transportation route, he thereby ceased to be a teamster and became a "freighter," this last term having been until well into the decade of the seventies interchangeable with "a professional." While still called a freighter, he might coincidentally be termed also either a "skinner" or "mule skinner," or else a "bull whacker," according as his tractive animals were mules or, as far more often in the earlier years than in the later, yokes of oxen; and if his outfit were a jerk-line one, he was apt to be termed exclusively a skinner. In Range English, one did not "drive" a jerk-line string, but instead "skinned" it.

Teamsters used all the cowboys' profanity, and in addition had "private cuss-words" of their own. Their "chariots," "sulkies," "barouches," "gigs," "buggies," or whatever else they chose to term their heavy wains, fairly reeked with blasphemy. Thus a "wagon outfit" was no silent cortege.

The teamsters, while on their trips, were apt toward evening to receive much flattery from attendant ranchmen. The reason for this was that each teamster had entire jurisdiction over the "sheet" of his wagon, and this canvas cover when laid upon the ground made a warm and wind-proof bed for several men. Throughout the Range, any custodian of a "tarpoleon" or "tarp," as the West termed all canvases not specifically entitled as either "pack covers" or "wagon sheets," was very popular after nightfall.

The paucity of bridges and the absence of decent roads imposed upon the teamsters in rainy weather many a halt, some of them each of several days' duration. Such compulsory stoppings were termed "lay ups," while voluntary delays, particularly in towns or at ranches, were called "lay overs."

The country might be too rough to permit the wagons to reach far-outlying stations, and for such places the "pack-train" of bundle-carrying horses was the only transporter of food.

But the list of daily chores is not finished. Horses had to be shod, work animals on all four feet, saddle animals, if at all, on the front feet only unless the beasts were to be used in very rocky country. In this latter event, they were usually shod "all round," *i. e.*, on each of their four feet.

Repairs had to be made to saddles and to wagons. Lariats and harnesses had to be mended.

In the shoeing of horses, the shoes employed were everywhere ordinary metal ones, except that in the far Southwest occasionally an Apache Indian habit was adopted, and green rawhide was wrapped about the hoofs, there to dry and become almost as hard as iron.

The shoeing of the average Range horse was disturbing to human tranquillity. The shoeing of some horses was a miracle or a devilment according as one viewed it. Bill Evans one morning said: "I'll shoe that pinto cayuse right arter breakfast, and I reckon I'd better pin shoes onto all his feet. Joe, you come down and help." Presently, from the corral rose snorts and the sounds of scuffling, the strident voice of Bill and the bellowing tones of Joe, all merged into a single hymn of trouble. One of the ranch owners, sauntering over that way, found an angry pony glaring at two perspiring men, and asked: "Shod him?" He was answered by Bill: "Guess so. Tacked iron onto everything that flew past. It sure is a heaven-sent mercy that broncs ain't centipedes."

The cloudburst, when it came, produced a real task.

There had been a long period of rainless weather; and panting cattle, for mile after mile along the almost dried-up bed of a high-banked, meandering stream, were drinking at the isolated, surviving pools. Black clouds gathered. They coalesced. Then lightning split the sky; and, between the sky and ground, the down-pouring water was so dense as to make breathing difficult. All of the deluge that fell upon the prairie, baked as it was like a tile, rivuletted into the main stream. In too few minutes for the cattle's realization they were in danger; and, merely seconds after that, they were the playthings of a brown, swirling flood.

At some sand-bar or sharp angle, the floating cattle jammed. Into that mess, which was here writhing, moaning, wounded, here struggling but unharmed, there motionless and dead, cowboys delved with lariats and tugging ponies.

Shots ended suffering. The next chapter was skinning of carcasses and drying of hides.

A clash with Indians was often no mean affair. After the government had forced the Indians onto reservations and thus had left the bulk of the plains to the ranchers, an Indian tribe occasionally "jumped" its reservation, and in a carefully planned "uprising" or "outbreak" went upon the war-path. Cowboys would be drawn into this so-called war, either through running foul of the belligerent Red Skins or being taken on by the army for auxiliary service.

But there was another and lesser form of Indian disturbance which was more frequent, and with which the puncher had more proximate connection. From time to time numbers of the Red Men in entire peacefulness and, either pursuant to shooting permits or in childlike defiance of regulations, wandered beyond their reservation's limits. With the unreasoning inability of the Indians to resist their desires, attractive horses were presently "rustled" and driven away, while fat cattle were killed and eaten.

A cowboy came onto the scene and attempted to save the white owner's property. Shots eventually were fired. News of the affair flashed through mysterious Indian channels back to the reservation, and out poured its more militant inmates. News of this leave-taking sped up the Range, carried by a galloping horseman and by three shots from a rifle. The ultimately concentrated cowboys advanced upon a group of the still bewildered and indecisive Indians; and, answering a single shot by a scattering volley, blew away all indecision and started an active fighting.

The soldiers arrived later, and brought to an end hostilities that never would have commenced had the military uniform appeared on the scene before the cowboy did. Once the soldiers arrived, the punchers present might be asked to assist as packers or guides; but often and because of their notorious lack of interracial diplomacy they were urged in the most forcible language known by the army to withdraw from the neighborhood. The directness and promptness of punchers' methods did not accord with Indian mentality, and to the cowboys' honest but ill-advised action in affairs of this sort must be laid many a subsequent, serious uprising by the Red Man.

The term "rustle" employed above had curious and inconsistent usage in that, when applied to live stock, it almost always implied stealing; but when relating to anything other than live stock it, with almost equal regularity, denoted a legitimate getting.

The much-used term "outfit" had similarly diversified meanings; and variously signified, according to its context, the combined people engaged in any one enterprise or living in any one establishment, a party of people travelling together, or the physical belongings of any person or group of persons.

The prairie-fire sometimes produced exciting duties. Fires were frequent; but usually were of small importance, and, if promptly attacked, easily exterminated. At other times, however, they were terrifying.

For successive weeks an arid heat and a lifeless air, at ten o'clock acrid whiffs and a blurred horizon, but at twelve o'clock a biting smell and the horizon gone. Out there, somewhere, was a line of grimy men desperately fighting to stop the march of the advancing flames that the latter might burn themselves out upon their self-selected battle-ground. Punchers with eyebrows and eyelashes gone, with wet handkerchiefs over mouth and nose, in mad haste but with cool reasoning, "straddled" the fire; two mounted men, one on either side of the flames, dragging behind them at their lariats' ends a green hide or wet blanket. Other men either mounted or afoot, scarred and intrepid like their brothers, beat upon the fire's side-lines with similar utensils or with bunches of brush.

The thickness of the grass or the velocity of the wind might generate heat or movement such as to make straddling unfeasible, and then the only remedy was to "backfire" across the enemy's prospective line of march. Along the zone selected for the "back-fire," a horseman trailed a bundle of burning fagots. The flames thus started were held in check on their homeward side by straddling them.

In the early stages of the contest, living warnings intermittently came out of the wall of smoke, for an occasional deer or antelope, a solitary horse or steer would rush, wild-eyed, past the toiling men. Thus the best experts on the subject of danger had advised human retreat, but such retreat was not to be considered.

The last of these fleeing animals had passed through the line of fire fighters. There was a sudden puff far in the rear, and in an instant the prairie behind the men was ablaze. It was mount and reach the shelter given by a projecting hill, by the bottom of a coulée, by a grassless, "buffalo wallow," or, in the language of the craft, it would be "fried gent," "no breakfast forever," and the "long trail to Kingdom Come."

With safety thus attained, the next and an immediate task was to gallop down to leeward, again to move out before the flames, and to re-engage the enemy upon the same tactics as before.

There was peril in the extensive fires, for they would sulk and make slow progress for a time, and then would leap forward in irregular frontage more rapidly than a horse could run. They, on occasion, would travel for many miles. The peril was particularly for such as had to fight the flames and so, having to stand their ground, could not materially shift position. But any one who merely sought escape would find that, through the average fire, ran here and there safe lanes made up of interrupted and quite dissimilar elements, a stream's bed, a rocky ledge, a bit of grassless earth.

Of these fires, some were caused by lightning or by sparks from locomotives, others had broken away from farmers who had planned a merely local burning in order to fertilize their lands or to rid the latter of annoying weeds, others had escaped beyond the tract in which cattlemen either were eliminating loco plants, or else, warring against sheep, had deliberately kindled flames for the purpose of "cooking mutton." Still others came from the carelessness of campers or of smokers, while, in the earlier years, still others represented Indians' attempts to drive game animals into strategic territory.

Within a forest floored deeply with pine-needles, one tiny ember from a negligently abandoned camp has more than once been the parent of a subsurface, incandescent mass, which days later has a quarter of a mile away gnawed out a breathing hole, and, tasting air, leaped into a holocaust.

For a while after the advent of the early farmers, the latter were employed to "run fire guards" yearly here and there in certain sections of the Range, that is, to plough two parallel sets of furrows, which were some fifty yards apart and had four furrows in each set. The grass between the sets was then purposely burned by men who were trailed by water-laden wagons.

At rare intervals, a cyclone whirled its way across the flat lands, leaving in its trail dead animals, and on either side of this trail living, crazed brutes still galloping in wild stampede. When such a tempest broke on a driven band, "hell was a-popping and a-popping hard" for the herding cowboys. Wind, thunder, and lightning in wholesale quantities brought out the hardest sort of riding before the survivors from the punchers' maddened wards could be headed back into orderly formation.

The cyclone's prelude was awesome. Its arrival was terrific. A sky of inky blackness suddenly in one quarter suffused with tones of copper and dark green. Whatever wind had been blowing ceased, and there fell a silence, death-like save for the nervous lowing of the cattle and the subdued conferring of the men. Presently from the sky came a long-drawn moan; and next, with a roar, a screwing, lightning-capped funnel, point down, lined with dust, bushes, and trees, rushed out of the copper and green, and tore across "the flat."

The punchers, with but seconds in which to act, strove to guess the funnel's prospective course and to throw the cattle from it and, if possible, into protecting gullies. Despite the limited time, there was some opportunity for manœuvring, because the funnel was usually of comparatively small diameter, a few hundred yards at the most. Moreover, it occasionally would "hang," which is to say, would, for a moment or two, slow or even halt its forward progress, though still maintaining its dervish whirl. Then, too, the awful contrivance might have the decency now and then to "skip," "lift," or "raise," that is, for a while to retract its tip from contact with the earth, and thus to sail along harmlessly until the tip again dabbed down to earth and resumed its murdering.

The funnel, as though repentant of all this generosity, would on occasion make frequent and erratic changes in its course, and stab in unexpected places.

The hurrying punchers clung to the fleeing cattle until the last possible instant, then spun their horses into facing the storm, leaned flat upon their animals' necks and, at topmost speed, smashed headlong through the thin but seemingly solid wall of wind that flanked the cyclone's funnel upon its right and left. It was not a comfortable impact. It savored of colliding with a pile of bricks.

Taken sideways by the wall of wind might mean a horse blown over. Taken in any position by the funnel almost surely meant death.

Reputable witnesses have in seriousness reported cattle and horses as picked up and carried more than a quarter of a mile through the air before nature tired of her playthings and dropped them.

Other men, equally reputable, have with less seriousness given other details. Johnny Nealan, a much-respected rancher of Oregon's John Day country, recounted that he, when lifted from the ground by the wind, had in his hand a twenty-dollar gold coin, but that, before he returned to the earth, the money had been blown into two fifty-cent-pieces and one plugged nickel.

Snuffles Jones solemnly averred that a certain Kansan tornado had swept all the earth away from around the badger holes, and left these holes sticking up into the air. Asked how he could have seen them, he retorted: "Didn't see 'em. Ran into 'em."

However, the cyclone had unpleasant elements in addition to that of wind.

Vivid lightning, tossing itself about with constant flash, and just above a treeless plain, was in no way soporific to rain-soaked men astride of rain-soaked horses.

After each particularly blinding streak and the crash of its thunder, at least one dripping puncher saucily would implore nature to "raise your sights, raise 'em a lot," and thereby far to overshoot him. Though not affirmatively afraid, the puncher sometimes had a sneaking suspicion that his invocation might not be heeded, because, as a rider from Billings, Montana, once observed: "Nature is a skittish beast and no ways bridlewise." Occasionally, to sustain good-nature amid a huddled, physically uncomfortable group of men, one of the group would resort to blithesome foolishness. Thus the rigmarole "She loves me, she loves me not" was in more than one instance used to count off recurrent streaks of awesome lightning, just as that same rigmarole, at another time, followed the drone and spang of

Indian bullets which were arriving successively and with unpleasant neighborliness.

On still another occasion three ambushed punchers took to cover. Their range presently was found, and dust began to spurt around them. The bullets, coming with the crescendo, acid whine that sometimes they affect, produced no comment beyond "Merskeeters is gettin' thick."

Winter brought hard work upon cold ranges. Though the tasks were few in kind, they were strenuous in performance. Inspection trips with the thermometer at forty degrees below zero, night-herding under like conditions were not amusing, but the stock had to be guarded, however loosely, night and day.

Upon a large ranch the work was performed in part by punchers operating from the main buildings, in part by punchers who, stationed in far-off outpost cabins, so-called "line camps," patrolled as "line riders" prescribed boundaries. These men were interchangeably called "line riders" or "outriders," though, strictly speaking, a "line rider" had a regular beat, while an "outrider" was commissioned to roam anywhere.

Effort was made to minimize the duration of continuous work, and the men served, so far as possible, in shifts each of twelve hours. But the West stuck to its job until the latter was done, and never quit at any mere clock strike, as do adherents of the modern eight-hour principle.

The riders had always to know where grass was plentiful and the snow above it reasonably shallow, and constantly to keep their wards shepherded within such happy territory, for the animals' only food was the grass, and they could reach it solely by pawing through the snow. Horses could obtain their provender through even four feet of covering, if the latter were powdery; but let an ice crust form, and the story would be very different. A thaw, immediately followed by a freeze, spelled disaster on the Range.

Even in snowless stretches danger lurked, for rain, promptly succeeded by tremendous drop in temperature, turned each grass blade into an icicle so armored that the live stock could not eat it.

The winds however cold were friendly to the stock in that they swept away the snow from wide stretches of grazing-ground.

In the Far Northwest blew a specially amiable wind, the Chinook, born above the warm current of the Pacific Ocean, and intermittently coming to save the Range in its hour of peril. In the early morning one saw the mountains dazzlingly white, the lowlands spread with snow; then came advance couriers in little puffs of air, and next the wind itself. The stout air-current wiped the white from the hillsides

A LINE CAMP

From a photograph by Philip A. Rollins

as a handkerchief clears a perspiring forehead, and freed the plains from their murderous covering. The transaction was so rapid that the snow did not seem to melt. One moment it was visible, the next it had gone.

Although during the winter the horse herd pretty well could take charge of itself and needed little guidance, the cattle throughout that period were a constant care.

When snow fell the cattle frequently lacked initiative to search for food. Bothered by the wind, they at times left the hillsides, where the grass was within pawing reach, and sifted to the valleys' bottoms, where the drift-covered forage would have been insufficient for the many brutes even if they could have reached it.

One of them, becoming thirsty, started for a hole in the ice formed upon the waters of a lake. The other animals mechanically followed. Ton after ton of weight stupidly, uselessly moved out from solid shore and the inevitable happened—loud, cracking sounds, wild bellowings, tumultuous splashings, and then new ice, marred here and there by a projecting horn or tail.

Upon sign of an impending storm, were it day or were it night, off went the riders to hustle their charges behind the protection of trees or projecting rocks, or else into valleys or swales, which, at right-angles to the blast's promised track, were less likely to be buried deep in snow and, above all, to keep the stock from "drifting."

Throughout the winter, numbed, ice-clad men sat night and day atop exhausted horses, fighting the tempest, were it Texan "norther," or Northern "blizzard," that "away back East" might eat roast-beef and ride in street-cars. For such a life the maximum monthly wage in the decade of the eighties was for a first-class or "top" rider forty dollars, with ten to forty dollars additional if he were a competent ranch foreman; for a rider of less than top rating twenty-five dollars and upward; in each case with board and lodging free. Of course, there were exceptions, and some of the large ranches paid monthly as much as two hundred dollars to an able foreman.

The "drift" was often tragic for both the animals and their owners. It might send to death practically all the cattle of a range. Cattle were its usual prey, for horses almost always had sense sufficient to avoid it, and to find shelter for themselves.

The drift was the live stock's marching in wholesale numbers away from a particular locality, either to avoid the local conditions or to seek better conditions elsewhere. Deep snows having covered the grasses, the discouraged cattle would assemble just as they did for the already described, unintentional drownings in a lake, would suddenly in compact formation begin their trek toward their self-selected, unknown land of promise.

Were the weather not stormy, the beasts would march along for miles and until stopped by some insurmountable obstacle, all the way unwittingly bettering themselves by ploughing a wide cut through the snows. Stopped by the obstacle, whatever it was—a hill, a canyon, or aught else—the beasts would about face, and, retracing their former trail, would browse their way along its partly cleared bottom and back to their starting-point.

But stormy weather might produce a very different result. A bunch of cattle were pawing through the snow and eating their hard-earned ration, when a storm broke upon them. As the air became filled with blinding flakes and the killing wind increased, the beasts uneasily stirred about, then, seeking protection, huddled themselves into a compact mass. With the water from their eyes freezing, with long icicles hanging from their lips, with their backs rime-coated, they stood, head down, moaning, hopeless. Abruptly, in sodden despair, with brain entirely dormant but muscles automatically working, some forceful steer started down to leeward, and behind him, in like condition, straggled the staggering herd. Each animal, keeping true to the wind's course, fought on till the animal dropped; and where it dropped it died.

The numbed brutes fell one by one, first the weaker calves, then the stronger calves, each little tumbling body causing its attendant, anxious mother to stop and wait and perish beside a diminutive mound of snow. Next toppled the weaker steers, then the more virile animals, until the final sacrifice appeared in the frozen bodies of some grand bovine monsters, lying piled before the impassable barrier of a high snow-drift, a deep cut, or a rocky wall.

Material was plentiful for the skinning knives and for the birds and beasts of prey.

Could mounted cowboys, like a flying wedge, have plunged their horses into the mass before the leading steer began the hypnotic march to death, the herd might have been driven to safe cover; but, once the fatal procession started, the doomed animals would obey no order except the summons to destruction and, in the frenzy of hopelessness, would savagely attack whoever sought to rescue them. "Might have been driven to safe cover," but not assuredly. Many a puncher has galloped into a "drift," and, exhausted by his futile efforts, perished with the beasts he tried to save.

A "drift" might occur in summer weather and be the aftermath of a stampede or the result of drought-made scantiness in local drink or herbage, but such a drift would mean no more than that a group of cattle had wandered far afield. It had no terrors.

In snowy weather the punchers had also to keep the stupid cattle from self-immurement in "box canyons," which were gorges with but a single open end, the inner terminal being against a wall of rock within the mountain's mass. A high snow-pile across the entrance might insure starvation for all hoofed beasts within the prison.

Even when unhampered by any responsibility, mere facing of the blizzard offered sometimes to the cowboy a very material hazard. More than one man, leaving his door for the purpose of obtaining wood from a pile fifty feet away, has been so confused and blinded by the shrieking wind and the hissing, stinging snow as to lose all sense of direction, and, devitalized by aimless, unsuccessful searches for some familiar object, has wandered down to leeward, the course instinctively adopted by all storm-numbed wayfarers when headed for the grave. To leeward was whither rescue parties first gave attention in their sad search across a waste of snow.

In particularly storm-swept areas, occasional prudent men, before plunging from their house-doors into the flake-filled air, tied one end of a rope to the door-jamb, and, as they went forth, held grimly onto the other end of that bit of saving hemp.

In the open stretches of the colder sections of the country, there would form crust, often strong enough to support a bronco, sometimes even a wagon with its draft teams. Over such a surface ponies with sharpened shoe calks could be ridden with impunity; but, under average wintry conditions, the local riders were compelled to do considerable navigating in order to avoid soft drifts and deceptive, snow-filled hollows.

At times horses were useless, and for locomotion the men were restricted to the ski. This form of snow-shoe was carried into the West by the Scandinavian linemen whom the telegraph companies employed.

While at times horses were useless, such times were few, for, broadly speaking, the bronco could go anywhere that a man could, save only where the latter in climbing was forced to use his hands, and save only where bog covering or ice too frail for the horse's weight would yet support the lighter human being. Up or down dizzy, trailless heights, over rocks or snow, the wiry, sure-footed cayuse would pick its way and carry its rider, occasionally pausing at some turn to gaze with nonchalant curiosity into the valley a thousand foot almost vertically below.

When descending particularly steep and dangerous slopes, some animals sat on their haunches, and, stiff-kneed, using their front feet as both rudders and brakes, contortingly slid themselves along. To a tenderfoot such an approach to a canyon's rim was decidedly nerve-racking.

Upon ascents however steep, the cowboy usually remained in the saddle and, leaning far forward over the neck of his horse, aided the enterprise by a series of violent forward swings, each in time with one of the horse's upward lunges.

Nevertheless, upon long up grades over shifting gravel or soft snow, the puncher might dismount, and, by seizing the end of his animal's tail, obtain a powerful tow-line. Prudent users of this tractive method cast loose just before the steed passed over the summit, for a horizontal bronco and a human head on a level with the beast's heels might prove an irresistible combination. On the up-hill journey the towed puncher was free from danger, since he was below his beast's kicking plane.

An open winter made life physically comfortable; but it caused worry about prospective drought, because summer's waters came largely from the melting of the previous winter's snows.

The subject of ice and snow suggests what has amazed many an Easterner, the bronco's ability safely to drink the coldest water. A ridden horse in a lather of sweat would fairly fill himself at a semifrozen stream, and afterward happily go on about his business. He never had lived indoors, never had been blanketed, and so he had no fear of being foundered or of catching cold from drafts of air.

Incidentally, he never had been groomed by any man. Whatever person had touched a bronco with currycomb and brush would have had immediate use for a tombstone.

The Western horse groomed himself. He would roll in the dust and the bunch-grass, would shake himself, and, if in good physical condition, would thereafter shine as though hostlers had rubbed and waxed him.

This lack of acquaintance with currycombs was no more marked than was the absence of all familiarity with oats. Many a pilgrim, at the outset of his initial Western visit and with best of intentions, has poured oats onto a bit of canvas, and has led his pony up to what humanly was planned to be an equine feast. A few suspicious glances would be followed by an inquisitive sniff or two, by an inhalation that drew some prickly oat-grains up the pony's nose, by a strenuous and disgusted snort, and by a shower of oats. The cynical little cow-horse, knowing whence his saddle came, had small confidence in anything else man offered him.

There has been mentioned, as being one of the puncher's functions, the laying of poisoned baits for wolves. The cowboy was relied upon for this service only when the animals were not uncomfortably numerous; as soon as in any locality they materially increased in number, and their toll of murdered calves and colts became unduly large, there was temporarily hired a "wolfer." He was a professional killer of wolves; was a man usually very "sot" in his ways, and who, by instinct or training, could outwit the "varmints" and cause them to walk into traps or to eat mortiferous meats when none of the ranch staff could entice them to do more than emit derisive howls. The wolfer had the uncanny habit of stuffing his loose tobacco and cigarette papers into the very pocket that contained a pound of unwrapped strychnine crystals, of smoking all day long, and of being well at supper-time.

Some ranches maintained packs of dogs for the purpose of wolfing; though the majority of cattlemen, doubting the hounds' willingness to spare the live stock's young when the wild animal was absent, and also realizing that, should the dogs, unattended, wander from home the brutes might be shot, preferred wolves to a Range war, and accordingly forewent canine protection.

The wolves throughout the Range did not begin wholesale eating of calves and colts until after the buffalo with its calf had passed into history, or, more definitely speaking, into sleigh-robes and fur coats, and into the stomachs of the men who built the Union Pacific and Northern Pacific railways.

The Western railroads, through their cattle trains, enabled ranching to become a national industry; thereafter, through their eating buffalo, unloosed the wolves against the commercial live stock; and finally, through their wheat cars, took the farmer westward and enabled him to slay the Range.

The wolves fell into two classes, one, a small animal, the coyote or cayote, popularly known as "kiote," the other a large beast which, without regard to possible scientific subdivision, interchangeably was called "timber-wolf," "gray wolf," "big gray," "buffalo wolf," "traveller," "loper," "loafer," "lofer," "lobo," or else "wolf," with any one of the last-mentioned five words as a prefix, as, for instance, "lobo wolf."

The lobos were often very hard to capture; particularly when in rare instances they added to their own extraordinary sagacity the cunning of a pair of coyotes which had attached themselves to the great wolf's presence, and, as sycophantic pages in waiting, accompanied him on all his travels, and scouted one on either side of him.

CHAPTER XI

LIVE STOCK

THE stock, turned loose upon the Range and able to wander whither it would, and that is what happened to all of it, assembled itself through process of natural selection into small groups widely separated from each other and each headed by a dominant leader. There were here and there, as exceptions, individual animals, which as Ishmaelites lived a solitary life and ranged alone. All the beasts, whether in groups or out of them, were in instinct and habit almost as wild as the deer.

The average group of horses contained from ten to fifteen animals, very rarely more than fifty of them, and tended to remain in compact formation. The average group of cattle had a smaller membership and, particularly when pursued, was less cohesive. Each group, whether of horses or of cattle, and each Ishmaelite, pre-empted for itself a particular section of the feeding-grounds, and thus the entire Range was subdivided into tiny equine or bovine principalities.

Each group commonly was called, according to the nature of its component animals, a "band of horses" or a "bunch of cattle," though this distinction between "band" and "bunch" was not always made. For purpose of combination with either of the two terms "stock" and "live stock," "bunch" was by tacit consent the correct word, and not "band." Thus a "bunch of stock," not a "band" of it.

Because of the usual sparseness of the live stock, the Range was to tenderfoot eyes on most days a lonely-looking area; but semiannually the picture would for a short time completely change, and show the great herds of the roundups and of the drives.

Regularly in the spring and again in either the late summer or early fall, as also at any other time that special cause required, there was held a so-called "round-up," or, as it was termed on the Mexican border, a "rodeo."

A round-up attempted to herd to a single point all animals within the territory over which the operation extended.

Little escaped its mesh, though occasional animals, through accidental screening or intentional hiding in boulder fields or clumps of trees, might elude the trap for several successive years. "Man-killing" horses traditionally were past masters at thus concealing themselves.

161

The round-up might cover only such lands as were apt to be grazed by the animals of a particular ranch; and, if so, was conducted primarily in the interest of that ranch, although other ranches benefited to the extent that stock belonging to them turned up in the shuffle. Or it might embrace the several feeding-grounds separately used by a number of ranches, and in such case was principally for the advantage of the ranches thus immediately interested, though, as before, distant owners of visiting animals profited through the unearthing of their errant stock.

The extent of the tract thus to be combed over was determined by conditions. It might be an entire valley, or the lands this side of a desert, or the space between two converging rivers, or, in default of natural boundaries, merely such particular square miles as in all probability would contain all the interested owners' animals inclusive of those with a touch of wanderlust. Although in later years Wyoming by formal law divided itself into definite "round-up districts," which severally averaged about two and a half million acres, the exact field of any operation in Wyoming continued to be determined, as in other States, by the people of the operation's locality. The size of the tract to be covered, the number of the ranches financially concerned were fixed automatically by the situs and quantity of the local water-supplies, for water regulated the extent and ownership of the stock on every range.

Frequently only part of a large range was "worked" on a single day, the entire task being done in instalments. In such a case the field of each such instalment was fixed, as in the instance of the round-up as a whole, either by nature-made limits or by mere square mileage. Each such instalment's field might have its own point at which to concentrate that field's yield of live stock, or several of such fields might use in common one such point.

The number of animals picked up in a day's operation might be ten thousand. It might be only fifteen hundred. In a "little" country, it might be even less.

All the ranches directly interested, called upon by custom to contribute men in numbers proportionate to the extent of the interest, actually threw into the adventure their entire active personnel; while, from distant ranges, appeared volunteers, the latter realizing that their services would be repaid in kind when their own home round-ups should occur.

The men participating in the affair elected from among themselves the various necessary leaders, these being the "round-up boss," the "tally man," etc.

Twice a year the West climbed into the saddle, and a human drag-net in intermittent motion swept all of the area bounded by the Missouri River, the Sierra Nevadas, Canada, and the Mexican border.

These doings permitted the stockmen to ascertain the extent of their possessions and to compute their financial gains or losses, to impound the beasts desirable for sale, to register marks of ownership upon the animals that were to resume their nomad life, and to gather in strays that had wandered far afield.

The "spring round-up," which was primarily for the purpose of branding and thus among cattle-raisers was often called the "calf round-up," occurred after the vernal grass had come, and took place in March throughout the South and on correspondingly later dates in the more northern latitudes. Because of the time of its happening, it yielded no cattle for the market, though on the horse range it produced, as did every round-up there, horses available for sale. This spring herding provoked much discussion of stock that "had not wintered well," and of "dogies," or "dobes," these last being calves or yearling cattle that were still scrubby and anæmic from the scant food of the cold months.

The next regular round-up, the so-called "fall" one, took place in Texas in August or late July, and moved its date later into the calendar in accord with the farther northing of its scene.

This latter round-up gave forth kine fat for the abattoir, sleek cows, and heavy steers. It frequently was termed on a cattle range the "beef round-up," although technically a "beef" was only such a beast as was both four or more years of age and also not a bull. As a matter of fact, most of the animals sold to the packers were "beeves"; but, because weight rather than age was the controlling factor, large younger animals often were included in the procession headed for the slaughter-house.

An animal of the cattle family, whatever its sex, was born a "calf." If a male and reserved for breeding purposes, the brute later became successively a "yearling bull," a "two-year-old bull," a "three-year-old bull," a "four-year-old bull," etc; but, if not so reserved, he, at the end of his first year, passed into the class of "yearling," to remain therein for twelve months, to be termed, for the two successive years immediately thereafter, a "steer," and then to become a "beef." But if the beast were a female, she at the end of her one year's calfdom, became a "heifer," a "yearling," or a "young cow," according as her biographer happened arbitrarily to entitle her. After she successively had served as a "two-year-old cow" and a "three-year-old cow," and meanwhile had by whoever wished to flatter her still been called from time to time a "heifer," she was promoted into the "beef" grade, wherein, with no regard for feminine susceptibilities, her age was blatantly advertised.

The West, despite its creating of all these technical distinctions, was quite apt, when speaking colloquially, to use the word "cow" as a synonym for the word "cattle," and thus not only the "bunch of cows," which the Westerner reported as in the distance, might in fact contain merely steers, but also he was very apt to call a cattle ranch a "cow ranch." Nevertheless, he never termed the Range a "cow Range," or the Cattle Country a "cow country."

The corrals used for a round-up were often far distant from the ranch buildings, and then "chuck wagons," as mess wagons were called, took aboard their cooking outfits and food supplies, and rumbled out to the work place.

A chuck wagon usually was made by imposing at the back end of an ordinary farm wagon a large box which contained shelves and had at its rear a lid that, hinged at the bottom and armed with legs, made, when lowered, a serviceable table. Some ranches, however, had wagons specially designed for restaurant use.

To the round-up corrals, strings of extra saddle-ponies were driven by hostlers whom the Northwest called "horse wranglers," this term being possibly a corruption of the Mexican's "caverango," a hostler.

An unreasonable distinction, often made in colloquial usage, caused these men to "wrangle" horses in daytime, and to "herd" them at night, although the services rendered were identical in nature, merely a keeping of the horses from straying too far away, and an ultimate production of them at the place and time desired. This same usage made the men wrangle the horses, and not wrangle *with* them.

The extra ponies driven to the round-up corrals formed an aggregation which the Northwest knew as the "saddle band," but which in the Southwest was called by this name, by that of "remuda," or "remontha" (this latter a corruption of Spanish "remonta") and also by that of "cavvieyah," "cavoy," "cavvoy," "cavy," "cavvy," or, if the dictionary were more closely followed, "caballada," "cavallard," "cavayard," or "caviarde." The West reserved control of its spellings and pronunciations, and cared naught that the lexicon gave the Westerner's two-syllabled "kiote," or "kiyote," as the three syllabled "co-yot-e."

The extra ponies were necessary, for the work at the rodeo corrals was done at so fast a pace as to force the cowboys to frequent change of mounts. The average puncher, to do his best work, had to have four horses resting while one was being ridden.

From a drawing by N. C. Wyeth, published in Scribner's Magazine

THE CHUCK WAGON

Each of these rodeo corrals was of a size sufficient to accommodate whatever animals a combing of the dependent territory might yield. Thus, while almost all of these corrals were more extensive than those at the ranch-house, they, as among themselves, varied much in area. Some were very big. In the more extensive structures, advantage often was taken of whatever conveniences nature had offered, and, instead of a continuous fence identical in character with that in the ranch-house corrals, fencing of this type would merely piece in the gaps between high piles of rocks, or would spring from each of two places on a forest's edge and leave the intervening space to be guarded by horizontal rails lashed to growing trees, or else would do no more than run across the open end of a favoring "box canyon."

In any event, each rodeo corral had an entrance which was closable by bars, and, from each side of this entrance, flared out for many feet "wing fences" to shunt the edges of the entering herd into the break in the pen's high boundary. Connected with this main enclosure might be subsidiary ones which had interopening gates and were thus convenient for sorting stock.

These preparations made, the round-up itself began.

Horsemen, widely separated in skirmish line, started miles from a designated corral, and, as "circle riders," converging on it, drove slowly before themselves everything that moved on legs. The animals thus gradually herded together would be, with a few exceptions, all horses or all cattle, according to what the local ranches raised.

The procession to some extent was self-constructive, for, although the riders frequently had to "round in" isolated beasts or groups of beasts and to urge them into the driven herd, the grazing brutes would in the main voluntarily join it. Stock quietly feeding would hear or scent the coming procession; would, for a moment, gaze inquisitively at it; and then, obedient to the instinct of gregariousness, would trot across country and fall into line.

The herding horsemen advanced with gingerly slowness, fearful lest sudden movement might cause the quarry to break and run; and, as they gradually converged, the creatures before them melded into a common herd. Quietly there moved in ahead of it one rider, the "round-up boss." He was the pacemaker, the general of the occasion. Possibly he had beside him a lieutenant-general or two. Quietly there ranged along either side of the herd and from among the circle riders a line of flankers, riders less strategic than the general in front or than the lieutenant-generals who "rode tail," and thus as "tail riders" stayed behind the herd and kept it to the pace the general from time to time might order.

Until the procession had come so near the corral that, if walking were abandoned, the higher speed assumed might continue surely to the end, the animals quietly were nursed along. It was true that they were more liable to break while walking than while moving at a swifter pace, for at the slower rate they had more time to think. But when under the excitement of recent, rapid speed they were reduced to a walking pace, they were almost certain to make a "bobble." Accordingly, the men all rode leisurely along.

A beast shot out to the side. If it were a deer or antelope, none of the riders did more than to hope that its departure would remain unnoticed by its late brute companions. If the beast were a single steer and the herd were of horses, if the beast were a single horse and the herd were of cattle, the decamping creature had relieved the riders from the prospective trouble of "cutting it out" after arrival at the corral, so in muttered tone they gave the quitter a profane benediction and hoped, as before, for inattention by its former comrades. If the fleeing animal were of the same stock as that of the herd, the brute probably would be let to go, lest an effort to "head" it create confusion disturbing to its crawling but nervous mates. But, in fact, numerous animals had started. They had to be headed at all cost, for otherwise the entire aggregation would pour out through the opening like water through a levee's break. The job was accomplished. The men and their charges quieted down and plodded along.

The general, with one of his eyes glued in his back, had followed tensely every changing whim of the beasts which he had held behind him, and from time to time had headed from a forward dash. He sensed that the herd no longer would tolerate quiescence. He knew that the corral was not, in distance, beyond the breathing limit of more rapid motion. He put his horse in trot. Rank by rank, the brute platoons behind him, in quick succession, increased their speed.

Near the goal, with his pony for days groomed for the effort, the general plunged forward, followed by the thunder of six thousand hoofs and by a blinding cloud of dust. The wing fences showed in front. He headed directly between them, but an instant before he otherwise would have reached their limitations he "whirled" his pony, darted to one side, and was out of the rush.

The insensate, now leaderless brutes had no opportunity to swerve, and, like a living avalanche, rolled into the corral, the pressure from the rear often sending the forward animals with horrid force against the farther fence. Occasionally one or more horses among these forward animals would wildly leap, and, as lightly as a scaling card, would sail over the corral's fence.

The "flank riders" also had drawn off to the sides and away from the mess, and no human was as yet within the corral. Up went the bars across its entrance; cookie and his crew having stood guard for this service.

Every horseman dismounted, dropped the handkerchief which had been about his nose and mouth, wiped at sweat and dust, said "damn," and congratulated the general. The latter had paced well and deserved congratulation. Nobody, of course, suggested that, had the general's horse gone down, a man and an animal would have been ground to pulp. That was axiomatic and was all in a day's work.

The tired ponies, for their reward, were unsaddled and allowed to roll and delightedly to writhe on their backs; each rider furtively watching his own steed, to see whether on its third attempt it went completely over, and thus, according to frontier diagnosis, proved itself physically sound.

Where did all this happen? Its scene and its action, as regards horses, was on any of the principal horse ranges at any time during the life of the horse industry. For a smaller range, the number of the corralled animals should be decreased. As regards cattle, the description is subject to a corresponding adjustment in figures, and, for the years subsequent to the seventies, must be modified in certain other details.

When, in the decade of the seventies, cattle customarily began to sell by the pound instead of, as theretofore, by the head, ranchers commenced to realize that with cattle rapid movement meant loss of weight, that the fat which dripped away in sweat was the same as the fat the packer would have bought. Consequently, cowboys were ordered to hold cattle, so far as possible, to a walk, a result obtainable by decreasing the number of beasts one man was expected to control.

Wherefore, to make the description accurately applicable to the majority of cattle round-ups after the decade of the seventies, one must alter the above recital so far as to have the live stock effect, at a far slower pace than is above denoted, both the traversing of the country and the entering into the corral.

And, for certain sections of the Range during the later years of the cattle industry, one must make the further amendment of doing away altogether with the corral, and having the final bunching of the cattle not within high fences but in an "open" round-up.

The selling by the head or by the pound, as mentioned above, relates to sales made to the public. Ranchmen, in such transactions among themselves as involved a rancher's disposing of all his live stock, sometimes sold "on range delivery." This meant that the buyer, after inspection of the seller's ranch records, and with due regard to the seller's reputation for veracity, paid for what the seller purported to own, and then rode out and tried to find it.

If we cease these digressions and return to the corral, we shall find that the men beside it had scrubbed at the black muck which sweat-mixed white or gray alkali dust had laid upon their faces, had gorged themselves from the results of the efforts made by cookie over his intrenched fire, and now were about to attack the second stage of their work.

If the corral were filled with cattle and the season were the spring, there would be much branding of calves to do, but there would be very little dealing with the older animals beyond sorting out and returning to their owners such brutes as were visitors from foreign ranges. If the corral were filled with cattle and the round-up were that of fall, while there would be scant necessity for branding, the older animals would be the principal subjects of the cowboys' labors.

If the corral knew only horses, there would be far more branding at the round-up of the spring than at that of the autumn; and, at each of these round-ups, mature animals might be gathered for the market.

But whatever the season and whatever the kind of animal involved, the punchers were now ready to resume their work. People, some outside the bars of the corral and others on its top rail, prodded the imprisoned animals back from the entrance sufficiently far to permit lowering of the bars and an entrance by some of the remounted cowboys.

These men's ponies, sending front knees high in air but taking mincing steps, impatiently waited for an inkling as to the quarry's identity and for a raising of the reins, this last the signal for a burst of speed.

These mounted cowboys, remaining ahorse, wormed through the herd, and separated the animals for which there was no immediate need from those which were to be sold or broken or branded, as the case might be.

This process involved "cutting out," which means that the rider, sighting an animal to be segregated, rode between it and the body of the herd. The animal dodged. The rider had barely commenced to guide his pony into pursuit before that knowing little devil sensed the entire situation. Highly trained to the purpose, like a kitten following a ball, he gleefully, and with lightning-like changes of direction, began with the quarry a game of competitive dodging. In and out through the herd, they twisted and turned. The cutting-out pony, learned in all the tricks of the contest, eventually got the advantaged position for which he had schemed; the quarry clear from the herd, with a panting, man-laden imp in between.

The quarry, once clear from the herd, was fair target for the lariat, and also, if moving, might be "tailed."

Amid this whirligig, the rider, if in playful mood, very likely kicked his foot free from his stirrup, and dug his spur into an animal galloping past. The pony under him, equally joyous, would from time to time slyly nip at passing beasts.

When the objective for the lariat was a particular calf or colt, usually the cutting-out campaign was directed principally against the mother; for not only was she needed near the fire, that her markings might show what should be imprinted on her offspring, but also she was easier to follow, and confidently could be expected to sweep her youngster along with her in her rush. No matter how great the confusion, the mother never would mistake the identity of her baby, although the latter might fail to recognize its parent.

A saddle-horse which when galloping could stop short in his tracks, change his direction like a weather-vane, and instantly bound off on a new course was called a "peg pony," "peg horse," or "pegger." He was very dear to his cowboy rider, but he "dumped" many a novice.

The animal recently cut out was now to be roped.

The pursuing puncher lifted his coiled lariat from its home below the saddle's horn, his left hand holding, high in the air, such portion of the rope as was not to be included in the noose, that no part of this surplus rope might, when flying out, pass behind the puncher and do damage to his temper, if not to his neck. The puncher's right hand, gripping the "hondo," paid out through it, by a series of short jerks of the wrist, rope sufficient for the noose.

When rope enough for a circle of six or seven feet in diameter had thus been emitted, the puncher's right hand, palm down and twenty inches or so behind the hondo, grasped tightly both the side of the noose and also that part of the rope which had not already passed through the hondo and thus become a portion of the noose. Then the noose was started swinging. By the time that it had made its fourth revolution, it was in the shape of an oval, was in horizontal position over the wielder's head, and was sufficiently open for the "throw."

Until the throw was made, the noose was kept steadily revolving; but, an instant before the throw, the noose was for two or three revolutions whirled with tremendous speed, the puncher meanwhile twisting his right shoulder backward and forcing his right hand still further to the rear. Then this hand shot forward and released the noose. Forth with the latter landed, as the thrower wished, either over the victim's head or else on the ground, from the latter target to bounce up and catch whatever leg or legs of the moving quarry the thrower had selected.

The lariat then was jerked to semitautness, and instantly was snubbed around the saddle horn.

Coincidently with the "catch," the ridden pony stopped short, and squatted on his haunches, fairly sitting on the end of his spine. From that instant, his eyes stayed fixed on the fallen victim. As the latter rolled one way or the other, the pony, with front legs straight and braced stiffly before him, pivoted on his seat; and, moving his front feet in inch-long side-steps, sat facing ever squarely at the contents of the noose. So expert were some of the ponies, that their riders could dismount and leave the holding of the roped beast entirely to the management of the sitting little horse.

Sometimes, just as a lariat was to be thrown, a quarry on the rider's right doubled in its tracks, and the thrower, if of ability, instantly turned his right-hand palm up, which overset the spinning noose and let a rearward snap of the forearm make that throw admired in the "opera-house," the "backthrow," on the off side.

Also, by a similar oversetting, the noose could be brought down from its normal high level, and, by a backward round-arm swing which ended as the holding hand advanced, be shot forward upon a plane quite near the ground.

If, when a catch was made and the reata came to tautness, the roping pony were all sideways toward the quarry, over went the pony and its rider with a crash. Accordingly it was important, particularly when lariating heavy animals, that the rider should make his throw only when either the length of his pony's body was in line with the direction of the throw, or else his pony had itself so well in hand as surely to be able to spin into that position before the reata gave its terrific yank.

It was necessary, in deciding when to throw, to consider the possible movement of animals not directly concerned in the matter; for, should one of them rush between the roping pony and the caught victim, and the roper be unable to let go of the lariat, an unfortunate little mustang and the man atop him would be snapped heels over head.

If, as the throw was made, the rider sensed that the pony under him would not be in proper position when the prospective jerk should occur, the rider would not snub his lariat's home end to the saddle horn, but would let the lariat hang loosely from his hand. Usually whatever beast had been so inconveniently roped would soon shake off the noose; but sometimes, if the catch had been made outside of the corral, a chagrined cowboy would see his reata trailing across the prairie behind a galloping steer. Such a sight would mean a tiresome ride in order to head back the brute with its stolen property.

The roping pony, if it had confidence in its rider, forgave occasional spills; but, once there occurred an upset which the canny little beast considered inexcusable, that particular rider could never thereafter make a catch from the back of that particular pony. The beast's slight outward swerve at the instant of each throw would cause the noose to land just short of its mark, but short every time; and, throughout the whole adventure, butter would not melt in the little pony's mouth.

There were marked differences in the speed of the throw. The noose of some men settled slowly and lightly on the target, the rope behind in sinuous line. The noose of other men moved like a bullet, and stood at the end of a ramrod.

Save in Texas, few men attempted to lariat an animal which was more than twenty-five feet away.

One now sees, upon the theatrical stage, men and women who can vitalize a rope, and can make its noose move when and whither the actor wills. However remarkable the performance, it is not roping, for it is given from a platform steadier than the back of a rushing, whirling horse, omits all strategy to force a rapidly moving target into fair position, and calls for no nice instinct as to the proper instant for the throw.

Cowboys frequently threw from foot instead of from the pony's back, but these throws from foot usually amounted to no more than dropping a noose either over the kicking leg of an animal already down and held by a horseman, or else over the neck of some calf or colt.

Should a free animal of mature years be caught, the unfortunate puncher at the other end of the reata turned sideways, left flank toward the enemy, jammed the rope against his own right hip, gripped with his left hand far down the lariat, dug his heels and the edges of his boots into the earth, and leaned far backward, then to commence a series of jumps, each concluding with a like digging in and leaning back.

After the noose had lodged and before the lariat had tautened, this puncher might have transferred to the ensnared animal much of the puncher's share of the prospective jerk, accomplishing this by swinging the rope's home end in a wide, vertical circle at a right-angle with the line of throw. This would have started a "roll," a corkscrew, wave-like motion, which, travelling along the reata to its far end, would have landed with a jar. If the jar and the jerk had been coincident, there would have been a tremendous shock to the animal, and the latter pretty surely would have somersaulted.

But if, at any time that there was a strain upon the lariat, the cowboy had happened to be at other than approximately a right-angle with the course of the beast he had roped, and worst of all to be behind the brute, and so subject, in this latter contingency, to what was termed a "line pull," or "end pull," he would have been reduced to the relative position of the traditional man who tried to stop a runaway horse by holding onto its traces.

The roper, when working afoot, also might ameliorate his task by using the "snubbing post," which was a vertical, round timber some five feet high, firmly set in the earth at the centre of the corral, and stout enough to stand the strains to which it was subjected.

He could hitch his lariat to this post; make a successful throw; take the initial part of the strain in the acrobatic way described above; and then, letting go of his lariat, allow the post to assume the remaining stress. Or else, with a "free" reata, he could make his catch, and afterward snub his rope to the post.

However, the post could not with impunity be used or the throwing of powerful animals. The tremendous pull which their downfall caused might break a lariat so unyieldingly held.

The throwing of an animal with a particularly heavy crash was called, as was every other Titanic, masterful act by man to beast, a "busting wide open" of the abused brute.

CHAPTER XII

BRANDING AND THE ROUND-UP

TAILING—BRANDING FIRE—BULLDOGGING—BRANDS AND MARKS—BRANDING-IRONS AND BRANDS—BRANDING CUSTOMS—MAVERICKS, DERIVATION OF TERM—BRAND BLOTCHING—HOG-TIES—ESTRAYS—OPEN ROUND-UP—INSPECTORS—ATTACKS BY CATTLE—STAMPEDING THE BEEF ISSUE.

FOR the downing of an animal, "tailing" sometimes took the place of roping. Any member of the horse or cattle families could, when travelling at all rapidly, be sent heels over head by the simple process of overtaking the brute, seizing its tail, and giving the latter a pull to one side. This would throw the animal off its balance, and over it would crash, onto its head and shoulder. Though the slightest of yanks frequently was capable of producing the result, many men assured success through a turn of the tail about the saddle horn, this supplemented sometimes, in the case of cattle, by a downward heave of the rider's leg upon the straining tail.

Horses, unless patently worthless, were seldom tailed. The process offered too much risk of springing a knee or of spraining a shoulder.

Occasionally, under playful impulse, a puncher would tail a fellow rider's pony, but this act rarely was intended to accomplish more than to cause the little horse, by a sudden jump, to jolt its rider. With similarly jocose purpose, a lariat would land about a man or around the neck of the horse beneath him; though, under such circumstances, the noose never was jerked to tautness.

While we have been wandering far afield in general observations, the cowboys have been sticking to their business at the rodeo corral. Out of this corral, the undesired animals finally were weeded, to sift in twos and threes over the horizon, sooner or later to reform, so far as possible, into the very bands which had been so rudely disturbed earlier in the day, and to resume the very haunts from which the beasts had unwillingly been driven. As they one by one passed through the corral's bars, they received farewell slaps from lariats' ends, mere slaps, save in the case of a horse leaving a cattle corral, or of a steer or cow leaving one of horses. These latter departing and excepted brutes, however inoffensive, invariably were assumed to have invited themselves to the party, and venom was put into each dismissal blow and into the words accompanying it.

While cutting out and roping were progressing within the corral, there rose from it a cloud of dust; and out of this, if cattle were the stock involved, came a constant and pandemoniac chorus from bleating calves and bellowing mothers separated in the mêlée.

In due time all the unbranded animals were discovered. One by one, they were cut out, were herded to the vicinity of the bonfire which held the branding-irons, were there thrown by roping, or, if horned, sometimes by "bulldogging," and, when prone, not only were branded, but also were subjected to such surgery, if any, as might be necessary. In the case of cattle, if they fell inconveniently far from the fire, they, regardless of intervening sticks and stones, ignominiously were dragged at a lariat's end to the desired spot. Horses were given more considerate treatment, in that some care was exercised that they be not "dumped" so far from the flames as to require this skin-abrading haulage.

The bonfire, if in Texas, was required by local law to be inside the corral's enclosure, the purpose of the law being to prevent branding in unfrequented localities, and thereby to lessen stealing. In States other than Texas, the fire often blazed just outside the corral's gate.

Toward the fire at an important round-up, animals slithered every few seconds, sliding on their sides, their backs, on any part of their anatomies, all of the beasts highly indignant.

Some cattle landed there as victims of "bulldogging," and not of roping. Bulldogging involved throwing one's right arm over a steer's or cow's neck, the right hand gripping the neck's loose, bottom skin or the base of the right horn or the brute's nose, while the left hand seized the tip of the brute's left horn. The "dogger" then rose clear of the ground; and, by lunging his body downward against his own left elbow, so twisted the neck of the brute that the latter lost its balance and fell. It was a somewhat active performance, because, the instant the dogger took hold, the seized beast began to run, and the man's legs, when not touching the ground in flying leaps, were waving outward to avoid his maddened vehicle's knees.

An animal, thus to be thrown, had to be moving at high speed, for the beast had to be deprived not only of balance, but also of ability to regain it. The feat, though favored in public exhibitions, found little usage in every-day life; except occasionally it might be applied to a youngster which was of no great weight, was attempting to dodge, and, for the latter reason, had its neck already somewhat twisted. Roping would achieve the same result and was much less onerous.

In the bonfire were the branding-irons of all the ranches interested in the round-up. Beside the fire stood the "tally man," a person selected for the position because of his honesty and his clerical accuracy, or possibly because of his physical inability to render more strenuous service.

He entered on a "tally-sheet" a tally mark for each animal on which an owner's brand or mark was placed; and, while he worked his stubby pencil, he monotonously chanted somewhat as follows: "Star K Outfit, one calf, Circle Nine Ranch, one calf," etc.

As a sprawling beast was dragged up to the fire and its ownership disclosed, there was pressed against the brute the appropriate, red-hot iron, and there were added by the knife such additional "marks," if any, by way of cuts on ears, dewlaps, or other folds of skin, as the owner had adopted to further prove proprietorship.

These burns and cuts were permanent, and established everywhere the ownership of the brute that wore them, even though he strayed across the continent.

Each raiser of horses or cattle registered with the proper official of his State or county a written instrument wherein was claimed the exclusive right to burn upon a particular part of an animal, such as a specified shoulder or rump, a particular design made of certain numbers, letters, lines, or of combinations of these elements, or to apply specified cuts or chippings to a stated ear, both ears, the dewlap or other feasible fold of skin, or to do both these things. If nobody had made prior claim for the use of the design, the latter was formally allowed, was entered in the official "brand book," and became in effect the trade-mark of the the person who registered it.

To safeguard whatever cut or chipping was made, various States required that not more than half of each ear be removed, that neither ear be whittled to a point, and that no cut or chipping made by one owner be altered or obliterated by a later proprietor.

Ears, because of their convenient viewableness, were the usual seats of the cuts and chips.

Cattle commonly received both the "brand" and the "mark" of their owner; while horses, to avoid disfigurement, were subjected only to the brand.

A rancher of large affairs might, through absorption of other ranchmen's businesses, become the owner of numerous brands and marks; though, in many jurisdictions, he was limited to registering in his own name a single set of such emblems.

Likewise a man without capital but with definite plan of self-enrichment would in many instances procure the recording of a series of such signs of ownership, one in his own name, the others in the several names of his various dummies. He would do this because he would anticipate that, when he took to "rustling" and to "pasting his brand" on other people's animals, he would prefer not to have it seem that each of his four or five mangy cows had given birth to eight calves in a single season.

Although, strictly speaking, a brand was the product of a hot iron while a mark was a knife cut, both in colloquial usage were termed brands.

The branding-iron was in the form of a straight poker called a "running iron," used like a pencil, and producing a "running brand"; or else it was in the form of a solid block of type recording at one touch the whole design and thus creating a "set brand."

While the brand might be of any size its owner wished, convenience dictated usually seven inches as the maximum for both height and breadth, and two and four inches as the respective minimums for these two dimensions.

The letters, figures, or designs in a brand commonly bore some relation to the owner's name or to some event of either business or sentimental interest to him, and always were selected and placed in combination only after careful consideration as to the extent of their immunity from forging alteration. A thief readily could retouch a letter C into a zero or a letter O; while the letter I as readily could be changed to any one of twelve other letters, or, with a numeral placed after it, be transformed into the figure one. Slight effort would change a 3 into an 8 or a B, would shift a 4 into an H. Crowding letters or figures together, surrounding them with framing lines, placing short, horizontal markings across their open ends, all tended to prevent improper alterations. So did the filling out of geometrical diagrams in such way as that there should not remain strokes, capable with slight additions of forming very different-looking markings.

The designs ordinarily used were simple, because complicated ones, when the brands healed and their lines somewhat shifted position, were apt to become confused.

When the brand's design bore framing lines, it was said to be "boxed." In the absence of such enclosure, it was called an "open brand."

Consideration was given also to the location of the knife cuts, and to the advisability of having them in straight or wavy slits, and with or without discard of a narrow wedge of cartilage.

Having designed his brand, the ranchman next decided and announced how he wanted it to sound when orally described, and thus fixed the order in which the component elements should be mentioned. In so doing, he rarely exercised caprice, but almost always was obedient to the reasonable limitations of common usage.

When a ranchman sold an animal imprinted with his, the selling ranchman's, brand, there was given to the purchaser a written bill of sale; and the already decorated animal might receive one, if not two, additional brands. Thus, the brute might be given one which was known interchangeably as the "vent brand" (from Spanish "venta," meaning a sale) or "counter brand," and which was the seller's admission of the fact of sale; and might be subjected also to the purchaser's ownership brand. Wherefore a thoroughly etched side upon a cow meant that she had had successive owners. The vent brand ordinarily was a facsimile of the seller's ownership brand, though it might be reduced in size.

While members of the cattle family obtained, save in rare instances, all the decorations mentioned in the preceding paragraph, horses ordinarily graduated from liability to branding as soon as they received their initial ownership impression, and their subsequent proprietors commonly relied upon possession of bills of sale. Branding somewhat injured the horse's appearance, so he was spared from an overdose of hot iron.

Upon a cattle drive in which variously branded animals were to participate, and which was to extend beyond the limits of a single county, a special brand, known as a "road brand," was applied for the purposes of the trip. This brand assisted the herders in identifying their stock, and also tended to prevent these herders from improperly merging in their herd, and spiriting out of the jurisdiction, animals of uninterested owners.

Lastly, there was in Texas for the benefit of its ranchmen a statutory series of so-called "county brands," a separate, prescribed letter or group of letters for each Texan county. Thus a Texan, if he wished, might place upon his animal not only his individual brand of ownership, but also the county brand of the county in which he ranched; this latter brand, if used, going by legal requirement onto the animal's neck. Thereafter a thief, seeking to alter brands, would be compelled either to change both the brands, or else to change the ownership brand to one recorded in the particular county to which the county brand related.

The road brand often was applied through openings in the fences of a "shoot," for, if the animals involved were numerous and mature, their roping would be unduly onerous.

At the round-up, upon each such unbranded animal as was attended by a mother went a duplicate of the most recent ownership brand the mother bore, unless the following condition obtained. If the mother were locally owned, and if also her brand were one of a distant State and did not, upon the local range, appear upon the animals of another rancher, her local owner, through desire to protect her from undue distress or for other reason, may have refrained from imposing his own brand upon her. In such event, her attendant offspring would receive the brand of its mother's local owner, and not a duplicate of any brand the mother carried.

Furthermore, if a mother should display an assortment of ownership markings so hopelessly confusing as not to disclose the identity of her then owner, her attendant youngster would be dealt with as though it were a "maverick," which latter, conscience-destroying and trouble-creating object will presently explain itself.

In the absence of such excepting conditions, the infant received, as a matter of course, a duplicate of its mother's most recent ownership inscription, whether burned or cut or both. She might have strayed with her child from southern Texas but, nevertheless, northern Montana was bound in honor to protect the presumptive Texan owner of many hundred miles away.

Any person having in mind these rules and customs and watching the branding at the corral could confidently read the branded inscriptions. He would know that "4-28," meant "four bar twenty-eight," since a hyphen always was called a "bar"; that, because a capital letter of size was commonly termed "big," "A2" was translatable into "big a two"; that, because a letter or figure lying on its side was termed "lazy," a prone letter "m" underscored was the "lazy m bar." This person would know also that, because a ring was dubbed a "circle," a letter "g" enclosed within a ring was the "circle g"; that, because a circle's are was, according to its length, designated as a "quarter," "half," or "three-quarter" "circle," a scant bit of a curve followed by a letter "r" was the "quarter-circle r," and that, because anything looking like a diamond or even its cousin was called "diamond," a figure "5" within a lozenge should be interpreted as "diamond five." This person would know also that any parallelogram, regardless of the ratio between its length and height, was a "block," a "box," or a "square," whichever its owner cared to term it, that the faintest resemblance to a pair of wings gave the prefix of "flying," so that the numeral "9," between two misshapen bulges was the "flying nine," and that other designs were attempted pictures, and should be entitled "broken pipe," "sombrero," "spur," "bit," "elk horn," "two star," "wheel," or whatever. Finally, this person would know that still further designs had arbitrary, slangy designations such as "wallop" (a wide letter "U" atop another letter "U" equally wide but inverted), "whang-doodle" (a group of interlocking wings with no "flying," central design), and "hog pen" (two parallel lines crossing two other parallel lines at a right angle).

Sometimes a design had foisted upon it by a naïve local public a designation unexpected by the design's creator. The late ex-President Theodore Roosevelt, when a ranchman, registered in Dakota three brands in the respective forms of an elk horn, a triangle, and a Maltese cross. The last of these promptly became on his neighbors' lips the "Maltee cross," these neighbors supposing that "Maltese" was of the plural number.

No Easterner should too patronizingly smile at this innocence, for did not New England, years before, not only share the mariners' belief that one lone Portuguese was a "Portogee," but also, having assumed that "chaise" meant at least two carriages, call a single one of them a "shay"?

All of the pictures used in a brand were of sufficiently open drawing as not to hide prior brands; because, early in the industry, it had been found necessary to frown on cross-hatched markings, as also on burnt spots of abnormal size, and thus to forbid the use of the "sash," or "window-sash," the "frying-pan," and other like designs, all capable of effecting a general obliteration.

The marks produced by knife cuts had no technical or picturesque designations. The latter ran in this typical manner: "One straight-edged, wedge-shaped slit on left side of right ear," etc.

The spectator at the corral could find interesting history on the skins of many of the animals. Over there was a beef which bore upon his neck "BZ," the county brand of Brazos County, Texas, and upon his hip the ownership inscription of a rancher in that county. The brute's sides, scarred with signs of proprietorship, of sale, and of the road, declared that he now belonged to the Double Triangle Outfit of Montana; that, before passing into this ownership, he had been an asset of successively the Three Flags Ranch of Wyoming and the Diamond Bar K men in Colorado; and that he had come northward "on the hoof," and not by rail. Beyond him, was a steer which showed from his markings that he had been either a maverick or the child of a too gaudily decorated mother, and also had walked from a Southern State to the spot at which the spectator saw him.

Of course, no ranchman attempted to remember the ownership of all the numerous brands and marks. While those of the larger, established ranches were widely known, those of small or new outfits often forced inquirers from beyond the local range to apply for information to the various registering officials.

If, during the transaction at the fire, a wrong brand mistakenly were applied to an animal, the beast, nevertheless, was turned over to the owner of that brand; but, as soon as an animal of his appeared for marking, it was "traded back" to the owner of the first brute, and, onto this last arriving beast, the "traded" animal, went the marking of the man who had borne the original loss. Thus ultimately nobody suffered privation from the error. True, for a year, mother and offspring would carry inconsistent inscriptions; but the official tally-sheet would explain the cause. At the year's end, parent and child would separate, and no apparent evidence of "rustling" would then exist.

However, it might be that no animal would appear for trading back, in which event the gainer would settle with the loser by paying cash, by giving an "I.O.U.," or by delivering an already branded animal, which beast now had to accept both a vent brand and a second ownership brand.

Pursuant both to long-established custom, and in some localities to formal edict, branding other than that performed by "rustlers" was done usually in the presence of men from several ranches; but, whether it were so done or instead were carried on by the men of a single ranch, it generally was intended to be conducted honestly. Even so, upon a range dominated by a single ranch that treated well its employees, the home brand had, through the enthusiastic loyalty of the punchers, a careless habit of wandering, at a round-up, onto an orphan's prostrate form.

There rarely was from overt stealing as much loss as the novelists have set up, for the thief ran too much risk of detection and faced the severest of penalties. Thievery indirectly accomplished through the altering of brands produced very considerable seepage; but its extent, except in Wyoming, has never been ascertained, even approximately.

In the earlier years, whoever anywhere found a "maverick," or "sleeper," an animal unbranded and without maternal escort, might impose on it the finder's ownership brand. Later, and by successive steps, this broad principle was greatly restricted. First, it was unofficially decreed that a man might place his brand upon only such mavericks as he discovered upon his own range. Next, there was added to this limitation a further one which not only forbade any cowboy to place his own brand upon any maverick, but also required him, in return for a cash bonus awarded him for each maverick which he discovered upon his employer's range, to turn over his finds either, as in some localities, to his employer or, as in other localities, to the stockmen's association or stock commissioners of the local State.

But even this amendment left the door open to grave abuses by unscrupulous persons. The latter, whether rancher desiring more live stock or puncher seeking a bonus, easily could convert an attractive colt or calf into an actual orphan. One shot would do it. Because of the activity of these so-called "maverick factories," as the Range termed all exterminators of parents with their inconvenient brands, still further amendments seemed necessary. Accordingly, the bonus system was abolished, and on some ranges, it was prescribed even that no cowpuncher might own live stock. Furthermore, the law ordained that everywhere, except in such localities as locally agreed to retain the earlier method of permitting a rancher to brand whatever mavericks he or his men found on his own range, the unbranded waifs should be sold at auction by the local stock commissioners or association, the buyer then to have right to add his ownership brand to the vent brand of the selling official body, and the cash proceeds from the sale to go either to the support of the stock inspectors and detectives of the State in which the transaction occurred, or else to some other designated public use.

Maverick, speaking from the dictionary, applied to both horses and cattle; but upon the Range, the term was restricted to members of the cattle family, and brandless colts were termed either "slick ears," or else, more commonly and in plain English, "unbranded colts," though they were dealt with as if mavericks.

"Slick ear," was sometimes applied as well to cattle; and, in such case, used as a synonym for maverick, it denoted a wholly unbranded and unmarked animal. Nevertheless, in strict usage, it meant merely an animal the ear of which was "slick," i. e., not slit with any ownership mark.

In some localities, maverick was limited to animals which were at least one year of age, although, in other localities, it took in every unbranded calf the moment it ceased to follow its mother and began an independent life.

When Samuel Maverick, a Texan rancher of long years ago, refused to brand his cattle and continually bedevilled his neighbors with questions as to the whereabouts of his straying animals, he little knew that he thereby was forcing his name into the English lexicon.

Such is the kindlier of the two traditions as to how his name crept into the dictionary. His detractors insist that he arrived in Texas with no assets except a branding-iron, a morality which was blind in one eye, a far-sightedness for unbranded animals, and a tireless perseverance.

The honesty of the West was not so complete as to exclude the existence of so-called "brand artists," "brand blotters," or "brand blotchers," these being gentlemen who, with ingenuity and a piece of hot metal, added marks to those already on a beast and made the final result identical with the "artist's" registered brand.

So flagrantly did these gentlemen miswield the "running iron," that several States eventually forbade its use by anybody, and everywhere its mere possession gave rise to suspicion.

Not only was this poker-like implement inducive to its transporter's disrepute; but also it was heavy and was awkward to carry on the saddle. Of course, honest men had but infrequent need to carry irons, but the rustler felt himself constrained never to be without one. He had always to be prepared to "pick up manna," that is to say, to steal, even though he might thus describe his loot as a gift from heaven. For a while after running irons became unfashionable, he affected broken horseshoes or the sidebars of riding bits, as being both portable and inconspicuous; but they, when heated, proved hard to manipulate.

Baling wire or, with the majority of thieves, telegraph wire took the place of all these appliances, and were much more convenient. The wire could be folded and hidden in the pocket, was light in weight, could be twisted into the shape of many set brands, and, from its small diameter, made lines such as best melted into the already healed scars of whatever legitimate brand was being "doctored."

Interposing a wet blanket or wet buckskin between the beast's side and the hot iron or wire tended to make the artist's work look, from the time he "painted his picture on the cow," like a fairly old brand.

The artists' harvest days were those immediately following the round-up when the legally made scars were still fresh upon the animals.

During the progress of branding, the punchers often subjected cattle to two humiliating actions from which horses were spared. Though a horse, when roped and thrown, was accorded the dignity of being held by lariats until all work on him had been finished, a calf was promptly deprived of the reata as soon as the infant struck the ground. Thereupon the little brute, through a most impolite seizure of its ears, had its head so twisted as to lie flat on the earth and to offer a seat to one officiating puncher. To effectually stifle any kicking, a second puncher, with one of his feet, pushed one hind leg of the squealing victim well forward, and, with both hands, pulled the other hind leg far to the rear. The little calf thus lay helpless, its bulging eyes wildly rolling, while still two other cowboys, one with hot iron, the other with knife, made brands and cuts.

Then too, very frequently mature cattle, after being thrown by roping or tailing or bulldogging, had their legs (usually two hind and one front) fastened together by a short piece of line; whereupon the lariats, if any, were cast off. Thus "hog-tied," the victim was wholly impotent. As he was reached by the cowboys on their rounds of the prone animals, he received such treatment as he was to have, and then was released. Punchers of Mexican blood frequently used for the tying, not a section of rope, but the sashes which these men customarily wore.

A horse was never hog-tied, and rarely, save by accident, was roped on a hind leg. Doing either of these things might cause such a strain as permanently to injure him for riding purposes. With any member of the cattle family, the rear legs were favorite targets for the lariat. A catch above one or both hind feet sprawled the beast out with ungraceful elongation, and deprived him of tractive force. After all, a horse was a horse, but a steer was only meat.

So expert were the punchers that often has a single, unassisted man accomplished, in terms of seconds, not of minutes, the entire task of first "spilling" a fully grown steer by roping or "dogging," and of forthwith hog-tying it.

Eventually at the corral all the unbranded animals were cut out, and all of them were branded, excepting possibly some "strays," which belonged on a distant range. As these vagrants were to be started immediately on their homeward journey, it was decided by the people present not to hamper them with burns and cuts, but to leave the making of such decorations to a home-welcoming by the vagrants' owners.

All brute visitors from other ranges, whether such visitors were cattle or horses, were technically termed "strays," or "estrays," though, in colloquial usage, these technical terms were usually reserved for the cattle, leaving errant horses to be called "stray horses." The beast's wandering from home might have resulted either from individual likings for travel or else from the dispersion of animals involved previously in a drift.

The term stray was applied to a single beast or to the brutes in a small group. When a large number of animals "bunched up" or "banded up," and marched away from their home range, they, so long as they clung together, were referred to, not as "strays," but as "drifting" or "drifted" animals, this last according as they were still migrating or had reached their goal.

As one by one the strays were discovered in the corral, they, whether branded or not, were segregated into separate lots according to their several home ranges, and, at the conclusion of the round-up's work, were "thrown over" to those ranges. This throwing over was accomplished through the beasts being driven homeward by men from their own ranches or ranges, or, if none such were present, by other punchers assigned to the task.

If cattle were to be shipped to market, such as were cut out for the purpose and thus formed the so-called "beef cut" were herded into isolated groups, there being one such group for each interested ranch, and each such group being termed a "cut," unless some Texan happened by and chanced to call it a "day herd." When any such cut had received all its members, it automatically was, in nomenclature, transformed from a "cut" into a "bunch" or "herd," and was ready to begin its active progress toward the railway and the slaughter-house.

When the last estray had been cut out and segregated, when the beef cut had been completed, and when the last animal to be branded had emitted its odor of burning hair and singed skin, had scrambled stiffly to its feet and gone in search of maternal sympathy, there ceased all dealings with the original herd. It had, in technical language, been "worked." In other words, the job was done.

Though the round-up described in the foregoing pages made use of corrals, and this was the prevalent method, the final handling of cattle in some localities during the later years of the ranching industry was done, not within fences, but in an "open" round-up. This modification came from realization that corrals were not necessary adjuncts for cattle, and from discovery that the ones already built were being used by thieves, particularly in their nocturnal work.

Horses, if in quantity, still called for a corral. Without it they were too difficult to manage.

For the open round-up there was agreed upon in advance a "holding spot" at which the cattle herd should be stopped and worked. This place would be a valley's end or lateral extension, or a wide-spreading, shallow depression, or, if nature offered no such aid, then merely certain acres on the flat plain. When the designated spot was reached by the herd, the cowboys headed the cattle and started them to "milling" (*i. e.*, marching in a circle). From the mass thus "held" by these men, were cut out, as they were needed, the desired animals.

If the primary task in hand were branding, the brutes cut out for that purpose were free to wander whither they would as soon as the hot iron had performed its function.

Then, too, strays required to be thrown over to their home ranges would be collected and started on their journey.

Meanwhile, other and long-since branded animals, if showing contagious nervousness, would be cut out one by one and chased away; but, if reasonably placid, they would be kept as decoys to lessen the chance of a general stampede. When the last animal to be branded had received its burn and all the strays had been disposed of, whatever beasts still were "held" were forthwith released to their own devices, for the herd had been worked.

But if cattle were to be shipped, such as were cut out for the purpose were driven to a second holding spot which was a little removed from the first, and there, as the "beef cut," were held by mounted men employing the same methods as those above described.

When, at this minor rendezvous, had been collected all the animals qualified for it, the bunch assembled there was ready to be started toward its destination.

There would be as many of these separate concentration stations as there were separate destinations for the cut-out cattle, and each thus segregated lot of animals was termed, as in the case of the corral employing round-up, a "cut" or "day herd." Not only would each interested rancher have at least one such rendezvous, but also there likely would be one for each lot of strays which was to be thrown over to its proper Range.

Very possibly during the progress of any round-up, quite probably while the resultant product was being driven to the railway, and assuredly from the instant it reached the railway until it was slaughtered or otherwise disposed of, all the beasts involved were under the active espionage of Range detectives and of stock inspectors.

Those tireless men glided like shadows about the Range and along the routes of shipment.

At any moment between the time that, on the plains, cattle were started for the railway and the time that, in Chicago, Omaha, or Kansas City, they were confronted by the butcher's poleaxe, it might be discovered by one of those official detectives or inspectors, by one of the shipper's men, by an outsider, that in the herd were scattered strays from ranges other than that of the shipper. If suitable for beef, these beasts were not discarded, to resume a life unprofitable to their owners or to pass permanently beyond their owners' advantage; but were sent through the ordinary channel of shipment, sale, and slaughter. Although in the earlier years the profit was to their shipper, in later years their money proceeds were forwarded through routine channels to their proper owners by the market inspector maintained at the abattoir by the stock commissioners or association of the State whence the brutes were shipped.

Such an inspector might find, amid a consignment, beasts with brands that belonged on the shipper's Range, but not to the shipper, or else might find beasts with suspicious looking brands suggestive of "artist's" altering. It was his duty to ascertain if possible the actual owners of the questionable stock, and to remit to them the selling moneys; or, if such owners could not be found, to pay over the funds to the stock commissioners or association of the State from which the animals had been sent.

If, in the case of an "altered brand," an official could not, by external inspection, ascertain what had been the original design, he might kill and skin the animal in order to read the inner surface of its hide.

Immunity from stealing was so utterly dependent upon strict guarding of the branding system that, in Wyoming, no person might slaughter unbranded cattle and, in every Western State, butchers were required to retain on public view, for a specified number of days, the hides of all cattle killed by them.

When branding a calf, the group of men about it sometimes received a hurried visit from the little fellow's mother; which, unadvised that his wounds were so superficial as to lose their scabs within two weeks, and responsive only to his vealish cry for mama, eluded her human guards and arrived on the scene, head down and at considerable speed. If no readily climbable fence were at hand, escape was effected by a matadorlike wait till the strategic moment, by a handful of dust thrown into the charging animal's eyes, and by a coincident jump or roll out of her course. This dust tended not only to prevent the cow from dodging with the dodging man, but also to discourage her from promptly wheeling and returning to the attack.

The cowboy feared the Range cow more than he did any bull or steer. Except when "dusted" she kept her eyes open, her mind on her job. She was exceedingly quick of motion, for all Range cattle were, for short distances, practically as fast as ridden horses. With horns in lieu of a broom, she went about her house-cleaning with considerable enthusiasm and thoroughly feminine persistency.

The bull or steer, on the other hand, lumberingly moved himself into battle position, horns to the enemy, roaringly advertised that he was about to annihilate, lowered his head, shut both eyes, and came on like a runaway coal-truck. The intended victim had merely to bide his own time, and, taking a short step to one side, to watch a blundering, conceited mass of flesh pound harmlessly by.

The cowboy's intimate knowledge of animals' natures and his alert observation repeatedly saved him from situations which otherwise would have meant disaster for him.

Some ranchmen's knowledge of animals' natures occasionally worked to the disadvantage of the Red Man who was expecting to eat governmentally furnished beef. These ranchmen knew among other things that cattle, removed from the latter's Range but released within a few days' journey of their former haunts, would promptly journey homeward. This homing instinct and the legal effect of the brand together laid the foundation for an abuse practised in connection with the Indians' affairs and known on the Range as "stampeding the beef issue."

The United States Government, as an incident of its care of its Indian wards, issued to them at stated intervals, beef on the hoof. This beef was in the form of live cattle bought from the lowest bidding ranchmen and herded into a corral at the Indian Agency.

Each so many Indians was entitled to one animal, each such Indian group being given for the purpose a serially numbered claim ticket. As a ticket's number was announced, the group holding that ticket ranged itself at the entrance of the corral. The bars were lowered, and there was let out one animal, which the Indians of the group might, as they elected, kill on the spot or drive away.

Thus animals were successively released from the corral. Meanwhile, within it cowboys were urging up to the bars two or three renegade steers which studiously had been teased. Another ticket's number was announced. Up stepped expectantly an Indian group. Down went the bars, and out shot the renegades, with the whole herd, obedient to cattle's gregarious instinct, galloping behind them.

The stock, thus freed, headed for home; and by reason of its brands, became for all practical purposes, once more the property of the very persons who had sold it to the government.

As regards this abuse, the government would do nothing, the Indians could do nothing, and the dishonest, benefited ranchmen kept quiet.

The "beef issue" was of so unsavory a reputation that many ranchmen would make no tenders for it.

CHAPTER XIII

THE CATTLE DRIVE

CATTLE DRIVE—SINGING TO CATTLE—STAMPEDE—BURIALS OF DEAD MEN—DEFINITIONS—WATERING LIVE STOCK—MORE DEFINITIONS—RAIL SHIPMENTS—SHOOTING GAME FROM TRAINS—MORALITY OF WEST—FURTHER DEFINITIONS—TEXAS TRAIL AND OREGON DRIVE—SWIMMING CATTLE—QUICKSAND—MILLING—CROSSING A RAILWAY—QUARANTINE—FINANCIAL RESULTS.

IF, upon the completion of a round-up, the saleable stock thereby yielded to a rancher were cattle, the next task for this rancher would be to start promptly toward the "shipping point," the animals that were to be sold. But, if the stock were horses, the terms of sale might require that the beasts be well broken, an obligation which, on the Range, was summed up in the single word "gentled," and which would take the animals, in their first movement, not to the railway but to the corrals near their owner's home ranch-house.

Assume that the stock was cattle. Accordingly, when all confusion about the rodeo corral or holding spot had abated, the brutes were herded into a ragged column and were headed toward the distant railway.

The men accompanying the beasts were in number such as, for a large herd, allowed—not counting the foreman (usually termed "trail boss"), his assistant (sometimes called the "segundo") and the cook—one puncher to each two hundred and fifty cattle. A large herd was controlled more easily than was a small one.

No puncher rode directly in front of the column, the theory being that, the less the herd realized that it was under constraint, the more disposed it would be to behave itself properly. Nevertheless, on each side of the column, parallel with it, and at some distance from it rode a line of cowboys with long intervals between the men. The foremost one of the punchers in each of these lines was slightly more advanced than the van of the herd and was called a "point man" or "lead rider." Each of the men in line behind him was termed a "swing man" or "flank rider." At the rear of the column came the tail riders, the remuda and the men in charge of it, and finally the chuck-wagon.

The function of the swing men was not only to block their own cattle from sidewise wandering, but also to fend off all such foreign cattle as tried to merge themselves in the driven herd.

For the first week, the herd was "shoved" to the reasonable limit of its speed, that the beasts might tire into submissiveness, and thereafter willingly keep to the course which their owners had planned. During that week there was made mileage, but not all of it in one direction.

When eventually resigned to a single aim, the animals would make a daily sinuous progress of ten to fifteen miles according to the smoothness of the traversed country. But only the kindliest of routes permitted a day's march to exceed ten miles.

It was tiresome grimy business for the attendant punchers, who travelled ever in a cloud of dust, and heard little but the constant chorus from the crackling of hoofs and of ankle joints, from the bellows, lows, and bleats of the trudging animals.

The caravan started forth each morning at "sun-up," crawled on till late afternoon, and then, as a preliminary to halting for the night and as a preventive of entanglement with other travelling herds, was "thrown" or "thrown off" a half mile or more from the side of the trail, if at that point it were narrow and in general use. For the halting place, the so-called bed ground, the punchers, in order best to satisfy the cattle's inborn preferences, tried to find land that offered fresh grass to eat, old dry grass to lie upon, and, if the weather were warm, an elevation sufficient to catch the breeze.

The animals, throughout their day-long march, nipped at the grass that they passed; but at the evening halt they set themselves to a solid meal. This eaten, the cattle embarked, as did Range horses, upon the same regimen as that which wild animals pursued. Two hours after dark the cattle one by one sank down to sleep, to rise again at midnight and to browse until that depressing time of night, two o'clock, when all vitality ebbs and the Death Angel frequently calls dying men. Another hour or so of sleep, another browsing, another nap, and then the dawn summoned the cattle to their feet. But, with the full moon's light, the beasts would eat practically all night long.

All through the darkness men of the "night herd," working in shifts of from two to four hours, rode about the animals; and as the men rode they constantly serenaded the beasts by crooning to them songs or chants, which, when so used, were entitled "hymns." This serenading was done partly to hold the cattle under the compelling spell of the human voice, and partly to disabuse from the mind of any fearsome member of the herd suspicion that either a puncher's silhouette against the sky-line or else the noise of his moving pony might represent a snooping dragon. The rider, when "singing to the cattle," as his vocal efforts were styled, disgorged all the words he knew set to all the tunes he could remember or invent, but omitted any sound or inflection which might startle. Sacred airs were usual, for from their simple melodies they were easy of remembrance, and also they then still held the national popularity which since has passed to the tunes

From a drawing by N. C. Wyeth, published in Scribner's Magazine

NIGHT HERDING

of the music-halls; but the words set to these churchly airs well might have surprised the clergy. The proper words, accounts of horse-races, unflattering opinions of the cattle, strings of profanity, the voluminous text on the labels of coffee or condensed milk-cans, mere humming sounds, alike and with seemingly deep religious fervor, were poured on many a night into the appreciative ears of an audience with cloven hoofs. Herded horses might wish for an occasional reassuring word, but they lacked debased operatic taste.

Thus tired men, cat-napping but always crooning, were out in the black, their ponies steadily, slowly patrolling, though half asleep; but man and horse were ready to wake like a shot and to act the instant that a steer started to "roll his tail," or, in less technical English, to gallop with his tail humped up at its shore end, an infallible sign of confident expectation to disregard both distance and time.

There was for the men, throughout a cattle drive, no recreation except swearing, and the eating of the very dusty meals which the attendant chuck-wagon provided. But as for work, there was always the exacting labor of daily routine punctuated from time to time by such extra galloping tasks as, without warning, the temperamental natures of the cattle interjected. And also from time to time a "trail-cutter" might "cut the trail," which is to say might require the punchers to halt the marching herd, to reduce it to such form as would facilitate inspection, to permit an inspection, to cut from the herd and deliver to the trail-cutter such animals, if any, as he was entitled to demand. This cutting upon the drive was termed "trimming the herd."

Each ranch owner whose Range was being traversed by the driven cattle had the right to cut the trail, and might do so in person or through any duly accredited employee. Such a trail-cutter might demand from the drovers only the animals belonging to the cutter's ranch. Each official stock inspector and Range detective might also cut the trail, and might demand all animals which, though actually within the herd, did not legally belong therein.

Day after day the marching cattle sauntered down the trail. Presently, they encountered a second bunch of stock collected at another of their owners' corrals, and were "bunched up" or "banded up" with these brutes. So it went till all that the owners were to ship was in a single herd, and that ambled on by day and halted by night until the "our town," the "our shipping point" of the guarding punchers, and its pens beside the railroad track were reached and absorbed the expedition.

All through the journey the animals had proceeded quietly and rested decently until one moment when there came a snort, a bellow. What caused the snort and bellow nobody knew or could stop to ascertain. Merely "tails" had "rolled," and a stampede was on. From a common centre cattle were darting toward every point of the compass. It was "all hands to the pumps!" and into saddle and on the run for every man. Riders armed with saddle blankets, with doffed coats, hastily plucked sage-brush plants, anything that could be waved, holding pistols, the only attainable objects that would make a commanding noise, galloped out beyond the fleeing animals, headed and flanked them, "cutting in" all incipient, bovine meteors. Finally, the frayed edges of the mass constricted, and the whole was reduced to a ragged, narrow, rushing column, one set of galloping cowboys guiding its van, another, as flank riders, guarding its sides and endeavoring so far as possible to soothe the animals. The forefront of this column was, under the pilotage of the attacking horsemen, swerved into the shape of a shepherd's crook, and a moment later the herd was pouring itself into the form of a capital letter "U."

When its two ends came opposite each other, they were welded together by a yelling, waving, shooting set of madmen on the backs of flying, snorting horses.

This started "milling," a merry-go-round which kept up until the participating cattle quit from exhaustion. Of course, milling did not take place in a circle, an ellipse, an oval, or in any other geometrical form. It occurred in an irregular chunk of grunting, bellowing cattle, overspread and surrounded by an unbreathable cloud of biting dust, with cursing cowboys acting as satellites.

To the miserable humans in charge of the milling, its disadvantage was the discomfort which it caused; its advantage was that the cattle involved in it were, at its conclusion, at the place from which they had started, instead of miles away.

The milling stopped, the animals commenced peacefully to graze, and the men were where they began, but were very tired and very mad. In their next ensuing hymns, they definitely told the animals what was thought of them.

After every stampede there was made a careful counting and inspection of the rebunched cattle, since not only did all absentees have to be hunted for, but also there had to be cut out and chased away any foreign beasts that might have been absorbed into the herd during the sweeping progress of the stampede.

If riders were enmeshed in the stampede or the milling, as they often were, they hastened along with the fracas; and, as opportunity offered, worked their way through openings and shot out to safety. It was a dangerous game of checkers played on the run.

A stampede at night and in a country beset with "cut banks," *i.e.*, precipitous hillsides, beset also with deep canyons, with vertically sided arroyos, with gopher and badger holes, killed many a steer, broke many a pony's leg, left many a rider lifeless on the ground.

After every night stampede there was a counting of human noses. This was done with anxiety which always was as tender in spirit as it was flippant in form. The riders, returning one by one during the next day's morning hours, came into camp, and an atmosphere of banter—banter which, in joking phrases and with several participants, ran on one occasion somewhat as follows: "Hulloa, Shorty, where'd you come from? Thought you was dead. . . . Where's Baldy? Guess he's gone off to git married. . . . No, he ain't. Here he comes. . . . Everybody's in but Jack and Skinny. They must a ridden all the way to Omaha. . . . There's Jack now, comin' up over the top of that rise."

The banter suddenly ceased, for, as soon as Jack had come completely over the top of the hill and into clear view, he had begun to ride rapidly in a small circle. This was one of the equestrian Indians' two signals of important news or of request for strangers to advance for parley, and was often used by whites as a messenger of like import or of serious tidings. At the first circle, some one remarked "Mebbe Jack's playing with a rattler. No, he ain't. There he goes again. He's shore signalling," while some one else added "Jack wouldn't do that for no cows. It must be Skinny." The camp had risen to its feet and started for the tethered ponies.

Suddenly there floated down the breeze three faint sounds evenly spaced. The wind had shifted, and its new course straight from Jack to the camp giving promise that sounds would carry thither, he had used his gun. The camp gasped, "My God, it's Skinny," and then the foreman said, with machine-gun rapidity but icily quiet tone, "Pete, quick, get them two clean shirts that's drying on the wagon tongue. We may need 'em for bandages." Nobody mentioned anything about a shovel, but a collision at the wagon's tailboard and the sound of rasping metal showed that three men instinctively had sought for the sometimes sad utensil, and that it was in hand.

In rapid strides of exaggerated length the punchers approached their horses. One beast shied away, but stopped the instant there rang out with tinny sound, "Damn you, Bronc, quit that," and thereafter the brute crouched and trembled and made no opposition to taking its bit and saddle. Bits were driven into horses' mouths like wedges into split logs. No effort was made to gather in cinches and offside latigos, to lay them atop the saddles, and to place the latter gently on the ponies' backs. The saddles, each grasped by horn and cantle, were waved in air to straighten out the latigos, and were slapped onto cringing backs with a sound like that of a slatting sail on a windy day.

At times like this when men were fierce and in a killing mood, their horses seemed to sense the situation. The most chronic buckers would forego their pitching avocation, and, squatting low in tremor, would receive their load and never make a single jump.

The camp moved out to waiting Jack, and with it went the two clean shirts, each clutched against a rider's chest.

There were jerky, vertical single nods of heads, Jack supplementing his own nod by one later, slow, horizontal turning of his head to right and then to left. A gentle sigh rose from the arriving punchers, two hands impotently opened and let two shirts flutter to the ground. Jack's inquiring look was answered by Ike's slight raising of the handle of the shovel, which thus far he had endeavored to conceal. Then came the first spoken words. Jack commenced the conversation, and in part it ran: "He's up at the end of the big draw, right by the split rock. Went over that high cut bank, him and a mess of cattle. He's lyin' under 'em. He never knowed what hit him. . . . No, I warn't with him. Just now seen his sign as I was coming acrost. I seen it was headed for the cut bank, so I chasséd over there." The foreman added: "Well, boys, let's get at it."

Then the little funeral cortège, having silently smoked a cigarette or two, fell into jiggling trot and headed for the big draw.

The funerals of the men who died in this way, of many Western men, were deeply affecting from their crude, sincere simplicity. About the open grave, which was at merely "somewhere on the plain," would gather a serious-faced little group. The body, wrapped in a saddle-blanket, would be lowered gently into its resting-place, and then would come a pause. Each attendant strongly wished that some appropriate statement might be made either to God or about the dead; but each man felt himself unequal to the task, and stood nervously wiping his forehead. Perhaps the strain wrung from some one person a sudden ejaculation. If so, the requirement for utterance had been satisfied, and all the mourners felt a buoyant sense of relief. If nobody spoke, some wandering eye fastened on the shovel. Whether by the ending of the spoken words or by the recognition of the spade, the signal for the filling of the grave had come.

When the filled-in earth had been pounded to smoothness and had been overlaid with rocks, as a barrier to marauding animals, it was time to leave. That parting would not be accomplished or even begun until there had terminated the strained, awkward silence under which most American men cloak their deeper feelings. The silence usually was ended by an expression spontaneously emitted from overwrought nerves, and often profane in form though not in intent. Speech broke the tension, horses were remounted, and the world was faced again.

At the foot of one of the noblest peaks in the Rocky Mountains lies a grave. Its occupant died in a stampede. All that was said at the interment came out hesitatingly and as follows: "It's too bad, too bad. Tom, dig a little deeper there. Hell, boys, he was a man," and presently, when the burial had been completed, "Bill, we boys leave you to God and the mountain. Good-by, Bill. Damn it, Jim, look out for your bronc."

Out of the darkness during a wild, night stampede might vibrate the blood-curdling death scream of a mangled horse. It was no more merry in tone than is the shriek of a woman in the face of murder. Nature seems to have invented various horrid sounds for the final leave-takings of the several species of her animal subjects.

From the insensate milling of frightened bisons came that picturesque Range word "buffaloed," as a slangy synonym for mentally confused.

The term "stampede" too was picture-making, coming as it did from the Spanish word "estampida," meaning a crash or loud noise.

On various nights our punchers, bound townward with their cattle, had seen the distant camp-fires of other "cow outfits," which were travelling just as our men were; but neither our punchers nor those of these foreign "cow camps" had had time for social visits.

The punchers of one of these outfits caused, one day, our punchers much trouble and some anxiety through failure to "hold" the former's herd until our men's animals had finished drinking at a waterhole. The alien cattle, pushing forward, had overrun and so fully melded with those of our men that it had taken the active efforts of all the riders on the scene to cut the commingled beasts into their proper herds.

Competent punchers upon their galloping ponies required but little time for separating two or more herds that thus had tangled themselves, however confusedly.

But our men's anxiety had had real foundation. They had feared lest their weaker animals—these weakly beasts naturally had been the last to drink—might be crushed by the thirst-maddened brutes advancing from the strangers' bunch. Not uncommonly at drinking-places in dry countries driven cattle were crowded to their death or mortally trampled under foot by other cattle pushing in from the rear.

Cattle, when loose upon the Range, and on their own initiative seeking drink, performed somewhat curiously. They would suddenly stop eating, would raise their heads, start on a trot, steadily increase their speed, and finally would upon a gallop arrive at the waterhole. They quietly would drink; but, when satiated, would leave as precipitately as they had come.

Both the cattle and the horses in driven herds required, because of the sustained effort and the awful dust, more frequent drink than when the beasts were shifting for themselves. In addition, the farther they were bred away from the original "wild" blood, the more often they demanded water. Wild horses and wild cattle during a drought would wander about for days without drinking, and would keep alive even though thirst might both swell and blacken their tongues.

Range horses and Range cattle, when loose upon the Range, demanded, for keeping in good condition, access to water at least once in every forty-eight hours; but if called upon to do so, could withstand thirst for a number of successive days. Many of the beasts, for reasons known only to themselves, selected for their habitual grazing-grounds tracts far from any waterhole, and so had regularly to travel miles to and from their drinking spot.

The recently mentioned lights of "cow camps," direct attention to an inconsistency in American English whereby "cow camp" labelled a merely temporary stopping-place, although "mining camp," denoted a lasting settlement of some size. But should a "cow camp" attain a substantial, human population and decide to root itself in permanently, it automatically became a "cow town."

As our men's cattle were so numerous as to fill many railway-cars, the owners of the beasts would send, as caretakers or as not uncommonly called "horse pushers" or "bull nurses," two or three cowboys with the shipment to its ultimate destination, the abattoirs of Chicago, Omaha, or Kansas City, theoretically to tend the stock en route, practically to ride all the way in the caboose, and to compare the game of poker as developed on transportation systems with that evolved upon the Range.

But, had the cattle been few in number, the brutes would have been intrusted on the journey to some other outfit's punchers bound eastward with their beeves.

Perhaps, upon the journey, the engineer would sight game near the track, and would stop a few minutes that the occupants of the caboose might stock the larder.

Until the decade of the nineties, in the days when newly laid tracks and hastily built bridges not infrequently went to pot, and made the time-table a nullity, passenger-trains were not uncommonly halted for this same purpose. More than one now living person can recall that, even upon the Overland Limited, there has been a sudden stop, and that presently thereafter the conductor has announced in each car: "Gents, the dining-car is short on meat. The engineer has just 'raised' a band of antelope. If there is any ranchmen or hunting-parties present that has Winchesters, will they oblige?" With due warning of such impending famine, a prudent conductor occasionally would break the news that the dining-car was "ate out," and then add: "Will ranchmen and hunting-parties with rifles please oblige by moving forward to the baggage-car? We're just about entering the antelope country." This anabasis expedited stalking, and produced through machine-gun effect a more telling fire.

On one occasion, a Northern Pacific train, which had for several days been stalled by a washout, began eventually its hungry journey along a bank of the Yellowstone River. Above the river, flocks of geese for several miles flew parallel with the railway-track. By the conductor's invitation, the baggage-car had been temporarily converted into a moving shooting-lodge. Every time a shot goose dropped in shallow water, the train stopped.

Not infrequently ranchmen "obliged" by alighting from a train, and killing such cattle as had wandered into a railway cut and been injured by the train.

Punchers, when bound for the Eastern abattoirs, scorned to pack their spare belongings into gunny "war sacks," and provided themselves at the "general store" with "boughten" bags of carpet or of imitation leather, bags such as urban folk then employed. These new receptacles the punchers often termed "go-easters."

In the youth of the cattle industry, long railway trips were infrequent for the ranchmen, because at that time delivery often was made at the local railroad shipping-point. There the animals were received as so many "head," or, if on the basis of weight, then in terms of estimated pounds, and when once so delivered, passed out of the field of the ranchmen's liability and into the purgatory of foodless, waterless miles of bumping railway journey.

Then came the decent laws which required, upon the cars, fodder, periodical halts for drink and rest, and consequent necessity for human attendants; and came also the habit of requiring delivery to be made at the abattoirs, with weights determined by their scales.

Let us follow the punchers to Chicago or wherever. Hours, not days, after reaching the destination, there almost always arose ample basis for that moot subject of school-day debates: "Which can the better care for himself, the city boy in the country or the country boy in the city?" Montana, Idaho, Oregon, Wyoming, Colorado, Texas, New Mexico, Arizona, and old Dakota have seen their sons taken unawares, black-jacked and felled in the slums of the slaughter-house cities of the Middle West.

However, for this the Far West never attempted to retaliate upon strangers within its borders. Whoever hunted there for trouble could find it, but trouble usually was reserved for the exclusive use of such as sought it. The Range may have been untutored in Old World draw- ing-room conventions, but it was humanly decent and humanly gen- erous. It roughly hazed newcomers only when by superciliousness they impliedly asked for the treatment, though the askers received at least all they had requested. Such newcomers as, instead of having positive quality and being affirmatively disagreeable, were of negative worth and merely not agreeable were not overtly assailed. Simply they were ignored and were left to wither away from ostracism.

A stone went under the saddle-blanket of such only as did not meet the West eye to eye. The tenderfoot who could not ride, had the cour- age to announce it, and was a man, was given at the ranches horses ashamed to buck. A man, who was of the same manly ilk, who for moral reasons did not wish to drink alcohol, but did not make unctu- ous advertisement of personal piety, could walk into any saloon in any settlement in the Cattle Country, and, save in the rarest of cases, be as happily treated over his glass of water as he would have been had he asked for "red eye."

However, there was one thing which that tenderfoot could not safely attempt. This was peremptorily handing his coat to a Westerner to carry. Throughout the Range such an offer was construed as an affirmative attack upon personal dignity, and beyond that upon the very democracy of the West.

The phrase "humanly decent," when used above, bore no relation to the question as to whether or not the men of the Range were any more devoted to the urban "red-light districts" than were their Eastern brothers. They were not so, if the testimony of many old-timers be credible.

Admittedly, at the end of lengthy cattle drives, notably that of the Texas Trail, the attendant riders, as a rebound from protracted, gru- elling duties, were prone to engage in orgies. Dodge City, Abilene, Newton, and their sister cow towns standing at the end of the long trail were, for the dusty, tired, jubilant, arriving puncher, relatively the same as for years was Paris to the ocean-crossing American—license rather than a place.

Morality with many a man was local. He might refuse to foul his own nest; yet, when travelling far away from it, his restrictive decency was apt to decrease in ratio with the square of the distance. As Smoke Murphy said at Julesburg: "Many a virtuous polar bear raises hell on the equator."

But long drives were, for any given man, unless he belonged to the small coterie that specialized upon Texas Trail work, only an occasional function. For the most part of his time he stayed comparatively near home, and home as such, however simple, were it only a one-man dug-out, ever had compelling moral effect.

West was, as regards its eastern boundary, a relative term. For the purposes of this writing, the West is taken as the country "west of the Missouri River," *i. e.*, westward of approximately the meridian of Omaha, Nebraska; but that country also had its intersectional comparisons. With a peg driven into the ground at any point in the United States westward of the Mississippi River, one found, as one still finds, all persons living on the sunset side of that peg regarding all transpeg people as Easterners. Colorado has ever been "back East" to Arizona.

The interchangeable phrases "west of the Missouri River," "west of the Missouri," and "west of the river" (with simon-pure old-timers the Missouri was merely "the river") had a very definite meaning in the Cattle Country. The ferries from present Council Bluffs, Iowa, to the site of present Omaha, and from first Independence or Westport, and later "St. Joe," to the Kansan shore, were the means by which many of the westward-bound Forty-Niners and their followers crossed the Missouri River. It was there that these gold-seekers left their "States," and entered their "West." It was these gold-seekers who made that phrase "west of the Missouri." The point which they thus fixed as the one to mark where the West began stayed put, but presently there extended from it a north and south line that reached to Canada and to the Gulf of Mexico. All the area westward of that imaginary line was said to be "west of the Missouri River," even though Dakota for much of its territory was in fact eastward of the actual stream.

In addition to the almost constant driving of myriad northbound cattle along the Texas Trail, there were sometimes, within the North itself, prolonged movements "upon the hoof." These latter hegiras sprang out of exaggerated, though temporary, differences between the conditions in various localities. A drought-made differential between Oregon and, say, Wyoming, or between Wyoming and, say, Dakota, occasionally made it advisable to drive live stock many hundreds of miles in order to reach an unscorched refuge. Thus, for instance, animals have been herded out of eastern Oregon and into Wyoming or Montana, while again Wyoming's ranchmen have forced their thirsty herds out of the latter's home lands and across the map to western Kansas. When planning these intrasectional transfers, care was taken that, so far as possible, the animals involved should not finally be landed unduly far from the line of their normal course to market.

The bovine victims of a long, long trail were, when leaving Texas, known there as "coasters," but after they had reached the Northwest they were called in the latter section "pilgrims." No special name attached to the suffering animals that ploughed through dust to escape from a blighted Northern Range.

The brutes' plodding journey upon all these drives was in details like the already described trek from the round-up to the railway—like it, save in three regards. To make fair comparison, one must multiply by ten, if not by twenty, all the distances, all the fatigue, all the vexation accorded to the shorter expedition. It took five months to make a drive from the Rio Grande straight northward to the Canadian border. Then one, while recalling the Texas Trail, should at times increase the herd's size to four thousand, even to ten thousand, animals; should not forget those strenuous periods, each of at least two days, when below the Colorado River, again between the Stinking Water and the South Platte, and again below the Tongue River, the punchers, on leaving one river, deliberately prevented their animals from satisfyingly drinking there, in order that mad lust for water might hold these animals to a steady march through the semidesert that lay before the next encountered stream; and finally not only one should bear in mind the distressing possibility of having to drive, across a sun-blistered country, cattle temporarily blinded by thirst and frenzied in their blindness, but also one must remember the strain of "swimming" the charges across a swollen river.

Though the "swim" was not encountered on many of the shorter drives, it was met on some of them, as it was upon all of the long-distance hikes. It was no event for weaklings.

Hundreds of driven cattle were walking in a column nearly a mile in length, and of irregular formation like scattered leaves blown slowly across a lawn. Their van reached the stream's bank. Singly, in pairs, or in somewhat larger groups, the forward animals broke from their formation, lumbered down the bank, trotted across the sand-bar at its foot, and finally side to side stood to mid-knee in the water, muzzles immersed.

Cowboy strategists selected from the line of drinking beasts one or two steers that promised courage and qualities of leadership, rode quietly into position behind them, and as they raised their heads, urged them farther into the stream, thus into "swimming water"; and, by heading all attempts to deviate from the course prescribed, achieved the satisfaction of seeing brown bodies churn wakes which pointed directly at the opposite shore. A few adventurous brutes, of their own volition, followed these leaders; and, once all these pioneers showed their dripping, glistening bodies on the farther shore, the herd automatically and in tenuous line passed down the hither bank, into the water and across it.

The line once established, there was little risk that the marching column would rebound from the stream and scatter over the prairie. So, for the quiet, seductive methods necessary to institute the crossing, there safely could now be substituted more overt and violent means to speed the rate and to force participation by slothful or timid beasts.

"Starting the swim" was an anxious task, for if the selected leaders were to outwit the men and succeed in "doubling back," either before leaving the hither shore or after fairly entering the water, it would mean an immediate stampede, wherein the steadily arriving cattle, on reaching the water's edge, would swerve from it and pursue the brutes which, though a moment before ahead of them, already would have similarly turned and now would be galloping inland; or else it would mean at the riverside an interweaving jam of nervous animals steadily mushrooming from the forward pressure of the still-arriving column, and ready at any instant to "split," *i. e.*, to form like a capital letter "Y," and to launch a stampede from the tip of each of the prongs.

As soon as the continuity of the line was assured, a cowboy or two plunged their horses into the water, made their way to the opposite shore, and set about clearing it of its clogging cattle and marshalling them in marching order upon the plain beyond. The rest of the punchers so timed their own crossings as to make them in proper relation to the varying sizes of the two sections of the stream-divided herd.

Some of the men, preferring sureness to comfort, made while in the water no change in their riding position, and "swimming wet," landed with clothing dripping to half-way between knee and hip. Others, more finical, bent their knees and raised their feet to a kneeling pose with spurs touching the cantle. A rider of the latter type ran the risk of being unbalanced by an unexpected eddy or a bumping steer, and thereby of rolling his top heavily burdened horse directly upon its side; or else, upon like collision and through instinctive and unfortunate pull upon the reins, of rearing his horse, to have it madly splash its front legs and then flop sideways. A successful grab of a stirrup or, better still, of a tail's end would give this hapless rider an efficient tow to safety.

The men's familiarity with this "crossing," as the West termed a ford, as well as the act of traversing it, relieved them from any anxiety about possible quicksands. Had not every square inch of the shores been known to the punchers, they would have "scouted" both banks before the herd's arrival. The treacherous sands of many a Western stream have swallowed many a horse or steer, and many a solitary cowboy has been eaten alive by the very land he loved. The only remedy for quicksand was a lariat and a tugging pony.

Fortunately, during the crossing, there had occurred no untoward event to drive into panic the swimming portion of the herd and impel it to suicide through self-devised milling in midstream. No low-lying sun had shone directly into the animals' eyes. No Indians had attacked the operation, no bear or wolf had appeared upon the farther shore; no stick unexpectedly had cracked; no fantastically shaped log had floated down the channel; nothing had happened to check the nautical pioneers, to break the brown thread which they drew behind them, and to send the living contents of the river, first into a crazed, revolving mêlée, and next into brown carcasses which would bob in the current until disgusted waters spewed out the carrion upon a sandbar.

Had milling started in the stream, mounted punchers and the ponies under them would have done their best to struggle through the whirling mess, to break its motion, to resolve its participants into a sane, straight line, and to connect that line's front end with the desired shore. A pony might be crushed, might have his trappings entangled in the horns of a sinking steer, but the plucky little horse preferred excitement to ennui. A rider might meet with similar catastrophe. Yet, because of the self-sufficiency of punchers, usually the worst that befell a man in breaking a mill was to be capsized from his mount and to go ashore upon a steer's back or by holding the end of its tail.

Horses, save in the very rarest of instances, had too much sense to mill in water or even on land. When they, however, did embark on it, their action was technically called not "milling," but instead "rounding-up," just as it was in the case of their interweavings upon land when being forced by cowboys to shift from a scattered formation into a compact band. To the cattle was given a monopoly of the term "mill."

If by chance a railway skirted the river, either upon its farther bank or at but little inland distance from it, there very possibly was an occurrence such as one never sees in these present days of fenced farms.

The moment the first steer entered the water, the entire herd was, by inviolate custom, vested with the right of way over every train, and this right continued until the fording was completed. The locomotive's whistle was of no interest to the cowboys. They knew that the engineer, with eyes out for swimming herds, under strictest orders not to damage future freight or to antagonize its owners and their kind, would come to a complete stop so far away from the scene of ferrying as not to lend his train to the starting of a stampede. Thus railways frequently were blocked, and for hours at a time, because in days now past, "cattle was king."

The profanity which poured from the opened windows of the cars and from the engine's cab melted into the lowing of such cattle as had made the passage and into the bellowing of those yet to essay it. The cowboys, indifferent to the noise and their fellow man's impatience, stuck to their own swimming job.

A northbound, Texan herd, once clear of the Panhandle, had an excellent chance of being held temporarily at any spot upon its route by a quarantine against "Texas fever," "Spanish fever," or "splenic fever," according as the local veterinarian chose to entitle that endemic disease. Then the punchers in charge of the beasts had an enforced halt of not less than sixty days, and so for at least sixty days impatient men practised swearing.

The fevered Texan cattle, so soon as they reached a Northern latitude, quickly ridded themselves of their ailment; but if not held in quarantine, the beasts would seed mile after mile of trail with pestilential germs that would lie in wait for uninoculated animals.

Some States permanently maintained for their entire areas a quarantine of definite period. In other States, the quarantine was intermittent and sometimes was limited to a particular zone.

Commercial profit proved for the great majority of ranchers a term of purely academic meaning. Taxless grazing-lands made possible large profits, if—. High selling prices potentialized great earnings, if—. The "if" was the drought or the snow-storm. The profits of the fat years went into high living or into additions to the live stock. If into high living, they disappeared immediately. If into additions to the live stock, their days were longer but usually were numbered. In the latter case, ordinarily sooner or later the profits and capital lay side by side, parched bodies on the sand or bloated carcasses appearing from the snow according as the ranch was in the South or in the North.

But no man who ever lived upon the Range regretted later that he had had that residential privilege.

CHAPTER XIV

BREAKING HORSES

THESE pages thus far, though having seen the cattle rounded up, branded, driven to the railway and delivered at the abattoir, and though having also seen the horses rounded up and branded, have failed to watch the later doings with the horses, for, in a prior chapter, they wandered off with cattle, and left the horses imprisoned within the rodeo corral.

During this absence, the "stray horses" had been started on their homeward routes, and the remaining horses had been divided into separate bands according to their several ownerships. Each owner, from his band thus obtained, had selected the animals to be sold, and also a few choice specimens, the latter all "top" beasts, all suitable it was thought for training into cow-ponies to be used at home. Each of these choice specimens was small, patently sound in body and quick of foot, and apparently promised intelligence and a sporting taste. Well-trained cow-ponies were regarded as aristocrats. They brought prices three times that of well-broken but more commonplace Range horses.

The term "pony" did not necessarily suggest diminutiveness, because the Northwest gave the title of "pony" to almost every horse regardless of its size, and in fact exempted from the "pony" class only "work horses," and such brutes as by despicable viciousness merited the appellation of "that damned cayuse."

A horse that could travel notably far, particularly when at high speed, was termed a "long horse." Consequently, the best stayer in one's band would be called one's "longest horse." There was no such phrase as "long pony," though any given animal might coincidently be both a "cow-pony" and a "long horse."

Ponies have been mentioned as participating not only in cutting out and cutting in but also in roping. All these functions were exercised by members of the class of "cow-pony," or "cow-horse."

One pony might be particularly good at cutting out and in, a fast runner in a spurt, but either a bit shy of a thrown lariat, or not expert in doing his part after the reata had made its catch. Nevertheless, he might be invaluable in driving stock, despite his restricted usefulness in the game played in the corral. Another pony, perfect at the roping work, might be slow in a dash to head stock running in the open; but, notwithstanding this, he might be capital for business within the corral. Some ponies did all things well, and they were regarded as being of almost royal rank.

As a result of this lack of uniformity in the horses' qualifications, to an efficient cowboy on a large ranch were assigned several ponies, one animal for one class of work, another for another. To such a cowboy was assigned also a horse of less attainment, and this beast was used in the commonplace errand-running rides of the every-day. The various animals allotted to a man, however humble he might be, were left severely alone by all other men on the ranch; and the horses' assignee, so long as he rode for the ranch, was sole lord of his string.

Having ostensibly "gentled" at the rodeo corral the few inferior horses that it was desired should hurriedly be put through at least a faint color of breaking, in order to be able to make immediate delivery to a none-too-discerning buyer, the punchers landed these beasts at their destination, and drove the remaining animals to the corrals at the ranch-house. In and about these latter corrals would be selected and, during the ensuing months, would be more or less carefully broken such of the horses as were to be kept as cow-ponies or were to be sold as really "gentled" animals. They would stay in the corrals at night, and, when not being handled, would browse under mounted guards upon the open prairie during the day.

The hurried "gentling" at the rodeo corral brought out the nearest approach to "rough riding" that well-managed ranches would permit. The reason for this bit of laxity at the corral was that nobody seriously cared whether the second-rate brutes involved—all veritable culls— were spoiled or not. So the punchers, both local and visiting, made a bit of a lark of the affair, and somewhat reverted to the same active use of quirt and spur as that from which the wild horses of early days had suffered.

Because there were present men from various ranches, competition in horsemanship occasionally displayed itself, and then the rail-birds, with strong partisanship, wagered heavily on the various competitors.

There was not much spectacular roping of the horses driven for breaking processes to the corrals near the ranch-house, for the horses gentled there represented the best quality that the ranch could boast, and were not jeopardized. With a well-managed establishment, there never was anywhere more rough roping than had to be, except that occasionally at a round-up a puncher might for a while cut loose.

Grown horses in process of breaking were thrown by the lariat, only when necessity demanded. More commonly, with neck through the reata's loop, they pranced about at its extremity like kites in a storm. The reata was gradually gathered in and the man at its home end presently found himself holding a rope of controlling length and within handling distance of the captive.

Next the hackamore was shown the trembling animal, and was girt upon his head, to rest there a half hour or so.

That same day or later, similar exhibition was made of the saddle. It was placed as gently as possible upon a twitching back, and the cinches, after being circumspectly and successfully fished for, were as quietly as might be made fast. A long crooked stick was most convenient for this fishing operation, because at times the air was quite full of hoofs.

After the horse had become accustomed to the feeling of the hackamore and saddle, a matter of minutes and a solitary saddling, or of a day or two and repeated saddlings, a rider mounted him.

Later the beast was, with similar consideration, introduced to the bit.

The reason for this quasi-tenderness was that the object of most ranchmen was not to make horses buck, but to keep them from doing so. The cowboy was hired, so far as concerned horses, not to inculcate but to discourage pitching. He was paid to turn for his employer unbroken horseflesh into money, and the buying public ordinarily would not exchange its dollars for useless, vertical motion. Hence, one ordinarily saw about a well-managed ranch only the bucking that could not be avoided. One saw much of affirmative efforts to wean a horse from the habit. There were of course exceptions, but the number of "rough riding" men was comparatively small.

The foregoing account of breaking horses sets forth the method employed by the majority of the ranchers after the first years of the Range, when "busting wide open" by "quirting a plenty," and "shoving in the steel," were the accepted means of gentling, though it should be remembered that these later ranchers dealt principally with the "graded horse," while the earlier stockmen had little save the unmixed wild horse.

The rough rider's object was to "break the pony's heart," on the first riding; for, if then the idea of human supremacy could be impressed upon an animal physically exhausted by its own efforts to the point of staggering, mentally dejected from the failure of its confident expectation, it was almost a surety that the pony never again would make so violent an effort. True, it might buck again and often, but never again so fiercely. The latent dread of man would cloud every subsequent plan to pitch. To create this dread, the rough-riding buster brought down the quirt at every jump the pony made.

These rough riders usually were either owners of small ranches, or else were men who, as itinerant "contract busters," wandered about the Range and temporarily leased their services to such establishments as could not afford to maintain a first-class rider of their own. These busters received five dollars for each animal they "busted," "broke," "peeled," "twisted," or "gentled," according as one termed the operation.

The method of these men was to intimidate, first, by roping and violently throwing the brute entrusted to them, next and as soon as the saddle was in position, by wholesale use of the quirt, a lashing which on occasion was augmented by the whips and howls of assistant terrorists, sometimes called "hazers." When the men's arms grew tired and it was agreed that the pony was in chastened mood, the buster mounted; and, if the welted animal made serious effort to pitch, the quirting commenced anew.

The buster might do the initial riding with one of the cruel bits described in former pages, but he was more apt to use at first a "hackamore" rigged with a "bosal," and to reserve the bit for a later lesson.

The buster frequently extended his training beyond the moments that he himself was in the saddle, because, after dismounting, he was apt to leave or place upon the pony's head a hackamore, and to fasten its reins to the end of a long rope affixed to a peg driven in the ground, thus to the end of what was called by Southerners a "stake-rope," by Northerners a "picket-rope." With or without encouragement from the hazers, the fastened horse was wont to run to the end of his tether, to have his wind suddenly cut by the pinching hackamore, and, at the rope's terminal, to somersault onto his back. This action might be repeated several times before the animal desisted.

He very likely also sooner or later thoroughly entangled his feet in the rope, and so rubbed bits of skin off his legs.

By plenteous quirting and the stake rope's aid, the buster endeavored to inculcate "fear of leather," and dread of "running against rope."

If the gentled animal were to be sold to strangers, two days of such rough treatment might suffice to satisfy the conscience of the ranch, but if the beast were to be used at home, it would receive a week of training and abuse.

From a photograph by L. A. Huffman

"BUSTING WIDE OPEN"

The intelligent, orderly method which is first above described, and which did not avoid firmness though it attempted to abolish cruelty, should not be confused with the affectionate, misguided, and desultory schooling occasionally given by amateurs and productive of one of the meanest, most unreliable objects in the Cattle Country—a "pet horse."

Although the decent method of breaking was far more gentle than was the "buster's" riot with the steel and quirt, its relative softness did not wholly free the bronco from the lash and rowel, or rob him of a wholesome respect for the possibilities of "leather." A pony, once thrown, never thereafter outgrew the recollection of the lariat's spilling ability. This doubtless explains why "gentled" horses, however mean, could surely be corralled by an enclosure made of a single line of rope held withers high.

Upon the round-up, in camp, anywhere, lariats were tied end to end, and were stretched along a line of nondescript posts which might be wholly or in part trees, men, wagon-wheels, or the horns of saddles atop sedate old nags. A band of saddleless riding horses would arrive upon the gallop, and at sight of that one strand of rope would stop short to stand there and await the saddle. This effective though very loose corral needed not to have even three enclosed sides. A wide-opened letter "V" was an efficient form. A straight line would do. It was the compelling fear of the reata that held the animals. And yet a few years before, when as yet unintroduced to leather, they had rocked the sides of a log enclosure with its rawhide fastenings.

There was less of equine violence during the "gentling," process than some of the tenderfoot spectators had expected, for usually the animals were ridden by competent horsemen.

Impropriety in human conduct might send at any moment into ecstatic pitching even a horse which had long since been broken, and for years had been thoroughly docile; because, broadly speaking, no Western steed, so long as he remained physically sound, was so craven as surely to tolerate at all times incompetent horsemanship upon his back. As a judge of equestrian ability, the Range pony was both quicker and better than any riding-master that ever lived. Put your foot in a stirrup, and in an instant you had been accurately appraised by the horse you were mounting.

Some men, for a reason unknown to themselves and undisclosed to human observers, invited bucking. Women riders as a class were less apt than men to start a horse to pitching.

Breaking, as actually done by competent horsemen at a number of ranches, produced averages recorded as follows:

Practically every horse, at its first saddling when it was on the leash of a hackamore and before any attempt was made to mount the brute, "bucked the saddle." If the horse were not abused at this stage of its training, and, while held by the hackamore or by a lariat about its neck, were cajoled, it in eighty cases out of one hundred quieted down, and either eventually on that same day or else at the second saddling on the morrow, tremblingly, hesitatingly permitted itself to be mounted by a competent horseman, and this without offering to buck the rider.

A few of these pious eighty might for a while "crowhop," *i. e.*, jump about with arched back and stiffened knees, but this was bucking seen through the large end of an opera-glass. Any thoroughly competent park rider, if a real horseman, could have sat it, at least, if he had been warned as to when the hopping would commence.

There were left from the hundred animals twenty, all of which would buck more or less at their first riding, ten of which would continue to buck more or less at their second or even third riding, and but two of which could be counted on to remain permanently versed in the art of pitching.

Of these two, one could be so well broken that it would "go after" its rider only when long rests in pasture had lessened recollection of human supremacy. The other though rideable would buck whenever it became excited or irritated.

One horse in approximately each five hundred was an "outlaw," a brute that never could be broken and that would buck almost in its sleep.

One horse in, it was supposed, approximately each ten thousand was sufficiently like a "man-killer" as deliberately to jump on his thrown rider's prostrate body.

The actual man-killer, traditionally always a male, was a horse so rare that the average ranchman in his whole business life saw not more than one.

The beast was a very devil masquerading in the body of a horse, a devil that at sight of man cunningly planned to kill him.

Ensconced amid the stock placidly feeding on the Range, the brute would sight an approaching horseman or pedestrian, would gently disengage itself from its fellows, would trot quietly forward as though mild and friendly curiosity were its only incentive, and then suddenly and without warning would spring ahead in a frenzied rage, and strike down the man, together with the saddle-animal, if any, under him.

If one of the mad beasts, through enmeshment in a swiftly moving round-up, had no opportunity thus to stalk its prey, it would bide its time and would, in apparent innocence, hasten along with the driven band, meanwhile edging toward the intended victim. When the moment for attack arrived, the brute would wheel, and, with hard-set face, open mouth, and glittering eye would come on like a destroying demon.

While the man-killer at times would kill riderless horses, either in the corral or out upon the range, the favorite prey was the human being.

Although, during the peaceful moods of the insane beast, men usually could not distinguish it from a normal animal, ridden horses frequently diagnosed it from afar. It was traditional among riders that, when in the vicinity of loose horses their mounts began to quiver and to swerve away, the "six gun" should be drawn at once. "Kill him, the second he shows he's one, or he'll get you sure," was the slogan of the ranchmen.

The pedestrian while on the open range ran a danger from man-killing horses, danger, however, so slight as to be almost academic; but he was in constant risk from all the cattle, especially from the cows.

For a dismounted man, the Range cow was, under average conditions, a far more dangerous adversary than was the grizzly bear. Under those average conditions, the cow would always attack; the bear would almost always avoid a conflict.

No Spanish bull-fighter would have dared to fight, with sword, a Texan "long-horn" cow.

A man on foot would be far out in the grass. A cow amid a bunch of cattle would spy him and start toward him. The other brutes would follow.

The bunch, starting at a walk, would break presently into a trot, and finally would begin to move in a spiral about the victim. So far, inquisitiveness apparently had been the only stimulus. Suddenly "tails would roll," and, with savage fury taking the place of the prior motive, the herd would quicken to a gallop and sweep over the helpless victim. Hoofs would crush out his life.

The herd had never before seen a pedestrian in the open country, and seemingly had concluded that so unusual an object must be an enemy.

So great was the danger from cattle to persons afoot, that ranchers imposed heavy fines on such of their employees as, without valid excuse, dismounted on the range when within a quarter of a mile of a bunch of cattle.

Men had, of course, to work afoot always at the branding fires, and sometimes within the corrals; but these men constantly were guarded by watchful horsemen with ready lariats. No dismounted man dared to stay alone within a corral containing cattle, for he was convinced that the happy issue of Daniel from the lions' den could not safely be relied upon as a precedent.

Memories of the Texan "long horn" make many a white-haired grandfather of to-day, a graduate of the Range of long ago, intuitively cringe as under guidance of his little granddaughter he goes afield to come suddenly upon a placid mooley cow.

Cattle, save for occasional ones bent on "prodding," were little disposed to approach a mounted rider. Possibly they thought the man to be part of his horse.

Scattered about the West were "spoiled horses," animals which man, by kicks in the face or by other abuse during the breaking period, had ruined as to character, and which, engraving on their hearts the motto, "No one shall ever stay on our backs," held throughout their lives as closely as they could to their resolve and bucked and bucked and bucked. They were merely man-made "outlaws."

Bucking itself needs little description. It was in part the antics of an angry cat on a hot plate. Every one who is familiar with its component motions, can draw in his imagination a picture as accurate as the pen can make, can run the gamut from "straight bucking" through "sun fishing" and the "end for end" to the "back throw," can appreciate the significance of the Western phrase: "Bucking off a porous plaster."

Between "bucking" and "pitching," there was no difference except that of geography. The Northwesterner called the horrid motion "bucking" or "buck jumping," the Texan termed it "pitching."

A horse was doing "straight work," when he kept his body headed in one general direction, however high he might arch his back at one moment, however sway-backed he might momentarily be the instant afterward. In accomplishing this, he might land always upon the same spot, or he might "pitch a plungin'," otherwise called the "running buck," or "bucking straight away," that is, jump forward with each buck. An ingenious brute could embellish his straight work by either a seesaw effect wherein he landed alternately on his front and hind feet (this sometimes called "walking beaming"), or else by bucking not in the vertical plane but diagonally upward, and leaning first to the right and then to the left. He also could vary the motion by snakelike contortions of his spine, by shakes and shivers, by rearward jumps, and by sudden downward and sideway lunges of a shoulder or hip.

When a brute added ability to leave the ground while headed at one compass point and to land while headed at another, he was "pitchin' fence-cornered."

If he twisted his body into a crescent, with its horns alternately to right and left, he qualified as a "sun fisher," and, in producing this motion, he was apt to merge in it an exaggerated "fence-cornering." Going up headed, say, northeast and landing headed, say, northwest was the passing mark for this latter phase of the sun-fish degree.

If a beast substituted for these directions straight north and south, he accomplished the third degree in bucking, the "end for end," in which he effected a series of semi-revolutions, and so, as the West said, kept "swapping ends."

Bucking might be terminated sometimes by a "rear back," or "back fall," sometimes by a "back throw," sometimes by a "side throw," or on very rare occasions by a "pinwheel." Usually it was ended by the mere failure of the bronco to buck any longer.

The difference between the "rear back," or "back fall," and the "back throw," was one of speed and motive. In the "rear back," or "back fall," according as one termed it, the horse, attempting to stand erect upon its hind legs, quivered, unintentionally lost its balance, and fell. In the "back throw" the brute with rapid movement and affirmative purpose overreared and hurled itself backward and to the ground.

The "pinwheel" sent the beast on a forward and upward jump, to turn feet up in the air and to land on its back. The crest of a steep hill gave best opportunity for this awful gyration. Most fortunately, it was extremely seldom that a horse achieved this movement.

The direction of the "side throw" appears from its name.

Such were the outstanding, technical expressions which ear-marked the various specialties in pitching. They, though slangy in origin, were not intended to be slangy in usage, and they functioned seriously as an integral part of the West's legitimate English. The West, however, had its conscious slang, "cat backed" for "buck," any phrase human humor could invent as applicable to the several motions which the horse and the devil between them had devised. This conscious slang was ephemeral, because it came from word mines of the moment, from social and political sources that, vital for an instant, passed into history, and through it into oblivion.

Modern days have filched terms from modern sources, and applied them in slangy sense to modern buckers. At present-day Western riding competitions one hears of horses "aviating," doing "nose dives," "high dives," or "tail-spins," being "skyscrapers," having "six cylinders," and "skipping on two of them," "stepping on the gas," doing the "cake walk," being the "best pitcher in the baseball leagues," being a "side winder," and "good thrower to second base." But such phrases

From a photograph by L. A. Huffman

START OF A "BACK THROW"

are creations of the present, and were unknown upon the open Range of bygone years.

Every rider of a "bad actor," a horse that acted viciously, was on the watch for kicks and bites, and kept himself in hand for the dreaded rear back, back throw, or less dangerous side throw, but could dismiss the pinwheel from the list of prospective probabilities.

If a horse reared and threatened to fall backward, the "loaded" end of the quirt striking between his ears would knock him down to normal position, would make him do what the cowboys termed "come down in front," but if stunned he promptly might roll onto his side. Incidentally, the quirt's blow might kill him. This roll onto the side and the side throw itself each could crush the leg of the rider, but notwithstanding this danger the man had good chance of landing clear of the horse. If, however, the animal, suddenly rearing, threw itself directly backward, there was some chance, though very little, to escape crushing by the saddle's horn. There was no escape from the pinwheel, and no method of preventing it.

Motion was accompanied by music, for the average pitching bronco emitted grunts and snorts, and usually loud "bawls" of rage, while a bucking mule rarely forgot to bray.

This word "bawl," because the technical term for the bronco's yelps of deviltry, popularized throughout the West the slang phrase "bawling him out," which meant one man's vociferously scolding another.

In violence of pitching motion, the mule outdid the horse.

Bucking imposed sudden, pitiless strains upon the abdomen of a horseman, and viciously twitched his neck.

The shock of bucking was so severe that many a rider bled from the nose, the mouth, sometimes the ears; not a few men fainted in the saddle; they occasionally, through involuntarily, constricted muscles, insensately maintaining their seats until the horses surrendered. Many men were ruptured, and in very rare instances men fell dead from their animals' backs. An autopsy upon the body of a rider who had thus died, disclosed a liver entirely torn from its moorings.

Pitching horses frequently bled from the nose, and sometimes, though rarely, bucked till stopped by self-imposed death.

The average pitching animal far from attained the extremes of turbulence indicated above, but he always was, even for the best of riders, excessively uncomfortable, and at least latently dangerous.

An animal bucked till he unseated his rider, or sooner either was satiated or made to the man atop him an affirmative surrender of spirit.

With such a surrender, the rider was said to have "ridden it out," or have "ridden to a finish."

Bucking might last five seconds. It has been known to continue almost uninterruptedly, though with slight vigor, for an hour. If an average time be demanded, there is hesitatingly put forth three minutes, this covering groups of jumps, each group consuming some ten seconds, and there being, between each two groups a slight pause, during which the horse sulked or, as the West said, "sulled." This average of three minutes means the average for all bucking horses collectively, not the average for the very violent spasms of a single confirmed pitcher. This latter type of brute was ordinarily no time-consumer. He threw himself so whole-heartedly into his task, as to use up his vitality in from ten to thirty seconds.

The cowboy, except as an occasional outlet for over-bubbling vitality, "topped off" buckers only when duty required. It was not danger that deterred him. It was merely that such riding was inhumanly tiring.

Some animals, planning to unseat their riders, resorted at the instant of mounting not to the buck, but to more prosaic running away or to calmly lying down. The performance of this last-mentioned trick automatically, though however illogically, brought from all bystanders derisive advice to the cowboy formerly aboard the supine beast.

Such a prone horse very likely received uncomfortable treatment, for his erstwhile rider, now standing over him, might with steady, upward pull upon the reins keep the beast's head from off the ground, and with one foot press steadily downward upon the saddle horn. The horse thus was deprived of the leverage of its neck, the balance weight of its head, and consequently of ability to roll its body or to regain its feet. When the pony's neck had received sufficient cramping pains, the beast would offer to rise, and as it reached its feet the cowboy would land in the saddle.

Or else the rider, instead of following this course of affirmative action, deliberately kept his feet in the stirrups, so that one of his legs remained under the down-lying horse. The man, for the safety of this leg, confidently relied on the softness of the ground, the strength of his stirrup, the thickness of his chaps, and the light weight of his horse, and trusted that the bystanders would rope and hold the feet of the animal, should it attempt to roll.

When the horse became tired of its prone position, it would lurch to its feet and have the man still aboard.

As to whether or not a rider should so risk his leg was a question for his individual decision. Some riders endeavored under any circumstances to stick to their mount, believing that their quitting would give the horse undue confidence, and would retard if not annul his growing belief in the supremacy of man.

All the time that the horse was lying prone he would be talked to by his rider in soothing tones though profane terms. Throughout bucking, the rider poured a conversational volley at the pitching beast. The sound of the human voice was supposedly one means of proving to the horse that he had met his master.

Running away was often interjected by a hard pitcher as a special scene between the regular acts of his real performance. Runaway horses would go astonishingly long distances, and not infrequently would wheel at the end of the course they had selected, and return at high speed to the starting-point. Their riders customarily were showered with vociferous farewells from the human spectators at the outset of these lonesome races.

One puncher many years ago mounted, and in a moment was flying due westward, soon to disappear behind a point of trees. Unseen from the corral, he rounded these and made his next appearance some time later headed for the corral, and coming from the east. The instant of his arrival, he received, in addition to a circular bit of leather hastily cut from a wide strap, the greeting: "You shore has proved the earth is round."

The man on top of the runaway usually was willing to let the beast "run down its mainspring," but he could promptly stop the animal if he cared to jeopardize his own neck. If this man were to reach forward, grasp either the rein or the bridle at a point close to the bit, and, as the horse lifted its front feet, were to pull the brute's head sharply to one side, the horse would land on its flank upon the ground. A less strenuous method was to lean forward and to hang a coat, handkerchief, or hat before the eyes of the horse. In this latter case, unless the brute promptly fell or was a "locoed" animal, it would quickly cease its galloping.

There were two methods of riding the buck. One was to "sit it," or, as otherwise termed to "ride straight up," i. e., to sit uprightly and squarely in the saddle, shifting one's balance with every change in the horse's position.

If the man sitting the buck were an expert, a top rider, he kept his seat and legs so closely to the saddle as never to bounce upward, and thus, even for an instant, to "show daylight" beneath his body; and his hands, after he had mounted, never touched the saddle, much less felt for the buck strap. But a single hand held the reins.

Less accomplished men in large numbers might be willing to "hunt leather," "take leather," "touch leather," "pull leather," or "go to leather," as a hand hold upon any part of the saddle, its accoutrements, or the horse was interchangeably known, might be willing to "choke the horn," or "choke," or "squeeze," "the biscuit," as a hand hold upon the saddle horn was more specifically designated, but not so the jaunty top rider. He scorned such aid, as also locked spurs, tied stirrups, and other mechanical assistance; and thereby he "rode slick." Not only was the buck strap absent from his saddle, but his specialty was rolling and smoking cigarettes while on top of a living windmill. Frequent waves of his hat or its slapping on the windmill's sides, thereby "fanning" the brute, his withdrawing a foot from its stirrup and swinging this foot far forward and backward to spur or "scratch" the horse on neck and rump, thereby "raking" the beast, his refusal to use his spurs for the purpose of clinging were additional, conventional, if insincere, evidences of an ostensibly care-free state.

The other method of riding the buck involved the rider's seizing the horn by one or both hands, his pushing himself sideways out of the saddle and standing in one stirrup, with his knee on that side flexed, and his other leg at its midway point between hip and knee resting horizontally across the saddle's seat. His flexed knee-joint and his two hip-joints, thus collectively absorbed the shock. Some users of this system, sometimes called "monkey style," stood in the left stirrup, others in the right. But however they stood, their method patently necessitated "choking the horn," "taking leather," and "showing daylight."

In formal riding competitions, whoever, competing in a class reserved for top riders and in which "hunting leather," naturally was barred, gave merely an accidental, momentary, and slightest touch of any part of either hand to any portion of the saddle after mounting had been completed, received a demerit for each offense or, if the rules were such, was at once disqualified.

Indifferent horsemen, more fearful of pitching than of the taunting tongues of beholders, used when upon the range to "tie," or "hobble" their stirrups, in other words to connect them by a strap or rope passing under the horse. This had the advantage of furnishing a firm anchorage during bucking, but the disadvantage of imposing a social stigma. Bystanders were wont to insist that no real horsemen "tied," while "sheep-herders ride with tied stirrups and one spur." "Tying" was forbidden in the riding competitions, on the theory that the latter were a test of horsemanship and not a "test of string."

Occasionally some daredevil puncher rode with "slick heels," *i. e.*, without spurs, or else rode a horse, a mule, or a steer either bareback or with only a cinch or lariat about the animal's body. All this, however, was an "exhibition stunt," and was no part of ranching work. Some irrepressible youths have successfully accomplished the feat of sitting a bareback animal while facing its tail. This last mentioned method of horsemanship is not recommended for beginners in riding.

Bucking sometimes is stated to have had its origin in defensive kicking by the original horses against attacking wolves. This statement is not conclusive, for neither European nor Asiatic horses are apt to buck, and wolves have ever been present on those continents. The only explanation at all satisfactory to one who has just dismounted from a "beast with a belly full of bed-springs," is that offered long ago by June Buzzell, a puncher of the Dakota and Wyoming Ranges, and which was: "Bucking started from the back door of hell on a hot day, and came out on the run."

It was only the light weight of the American broncos that made their pitching humanly endurable. If the heavier European horses, as a class, had pitched, and that with jounce which, measured by bronco standard, was proportionate to their weight and muscle, riding would have been a rarely exercised accomplishment in Europe, because only an occasional man would have had vitality enough to stand the punishment. One of America's best cowboy riders accompanied a "Wild-West Show" to Europe some years since, and there met almost his death from the terrific thumps and strains received while upon the back of a bucking stallion that never had been outside of France.

Moreover, the importation of European horses into America, and their crossing with the bronco would sooner or later have eliminated most of the "graded up" broncos from the list of saddle animals. For commercial reasons he had to be "graded up" to increased size and weight. He was too small for the great majority of harness uses, and it was the harness and not the saddle that furnished to the Range its principal market. There very probably would have been continued, with animals in limited numbers and for riding purposes, a strain of bronco blood either unmixed or else crossed with such larger, imported beasts as had proved themselves to be non-buckers. In any event, Western horse-raising would have had a history quite different from its actual one. Buck Taylor and various other horsemen might never have ridden into fame.

The whole situation was saved by a fortunate provision of nature which, in the average case, while permitting the imported horse, on crossing with the bronco, to pass down the former's qualities, nevertheless prevented it from also giving mere exaggeration to qualities which the bronco alone possessed. Thus a six-hundred-pound bronco, with, say, six hundred pounds of bucking force inside it, mated with a nine-hundred-pound non-bucker. Their colt would eventually weigh, say, seven hundred pounds and would have at most six hundred pounds of bucking force. Successive generations would tend to increase the figures for the animals' weights and to decrease those for their bucking force.

The spectator at one of the present-day formal riding competitions at Cheyenne, Pendleton, Billings, Prescott, Las Vegas, Wichita Falls, etc., sees, in a single afternoon, a much greater number of violently bucking horses than in olden time he would have seen, during an entire week, at a ranch, however large. The reason for this is that no horses except "spoiled" animals or "outlaws" are employed at these modern competitions. The spectators at these competitions see punchers ride at least as well as the latter's fathers and grandfathers used to ride, but these punchers of to-day are spared one danger that their fathers and grandfathers had to risk. The puncher of to-day, standing in, say, Pendelton's or Prescott's arena, assumes that while every one of the horses he is called upon to "hairpin" will go to the limit of roughness in legitimate pitching, none of them will prove itself a deliberate man-killer. He assumes this, because present-day horse-raising is done in a populous country and so allows the idiosyncrasies of practically every horse to become known to its owner.

But the father and grandfather, dealing wholly with animals self-raised on the lonely Range, had no foreknowledge of any particular beast's peculiarities. Although the father and grandfather, entering the corral of years ago, surmised that but a small proportion of their prospective mounts would buck to the limit of roughness, these bygone men could not be confident that they were not to meet a "back throw," or that among the horses was not a professional murderer.

The "gentling" of the horses which had been gathered at the round-up was eventually finished. At last came the time to ship, and the punchers headed toward the railway with their charges.

The expedition travelled by day and rested by night in the same manner as though the men had been driving cattle. But it moved a bit more rapidly, and there was much less fear of possible stampede; though a horse stampede once started was far more difficult to stop than was the "bust up" of a cattle herd; and beyond all was that of mules. Horses had as much curiosity as had cattle; but, unlike cattle, would not feel impelled to run for miles because a rumbling brown stream of buffalo had flowed into sight (this of course only in earlier days), or Indians had been scented, or a wolf had howled, or a stick had cracked, or a tin can had been dropped, or a wagon cover had slatted, or any one of a thousand and one things had occurred. Any happening, however trivial, might, if unexpected, send the cattle into racing frenzy.

The expedition travelled onward, and eventually reached the railway. The horses were herded into the shipping pens, receipted for, and, as none of the punchers was to travel with this particular shipment, their work for their employers was for the moment finished.

But important business was ahead of the men. They had of course to visit their "our town," their "our shipping point," "the biggest little town in all the West," a typical little cow town that lay a half-mile down the track.

They had in their pockets the coins of six months' wages—coins, because paper money was unknown upon the Range, where coins of gold or silver were the only money seen, a half-dollar if not a dollar was the smallest coin used, and, in lieu of fractional currency for the making of change, cartridges of standard sizes not uncommonly functioned.

Thus opulent, the men, their foreman and top riders in accord with social usage leading, headed for town. Had they been driving live stock, they would have entered the settlement or skirted it at the slow rate demanded by the driven herd. But, being free from convoying cares, the party kept its horses at a rapid walk or mincing trot, the gaits usual for country travel, until there was reached the first outlying building, when instantly, and in accord with custom, all horses were sent into a lope.

The men clattered thus into a town such as countless writers on Western subjects have described, and forthwith embarked upon the ostensible joys and rapid roads to insolvency which those same writers have so repeatedly employed as themes.

But there was far from the quantity of exploding gun-powder and flying bullets that many of these writers have portrayed. Probably there was none at all.

When the men entered the settlement, they made considerable noise, but it was the sound only of kindly yells, of hoofs, of bridle chains, and of spur steel. They did not attempt to "take the town" by "shooting it up," or by otherwise threatening its inhabitants. There was no incentive to do this. Every one knew the men, so there was nobody to bluff.

At times such shooting did occur in larger cow towns, as at Dodge City, Abilene, Newton, Ogalalla, Julesburg, and Cheyenne, but it represented in the main, apart from occasional, serious drink-caused duels, little more than youthful prankishness, and an egotistical desire by passing punchers from distant regions to impress the local inhabitants with the fact of the visitors' presence.

Young, trained athletes had just completed a drive of perhaps four months of actual riding in the awful dust of the cattle herd, possibly had been delayed for three or four additional months by stock quarantines upon the route. Now they had reached their destination, and their task was done. "Whoop!" Of course it was "Whoop!"

At times their boyish ebullition was attempted to be checked and the punchers turned to violence; just as today the home-coming, cheering attendants of some sedate college's victorious football team, busy with collecting discarded boards for a celebrating fire and undiplomatically admonished by the single local constable, instantly acquire axes and right and left demolish gates and fences.

And yet the records of the cowboys' temporary incursions into deviltry have come down through the years, and falsely advertised themselves as being pictures of the average life of the average cowboy. The very picture that shows a day of drunkenness, of shooting and of brothel life, and puts itself in the lime-light, omits any portrayal of the three hundred and sixty-four days of hunger, thirst, stampedes, fires, cloudbursts, drifts, quicksands, of uncomplaining and complete filling of a job that it assuredly took a man to fill.

Our punchers not only did not take the town, but also did not even "buy" it. Had they felt unusually hilarious and been markedly well-treated by whatever goddess presides over faro, and particularly had representatives from any rival ranch been present, one of our punchers as spokesman for his party might have turned away from the gaming-table, might have laid from five hundred to a thousand dollars upon the bar, have given that all-including hand sweep practised by queens, prime ministers, and drunken men, and have announced "Gents, it's on us. She's opened up. The town is yourn." Thereupon the local purveyors would have syndicated, and, until the exhaustion of the money thus laid upon the bar, none of the restaurants and saloons in town would have made any charge to any customer for whatever food or drink he might consume. This patronizing gift of a town to its own citizens, this complete reversal of the European spirit in conferring the freedom of a city was known as "buying a town," or "opening" it "up." Tradition, true or false, relates that Cheyenne on one occasion was "bought" for thirty thousand dollars by a convivial English group.

Another phase of this recklessness with money, a recklessness which in those days of optimism was locally epitomized in the sayings: "Easy come, easy go," and "Spending next year's profits," found expression in the ordering of inordinately large and useless quantities of useful things. "Gimme a bottle of beer and fifty dollars worth of ham and eggs," has greeted more than one restaurant's waitress.

It may not be amiss to digress for a moment to later years and to Alaska in its booming days. Tradition there relates that a spurned suitor for the hand of a woman "took to the hills," dug out a fortune, and one December returned to her presence. Knowing her regard for what Alaskans conceived to be the greatest gastronomic delicacy, he quietly cornered all the packed eggs both in the territory and in the ships bound toward it; and, at supper-time during the Christmas ball and in the presence of his rival, proudly directed a waitress to "give the lady a hundred thousand dollars worth of scrambled eggs."

As still another phase of this same spirit, audiences at the little theatres which were boasted by some of the larger cow towns were apt to throw coins to actresses who had earned acclaim. Silver dollars were the conventional offerings; but, at Cheyenne, one lusty man became so enthralled at the way "The last kiss my darling mother gave," was described in coyote tremolo by a blonde soprano, that he hurled a twenty-dollar gold piece, which, accidentally hitting the songstress behind the ear, knocked her senseless.

But none of these spectacular things befell our men. They merely "went broke," in commonplaceness, though with rapidity. The following day, the members of the party made, in the order of their entering insolvency, announcement of their intended departure; and, after being donated a farewell drink, mounted and ruefully "hit the trail" for the ranch and six months more of work.

The men had come into the town boldly, but they faded out of it.

All of the party had gone except one man. He was leaving the Range forever, to go to some city "back East," and enter a prosaic but profitable office. He stood, gazing sadly at the distant rear-guard of his late companions. There staggered up to him a cowboy whom he never before had seen, a cowboy befuddled in speech but not in heart, a cowboy who, taking one look at a troubled face, asserted:

"Say, stranger, you're out of luck. I've got four bits left. Here's half of it. Hell, no. Here's all of it."

Such was the spirit of the Western Plains in the days when lariats were freely swinging.

CHAPTER XV

RUSTLING

EARLY STEALING—LINCOLN COUNTY WAR—NESTERS—BEGINNING OF RUSTLING—DEFINI-
TIONS—SENTIMENTS PERMITTING RUSTLING—RANGE-DWELLERS—THEIR SEVERAL ATTITUDES
TOWARD RUSTLING—RUSTLERS' METHODS—WYOMING'S RUSTLER WAR—ITS SIGNIFICANCE.

IN the earlier days of ranching, the stealing of live stock was accomplished by the simple and direct means of openly riding up to it and driving it away. The transaction might be thus unvarnished, or it might be "decorated with gun play."

This thievery might be effected by a single individual or by an organized band. In this latter phase, small, local civil wars occasionally were fought.

New Mexico suffered the worst of these belligerencies; as, after criminals had begun to gnaw at John Chisholm's cattle, the men of an entire county took sides, and at least two hundred of them in a struggle of slow, sniping attrition were "passed out" by bullets. An exact count was never made; and, for years afterward, here and there in box canyons or between high rocks, wayfarers would stumble on grinning skulls with a round hole between the sockets for the eyes. Such was the "Lincoln County War." The contiguous New Mexican counties of Lincoln and Dona Ana truly were splashed with blood.

The Rio Grande too knew murder. International robbery never has been good-natured.

In these civil wars, stealing or its prevention sometimes was the primary object. At other times, the stealing was tacked as an incidental matter onto a campaign against encroaching sheepmen or farmers or onto a feud between two ranchers of horses or cattle. Then a better class of men was drawn into it and the robber was apt to salve his conscience with the thought that he was merely collecting the money-cost of efforts made in support of a moral cause.

Thus arose the bloody, Texan struggle between the local ranchmen and the "nesters," sometimes called "nestlers." These nesters, individually small farmers, and in the main immigrants largely of Germanic birth, had obtained by State grant or by other means scattered parcels of farming land. Each of these farmers, acting on the faith of ostensible, legal title, threw about his little tract a fence that cut off from public use whatever waterhole was within the tract. The little farm so fenced was, by the local cattlemen, contemptuously termed a "nest." These cattlemen, with despotic lordliness, not only fenced their own lands; but also, ignoring both law and the theory of an open

227

Range, fenced where they chose; and not infrequently embraced in their enclosures one or more already established nests. This loosed the fence-cutter and the Winchester, and there began wholesale pilfering of live stock. Both sides were at fault, and so were compelled to compromise. Accordingly the ruction eventually worked itself onto a peaceful if jealous basis whereon each faction began to observe the law.

By the commencement of the decade of the eighties, the Cattle Country had grown tired of bald raidings, of the disciples of Slade, Watkins, Lacey, Arnett, Spillman, Henry Plummer, Bignose George, Dutch Charley, Opium Bob, and Billy the Kid. Wherefore it purchased additional cartridges and further hempen rope, "took" some criminals, "got" more of them, and quite thoroughly ended stealing done in flagrant, primitive form.

Promptly appeared the wiley "rustler," who by more indirect and intelligent methods increased the total of the annual pilferings.

But, before entering upon that subject, one well may turn to those two picturesque Western words, "took" and "got." The law sent out its sheriff, "took" a man, and tried him. The citizens "dug for their guns," "got" their man, and examined his corpse.

To understand "rustling," one first must consider the public sentiment which made its existence and scope possible; and, as a prerequisite to this consideration, one should weigh certain underlying principles which at first blush well might seem wholly unrelated.

Every Westerner was an intense individualist, and demanded exclusive management of his personal affairs. At the same time, having no curiosity whatever as to the private matters of other people, he was perfectly willing that these other people should do as they liked, provided they neither improperly interfered with his rights nor contravened such of the tenets of the Cattle Country's code of ethics as the West deemed to be vital and fundamental both to the maintenance of life and liberty and to the pursuit of happiness.

He was ready and usually willing, for his own actions, to account to the ultimate authorities of competent jurisdiction, namely his God and the officials of either State or federal government; and he assumed that, when his neighbors felt impelled to make a relatively similar reckoning, they would, without appeal to his advice, ascertain where confession should be made, and would act accordingly. It never occurred to him that he might be his brother's keeper, and he knew how he himself would feel, if any one, even an intimate friend, "butted into" his concerns.

So set was the disinclination of every Westerner to intrude into other folks' affairs, that he volunteered to the public officers practically no assistance, save in such matters as pertained to his own cattle and horses.

Even though a notorious robber had quizzically announced that the Union Pacific Railroad was running its trains too rapidly for public convenience, or that his "side pardner," Skinny Joe or Black Bart, either had a contract to revise the schedule of the Santa Fé Railway or else was to act as head flagman on the Oregon Short Line, it would not have occurred to any citizen of the Cattle Country to forewarn the sheriff or even the representatives of the threatened railway. The citizen's view-point would have been that these representatives "shore knew about it," or "shore would learn about it"; would notify the sheriff, and would otherwise sufficiently protect themselves, or, if unable to do so, would call upon the public for aid.

However, for a while the citizen idly would have scanned the headings of whatever newspapers he ran across, to discover if possible whether the robbing Squint-Eye had "pulled it off," or, instead, had lost his entire head before the short-barrelled, nail-loaded shotgun of some alert Wells, Fargo messenger. Whether Skinny Joe had "made good," or "had shore got his'n" would also have been worth making desultory effort to ascertain. But all these transactions would have seemed as impersonal, foreign, and unimportant as though Squint-Eye, Black Bart, or Skinny Joe had been an Eskimo, and, amid the Arctic ice, had attempted to purloin a piece of seal meat from an oil-soaked tribesman.

If any old-timer in the West had heard that there was about to be robbed a bank with the management or ownership of which he was not connected, he would not for a moment have thought of informing the cashier. The old-timer would have felt sure that if he gave warning, the bank's officials would have ground to complain that too many people were trying to "play in the game," and that he himself was "feeding off his own range." The old-timer's view-point would have been that, if he knew of the prospective "party," the officials doubtless either also did or else would obtain foreknowledge; and, if they wanted his aid, they would send for him.

If they ultimately had sent for him, he would have gone, as he would have gone at the call of the railroads when Squint-Eye or Skinny Joe "held them up," and this on the instant and, if need be, ready to die. But, if his assistance had not been requested, he would have displayed in the matter no more activity than some day to inquire how far the safe door had flown.

These men were not thus close-mouthed in order to conceal any crime which they themselves approved, had committed, or were about to commit. The vast majority of them had intentions of the strictest honesty. They merely had a dread of "horning-in."

The West was then not yet old enough to realize that universal protection came only out of concerted action.

This close-mouthedness, this non-interest in other people's doings was the principal factor in opening the Range to the rustler's trade.

This factor had a companion, full advantage of which was taken by the thieves, particularly by such of them as "did not come West for their health." This put-upon companion was the kindly, tolerant pleasure which the Cattle Country derived from seeing any "likely young man" "get a start in life" and "get ahead."

To any one in the West the government gave, without charge, title to lands, and use of grass and water, and also said, in effect: "I shall make you a gift of minerals, of firewood, and of all the wild meat you possibly can eat, if you but go and find them."

Under such conditions, there was not a brutally outstanding, brilliantly clear-cut line of moral demarcation between, on the one hand, a noble-looking wapiti that fifty million people had donated to whoever wanted it and, on the other hand, a scrubby, anæmic calf that claimed either to belong to a distant English earl who had no knowledge that he owned the beast, and seemingly did not care, or else to belong to a "snotty city chap," who patronized his fellow ranchers and deserved a "taking down."

The owners of the live stock fell into two classes, the locally popular and the locally disliked.

The latter group was made up in part of non-residents who, spending the major portion of their time in England or upon America's Atlantic coast, lived upon their ranches only during short and widely separated periods. Their visits frequently were restricted to the autumnal seasons when big-game shooting was at its best. Such men, because they failed to reside in the West, and, when there, used the Range largely as a shooting cover or private country club, were assumed to regard their holdings as an incidental luxury, not to be financially dependent on them, and not to feel the pinch if any of their stock were "borrowed" by acquisitive persons.

The West had the same mental attitude toward such corporations as, being of size, were owned by numerous and scattered stockholders. These corporations also lacked the cogent, tangible element of a man who stayed on the spot and "had his pocketbook in his herd."

The second unpopular group was composed of such local residents as both did not fit into the scenery, and also palpably were intending a stay of but at most a few years' duration.

The Old West lived in its then to-day, and planned for its then to-morrow, but, except for recollections of Range tenets and of human friendships, its yesterday was but vaguely remembered, while its last week was for it as remote almost as when Julius Cæsar lived. The Cattle Country recalled every word and comma of its unwritten code, it recalled the looks and statements of its dead friends, and right there it "plumb petered out," on any affirmative interest in history.

The graded Herefords or Short Horns before a youthful rustler's eyes bore the brand of, say, the English Middlesex and Montana Ranch. The young man probably restricted his reflections to calves, to pocketed telegraph wire, and to trails. But, if his thoughts drifted into scholarly channels, he foggily called to mind that the Spanish had abandoned a lot of live stock, and that it had spread about the plains, and he concluded that the Englishmen must have done a few years before a "right smart lot of roping." Then he hazily decided that, if the Englishmen had been so selfishly wholesale in their acquisitions, it could do no harm if he himself were merely to nibble at the herd which, though the English now claimed, the Spaniards earlier had owned and thrown away.

And yet, in the very locality where the only surely safe repository for a calf was a bank's deposit-box, a man's saddle, pistol, clothing, money could, with impunity and without guard, be left beside the trail.

The recital thus far has disclosed that, in a country where the government made almost all necessities free, there wandered about huge herds of animals, which in some part were recognized as legally belonging to people that were supposed to merit chastening, and in other part, thanks to the Spaniard, were assumed to pertain morally, despite the brands, to nobody in particular; that, in this country, were impecunious, virile men whose desire to arrive at honored position was publicly acclaimed, and whose path for travelling thither was little scrutinized, seldom fully known or much discussed.

For another purpose of this present writing, the inhabitants of the Cattle Country were separable into five classes.

Of these classes, the first represented men who were uncompromising advocates of law, were of absolute integrity, and who scorned either to aggrandize themselves through any dishonesty or to give consciously the slightest aid to others in the latter's wrongful doings.

The second class was composed of men who, while equally set against improper personal gain, would, because of less stanch admiration for law, extend a bit of passive or even active assistance to a friend who personally was engaged in "picking up a few ownerless animals."

Men of the third class were like those of the second, except that these men of the third class were more easy-going in character, and were willing to "skim a little cream" themselves provided it hurt no "real Westerner."

The fourth class brings us to the man who in more or less degree resented affirmatively the restrictions of the law, and who, if he wanted beef, "went and got it," though to his credit it must be said that he usually first visited the undesirables' ranches, and generally spared the widow, orphan, and poor. He commonly was as trustworthy to his neighbor as were the men of the two immediately prior classes, excepting only that he was constantly "sentimental about cows," and temperamentally "couldn't help making love to them."

The fifth class, numerically the smallest, was restricted to the thieves as the novelists depict them, and was comprised of men who would steal live stock from almost any one, and who would take "even a sheep."

But even many of these last-mentioned men had redeeming characteristics, and were treated accordingly. With the better of them, if they limited their peculations to reasonable quantity, the Range shut one eye and said: "Jim, you eat too much meat, and need exercise. Come up to the ranch, and I'll give you a permanent job." The Range did so, because it knew that Jim would be faithful unto death in everything except in matters of cowhide, and possibly also his treatment of stages and railway trains. If Jim's appetite in time were not duly curbed, he would be given the address of a distant State and kindly but firmly advised to "hunt it up."

A few of this fifth class were truly anarchistic, "had snake blood," in them, were in fact "bad men," and therefore had not the backing of the Range. Sooner or later they would go the way of all "bad men," and would disappear.

For the sake of subsequent brevity, the men of these various five classes will be hereinafter arbitrarily designated by the several letters, *A, B, C, D*, and *E*, the letter *A* representing the first class, *B* the second, and so on. For the sake of clear understanding, let us keep in mind the principles already discussed, particularly the one to the effect that "other people's business is none of mine." Then we shall be prepared to fathom the subject of wholesale rustling.

A "low down, snake-blooded" *E* started to "gather" from anybody's stock, and raided the widow and orphan. All of *A, B, C,* some of decent

D, and a temporarily regenerated *E* "went looking for him," for he had raised his hand against the Range.

A decent *E* began a modest "collection," from the herds of disliked owners, *i. e.*, from permissible sources. During the acquirement of so much of his "collection" as the public tacitly sanctioned, very likely *B*, *C*, and *D* helped him to rope animals and to alter brands; *C*, if a well-liked individual, reserving as a commission a single comely beast; *D* withholding on this score all that *E* would let him have. Very possibly the entire party, on its way to or from the piracy, stopped for a night at *A*'s ranch. Of course, there was made to *A* no mention of the expedition's purpose. It was none of his business, for neither he nor any other "real person" was to be or had been looted. But *A*, by Range custom, was ready to house all passing travellers, good, bad, and indifferent, and to ask no questions.

Presently the public, thinking that decent *E* had made sufficient acquirement, warned him to "throw on the brakes." If he obeyed, the matter was ended. If he did not hearken, he moved to another State.

D, in his own efforts, would receive still more extensive aid from *B* and *C*, and would be allowed a larger looting.

There was a generally popular *C*, who jauntily sallied forth on his own account and "picked some blossoms." *B* worked like a dog for him, while the Range smiled, said nothing, did nothing, for the Range knew that *C* would never "overplay his hand." But no disliked *C* or *D* could, without the Range's implied consent, be "careless with his branding-iron."

As already stated, overt stock-raiding, so-called "brass-band stealing," had ceased by the commencement of the eighties, to be succeeded immediately by the more finished methods of highly specialized rustling. For some ten years this rustling continued in a widely spread but somewhat desultory manner. During that period the operations in each State were largely confined to its own citizens, its members of our alphabet below the letter *A*. The herds of well-liked owners were left quite inviolate; but our letters *B*, *C*, *D*, and *E* modestly whittled away at the holdings of the English and other vacationers, and occasionally were killed while at their work.

In this period the owners sowed seed for future trouble, because they began the system of paying bonuses to cowboys for finding mavericks, and later not only abolished the system, but also, on some ranges, forbade cowpunchers to own live stock.

This prohibition against owning live stock was in strict accord with the tendency which the entire West possessed, and incidentally which obtained in various Eastern States, the tendency to enact remedial laws of sweeping effect and general application, and to expect the laws to enforce themselves, and also to enact laws without first considering as to whether or not they probably would prove enforceable.

The prohibition availed nothing toward checking stealing, because the punchers had, in their bonuses, already tasted monetary blood.

The pilfering methods used by rustlers were both the altering of brands, and also the wrongful branding of thitherto unbranded animals; followed, in either case, by separating from their mothers such of these misbranded brutes as were maternally escorted, this last to insure that there be no combination of close companionship and divergent markings wherewith to advertise that "bossy had a stepfather." This separation was achieved by impounding in isolated corrals such of the youngsters as showed filial affection, and keeping them there until weaned away from their mothers, or by searing or scarifying the soles of the mother's hoofs to prevent her from following her baby when it was led away, or else by the very direct method of shooting the mother and thereby "pinning crape on the kid."

Meanwhile, paralleling the Union Pacific Railway, another transcontinental railway, the Northern Pacific, had been built across the Cattle Country; but the buffalo had lasted long enough to feed the railway's constructors, so the cattle had not as yet been much cut into. Nevertheless, these very buffalo had created a menace, for they had called together numerous men of a curious type, the queer beings who earned their livelihood either by killing buffalo for their skins or by merely collecting the dead buffaloes' bones. When "skinning" and "bone-picking" ended, the men of those trades were ripe for the rustling of cattle.

Meanwhile there was pushing, in quantity and over the edges of the Range, a new type of citizen or prospective citizen, the small farmer, who frequently was fresh from Europe. He already was or quickly became sufficiently "Americanized" as to look with envy upon the wandering assets of the earlier settlers.

Soon still another railway, the Burlington's Western extension, was projected into Wyoming, and so into the very heart of the Range. It attracted to itself workers from distant places, and, in addition, unloaded at its advancing railhead not only legitimate farmers but also many of those unwelcome characters who haunt the rails yet shrink from steady or honest work. Of the men who came to fill construction jobs, some proved inefficient and were discharged.

There thus seeped out among the cattle a new lot of citizens containing a leaven made of persons possessed of then as yet dormant criminal instincts, made also of fugitives from the justice of far-off States, made also of men who, out of jobs, turned to rustling for intended temporary livelihood, but, once in the dishonest calling, would not quit it.

While the leaven of these human misfits was filtering into the country, the political leaders were stirring the newly arrived farmers to have active interest in citizenship, and to exercise its duty, the casting of the vote. Simultaneously, political demagogues were descanting upon the themes that all these recent comers were the "real people of the land," and that the herds which these recent comers saw represented wealth improperly withheld from them.

Eventually, in Wyoming, the small farmers, with the perhaps unnecessary, but nevertheless enthusiastic, assistance of the ne'er-do-wells, held all the public offices in an entire county, and thus controlled the issuance and disposition of all its judicial process, a process that was prone not to attack the rustlers but was disposed to deal curtly with long-vested interests.

But all the disgruntled of the small farmers and all the confirmed thieves within Wyoming could not have gashed the stock industry as it presently was gashed, if it had not been that such of our above friends from the alphabet as lived within that State had the moral attitudes hereinbefore described, and that the truly Americanized of the new immigrants already had distributed themselves among those various lettered classes.

The railhead of the new railway, the Burlington, pushed further into the Wyoming Range. There were no buffalo for the railway's builders to eat. Some unrecorded, enterprising youth, who previously had outgrown the tedious process of stealing calves, rebranding them, raising them to maturity, and then smuggling them into legitimate East-bound channels, who later had adopted the more direct method of shooting adult animals, skinning them, destroying either the telltale markings of the hide or else the entire hide, and delivering the carcasses to butchers in the farmers' little towns, now made a great discovery. It was that the layers of ties, the drivers of spikes, the shovellers of dirt, in fact everybody in the construction camps of the railway had unlimited capacity for eating fresh meat.

Immediately eastern Wyoming ran amuck. Except for such of the old-timers as were austerely honest, and except for such men of the absentee landlord type as happened to be within the State, the male inhabitants in an astonishingly large proportion madly turned to rustling. Such of the better element as engaged in it did so with a grin, sometimes with no more definite purpose than a lark, but usually as a means of "getting hunk" with some well-to-do but hated rancher. The other participants were actuated by resentment against wealth or by affirmative desire for gain, and, in the latter case, materially differed in the amounts of their cupidity.

Almost every man of strong dislikes and weak conscience joined with his more ignoble brothers in devastating such of the large herds as belonged to unpopular owners, and in selling to the railway contractors the meat of "slow elk" and "big antelope." This movement, among the more dishonorable rustlers, extended first to raiding any large herd and, later, on the simple theory that "beef was beef," to ignoring completely the question of identity of ownership.

The movement became so well established as to have a jargon of its own. The movement had also militant apostles in the "waddies," men faithful to the illegal art of rustling; and these, by the weapon of derision, tried to wean honest punchers from protection of their employers' interests. These honest chaps were taunted with willingness to "slave," to be "peoned out," to be "servants," to be "low down enough to carry a bucket of sheep dip," to be "sheep-herders at heart," and, if in English employ, to "shine coronets." They sneeringly were termed "sheep-dippers," "bucket men," "pliers men," "saints," and again, if in English employ, "royal crowns."

The more sober-minded citizens began to realize that the very life of the cattle industry was threatened.

Suddenly there happened an event which brought the whole situation to a focus and resolved it into sanity. In 1892, some of the larger suffering ranches launched from Cheyenne an armed expedition which was intended to exterminate certain of the rustlers. This expedition presently opened fire upon the ranch of a man accused of being a "waddy." Forthwith many of the smaller ranchers and of the farmers hastened to relieve the threatened thieves. Out came the local sheriff with a posse, which was exceedingly large, and in which were many "waddies."

Throughout the whole affair, but a few shots flew, but two men fell. United States cavalry cut short the hostilities. Yet the episode had affirmative result.

The relative numbers of the people aligning with the several factions showed conclusively that the old order had ended, that the Range had ceased to be a political entity and had been apportioned among the States, that the cattle kings had forever ceased to rule, that the control of what had been the Cattle Country had passed from the herd-owners and top riders to the farmer recently from New Jersey, the clerk just come from an Ohio village, the shopkeeper who, through unreasoning fear of Indians, had long delayed his immigration from Iowa, the settler newly arrived from Europe and armed with his first papers of naturalization.

The Old West had passed. The New West had come.

Thereupon such of the robbed ranchers as were not in entirety of old-time Western spirit disposed of the wreckage of their holdings, and retired both from the industry of raising stock and from the country where their animals had ranged.

The men who continued in the business came into closer mutual relationship with one another. They were joined by the better class of men among the rustlers; and, through a revitalized machinery for the guarding of the cattle industry, there was soon suppressed the stealing which the more confirmed rustlers had endeavored to continue.

Very presently, by reason of increased activity in policing throughout the West, rustling became everywhere there virtually extinct.

Those happenings in Wyoming terminated by that shooting, which was the so-called "Rustler War," or "Johnson County Raid," had a distinct political and social significance. That final burst of thieving represented, for some of its performers, mere robbing; for others, a reckless, rollicking lark; for others, opportunity for punishment or revenge; but, for the majority, an uprising against concentrated wealth; and, at the end, it signified an accomplished, social and political revolution.

Though Wyoming alone pitted armed man against armed man to decide a fundamental problem, all the other Western States sooner or later arrived at the same conclusion that Wyoming did in Johnson County in 1892. From the Missouri River to the Sierra Nevadas, the open Range as a dominant, political entity passed into history. True, thereafter cattle-owners as such had great political power; but, to obtain results, they often had to seek the assistance of the farmers, of the townspeople, and, at times, ye gods! of the sheepmen. It was a power which, though able still to make a legislature hesitate, was no longer capable of imperious dictation from a horse's back.

The open Range had everywhere overstayed its leave.

CHAPTER XVI

TRAILING

"RIDING sign" was one of the duties of the cowboy. This act of following the track which had been made by an earlier traveller, whether man or four-footed animal, was guided by the same principles as those that had been adopted by the scouts against Indians. The act was termed by the scouts either "trailing" or else "following sign," and by the cowboys "riding sign."

Some of the cowboys were extremely proficient in pursuing trails; but of course few of them rose to the highly specialized ability of the men who as Indian scouts devoted their lives to this one function. These scouts, as one of them, James Bridger, remarked, preserved their scalps by tying them to their brains, and as another of them, John Yancey, said, were taught in a school in which the Indians periodically conducted examinations, and in which any scholar who flunked was scalped.

Nevertheless, cowboys working upon the open Range had in the main to abide by the same methods as those which were employed by these Indian scouts, and had been copied by the latter from the Indians themselves. The principles hereinafter enunciated were those utilized by the scouts; and, save for so much of those principles as related to ascertaining the tribal identity of the makers of Indians' trails, were pursued by the more capable trailing cowboys, and were attempted to be practised by all cowboys even though they were called upon merely to ride sign after live stock.

Each of the various Indian tribes had individual and very distinctive peculiarities in its equipment and in the form of its camp. Usually a short section of an Indian trail, and always an Indian camp, or even the mere site of an abandoned one, disclosed definitely to the scout the identity of the tribe involved. But only in Indian-infested country did the cowboy have to acquaint himself with these distinguishing technicalities.

An underlying axiom gave to trailing practical results. This axiom was that no two species of animal, man included, left similar trails; and that no two animals of the same species, man included, could so divest themselves of their several individual peculiarities as to be able to leave trails that were wholly alike.

Trailing was no more or less than detective work. Sherlock Holmes of English fiction would have been a great Indian scout, had he lived on the Western plains. Trailing involved both intensive exercise of the powers of observation, and also careful reasoning from the facts observed, this reasoning taking into consideration at times human or animal psychology.

The powers of observation employed were, in the order of the importance of their services: sight, hearing, scent, and touch.

The trail might be so clearly blazoned as to be self-evident to any tyro. Then its pursuit was so facile as to amount to no more than, in the scout's vernacular, "sliding the groove." But, when the inductive facts were few and appeared at widely separated points, trailing rose to the level of an art.

The scout's work might have either one of two objectives, namely, the overtaking of a living fugitive or else the reaching of a definite spot upon the map. These two objectives called for very differing methods of procedure.

The first, the chase, required for probability of success that the quarry's course be in the main strictly followed; although not infrequently, when pursuit had continued sufficiently long to satisfy the pursuer's mind as to the quarry's intended destination, short cuts across country might safely be hazarded.

When the scout's task had to do only with the reaching of a geographical objective, his work was more akin to that of the engineer. The scout then was concerned with two propositions: first, how surely to attain the point; second, how best to avoid all intermediate obstructions. In this he was not interested, like the scientific explorer, in actually mapping the details of the intervening country, though the scout might have to give attention to them in so far as they might promise to be factors in the then present expedition or in some future one.

For the successful exercise of the art of pursuit, the trailer first concentrated his scrutiny upon the face of the country through which his quest was to lie, in order that, becoming thoroughly familiarized with the normal appearance of all the details, he might have his attention instantly arrested by any infraction of that normality. Once intimately acquainted with the usual appearance of things, the trailer thereafter could confine his observation exclusively to watching for the unusual. The unusual, the infractions which the quarry had imposed on usual conditions, wrote the story of the eluder's journey and prophesied his destination.

The simplest situation was the following of a fugitive which, until overtaken, kept himself in clear view; but so bald a "sliding the groove" deserves no consideration, for it involved no element of detective work. Not unless the pursuit were of a hidden quarry did the operation rise to the dignity of trailing.

An otherwise invisible fugitive might disclose his position by unwittingly permitting sunlight to reflect from some bright object worn upon himself or upon his horse. Upon brilliant days such flashing would, in the clear air of the West, be visible for miles. For this latter reason all law-abiding Westerners in either Indian-beset territory or the country of big-game shooting, and everywhere all law-breaking Westerners, eschewed anything that might throw off reflections. Bright nickel was at a discount, whether it were upon rifle, pistol, spur or bit. White handkerchiefs and shirts were not held in high esteem.

The flashing from a reflecting object was particularly noticeable when that object was in motion. Because of this the trailer, the instant he thought himself observed by his quarry, stiffened into immobility, to remain quiescent so long as he deemed himself or his location to be under observation.

Many a tenderfoot, riding alone and solemnly brandishing his shiny pistol during a self-imposed drill, has thereby sent to far-distant, grinning punchers advertisement of his coming.

The route of the man or animal pursued might be visually reported by impressions left underfoot or at the trail's side, by foreign objects dropped in the way, by the fugitive's routing of birds and animals from their stations and sending them scurrying into the pursuer's sight. It might be audibly reported by the fugitive's footfalls, his rolling stones, or his breaking sticks, and, if the fugitive were a man, by also his discharging weapons. Finally, it might be reported to the nose by identifying odor, and to the sense of touch by the temperature of dropped objects.

These memoranda of travel could be read; and, when accurately perused, they disclosed the identity of the quarry, his course, and, save in the instances of the audible messages, the time elapsed since he had made any given "sign," as each tangible memorandum left by him was termed.

The impressions left underfoot might show as more or less clear imprints of the foot, as mere scratches upon a rock, a frozen surface, or a sun-baked soil, as breaks in sticks or herbage, or as displacements of natural objects from their wonted positions.

Because the fugitive's footprints were the most satisfactory evidence of his identity, the first function of the trailer was so to acquaint himself with the impressions of his quarry's feet as to be able thereafter to distinguish them from all other tracks. To accomplish this, he might, until he came upon a set of complete imprints, have to rely, in the case of each foot, upon a composite construction made up of a heel's impress here, a toe's print there. A half dozen fragmentary impressions might be all an expert trailer had seen before he had formed an accurate, detailed conception of a foot's shape, size, and characteristics.

With the prints once clearly pictured in the mind of a competent scout, he, despite their infrequent appearance in complete form upon anything but moist soil or damp snow, would follow them from such surfaces across the sand, the rocks, the ice, through myriads of other and temporarily conflicting tracks, confidently recognizing telltale peculiarities which were from time to time disclosed, on this print a worn-over heel, in that impression a twisted toe.

If the trailer had not before his start been advised as to the physical peculiarities of his quarry's feet or their shoeings, he quickly learned them from the imprints. The size and shape of each foot, as also lameness, deviations from normal pointings of the toe, undue throwing of weight upon any special portion of a foot, length of stride, projecting seams, indented breaks, each wrote a memorandum. The form, size, and character of sewn seams, of a repairing patch, of an unmended tear or hole would, for the human moccasin or boot, leave a record as instructive as would a broken shoe or a malformed hoof for a fleeing horse.

Limping not only drove a lame leg's foot more deeply into the ground than a sound leg sent its foot, but also was apt to cause both a twisting on the sole and a variation from the normal length of stride. Drunkenness and physical exhaustion each were recorded by prints which showed successive staggerings from and to the course; as also undue indentings, here of the heel, there of the toe; and finally signal inequality in length of stride.

At the scene of an Oregonian "hold up," the footprints of the bandit evidenced a patched sole and a lame leg. A puncher, following the prints, ascertained promptly that the bandit had walked two hundred yards to a tethered horse, had mounted, and had ridden away. The puncher, by clinging to the horse's trail, arrived at a ranch temporarily emptied of its inmates. Earth markings showed that the bandit had dismounted before the door. The patched sole had clearly recorded its entering the building, but had made no record of its leaving. The puncher's study of all the local impressions soon offered the explanation. The prints made by an unpatched sole under a limping foot told of a change of shoes, led to the corral, and, in combination with the hoof-marks within the corral and leading from its gate, advertised that the bandit had saddled a fresh horse, and had trotted away upon it. That puncher within two hours caught that bandit.

Incidentally, all Indians toed in and wore moccasins, the sole marks of the latter frequently by their shapes establishing the identity of the wearer's tribe. Also no Indian shod his horse with metal; or, unlike the white man, let his fire, when not used for signalling, emit dark smoke.

Length of stride was, as between a man's two feet, apt to be unequal. Usually the right foot took the longer step, direction being maintained by twisting on the longer-stepping foot as the other was in the air. This twisting imprinted a distinctive swirl upon the track.

Some men, when walking, brought down their feet with even pressure. Others stressed upon either heel or toe. A running man rarely touched to the ground any part of his foot that was back of its ball. If he did otherwise, the heel print would be but slightly impressed. A man could run backward, but this only for short distances, and when he both was upon his toes and also was taking short strides. When he was walking backward, he would, after the first few yards, all done with great physical effort, throw his weight upon his heels, and also drive them into the soil accordingly. These simple, natural characteristics saved a competent trailer from being long deceived by that hoary subterfuge of thieves, walking backward.

A pedestrian, if heavily laden, would markedly indent his heels.

A Californian bank was robbed of some silver bars. A single set of human footprints, all of them showing deeply impressed heels, led from the bank's building to the hoof marks of a horse; and thence, with much lessened depth of heel impressions, continued to a second and dissimilar set of equine hoof-marks. The two sets of hoof-marks forthwith diverged. There came upon the scene a competent trailer. He reasoned and, as it soon developed, correctly reasoned that but one robber had dismounted, had entered the building, and had removed the silver; that this robber had carried the loot to a confederate who had remained in the saddle; that the dismounted robber then had mounted his own horse; and that, to confuse pursuers, the two men had fled in opposite directions. The trailer, on the faith of altered depths in human heel prints, guessed accurately as to which horse carried the silver; and the trailer made his capture.

A ridden horse clung to a fixed course. A riderless horse would wander hither and thither.

A horse, when walking or trotting, made two parallel lines of hoof-marks, one with his two right feet, the other with his two left feet.

In each of these lines were widely and regularly spaced sets of imprints; each set consisting of the closely adjacent impressions of the front and hind feet belonging on whichever side of the horse was the one to which the line related. Each set showed, for the normal horse, the hind foot's impression slightly in advance of that of the front foot; while a lame animal was apt on his infirm side to reverse this order of precedence. The intervals between the sets of normal prints would be for a horse, when walking, approximately five feet, and, when trotting, approximately eight feet.

The walking horses, when riderless, made with all four feet such indentations as showed the heels and toes equally impressed. But the walking horse, when ridden, acted as did any trotting horse ridden or unridden, and tended to accent the impressions of its toes. Trotting hoofs also scarfed up a bit the ground immediately ahead of them.

In the lope, and also in the gallop or so-called run (a horse does not run), all four hoofs tended to track in a single line.

A loping horse, if leading with his right front foot, made his hoof impressions in the following order: (1) right front, (2) left hind, (3) left front, (4) right hind, (5) right front again.

The length of the intervals between the several impressions depended on the individual peculiarities of each animal; and also, in the case of each animal, varied with the levelness or hilliness of the course, and the character of the footing. For the average, normal horse on level ground with good surface, the intervals, other than that between the marks of the left hind and the left front foot, would be approximately twenty-four inches. The excepted interval would be either very short or else non-existent, possibly one inch in length, or, perhaps, instead of this, the hind foot's print would cut into the front foot's mark.

In the gallop the order of imprints changed, and, for a horse leading with his right front foot, was (1) right front, (2) left hind, (3) right hind, (4) left front, (5) right front again.

The intervals would be much longer than in the case of the lope, and there would be no counterpart of the loper's single, inch-long spacing above mentioned.

In both the lope and the gallop, if the animal were to lead with his left foot, the serial orders above given would be correspondingly transposable.

In all these higher speeds, added to little mounds before the imprints were splays of earth thrown back from the prints; both the depth of the prints and also the lengths both of the splays and of the intervals, all considered in connection with the character of the soil, accurately announcing the rate of speed.

In 1894 the federal government's scout in the Yellowstone National Park came upon the hoof-prints of a poaching outfit. After following the trail a short distance the scout suddenly turned to the army officer with him and said: "No use. They've seen us and their horses are faster than ours." The scout had observed the prints of a walk continue into the prints of a gallop, and had recognized that the intervals were longer than the horses of his own detachment could make. That he had reasoned accurately appeared when, a day or so later, the poachers were arrested, told their story, and confessed their own horses' racing quality.

Hoofed animals other than horses left, within the limits of their several gaits, tracks open to an analysis like that already described.

Observation made from these view-points permitted accurate diagnosis between the hoof-print of an antelope and that of a mountain-sheep. Each of these animals had cloven hoofs of the same shape and size, the two sections of each hoof making collectively an impression somewhat in the form of a triangle. The apex of this triangle was, in the case of the antelope, at the forward end of the imprint, and, in the case of the sheep, at the imprint's rear end. A trailer would discover whether the track were that of a sheep bound north or of an antelope travelling south, the moment that there appeared the tracks which the beast had made after it had broken from a walk.

A given print seemingly might have been made by a steer, a large wapiti, or a small bison, but sooner or later there would appear upon the trail some sign that clearly established the identity of the animal.

Sometimes the surface trod upon was rock or ice, and thus incapable through hardness of taking a complete impression. Nevertheless it could, from an iron horseshoe, a stone caught in the hoof, or a nail in a boot's sole, receive scratches which, from their freshness, stood clearly forth to an observant eye. In granitic rock, recently scored mica shone like a galaxy of little stars. Ice-cuts would for a while display scintillating crystals.

Freshly broken sticks had evidential value as to both the fact of passage and the identity of the traveller. Except through occasional inadvertence or when in the recklessness of terror, wild animals never stepped upon avoidable sticks, particularly on such as patently would break. The Indian adopted this habit of the wild animals, and over-stepped branches and twigs lying in his path. It remained for the white man, the cattle and the horse to tread ruthlessly upon all wood within the way. These last two animals, the white man's only rivals in stupidity, outdid him merely in that they, from their greater weight, broke the wood into smaller pieces and pushed the fragments further into the ground.

Two broken branches overhanging a wide flat rock offered to trailers the first proof as to the direction taken by an Idaho horse thief in 1888.

Logs dropped across the trail were apt to receive scratches from the overstepping foot of a white man or of a large hoofed animal; and also were wont, through this same agency, to have broken from themselves bark and outstanding branches or stubs.

Grass or other herbage, trodden upon by man or a weighty beast, usually was so bruised as for some time to remain at least partly prone. While it remained depressed it, if long-stemmed, definitely told the direction which the traveller had taken. A man always kicked knee-high or taller grass away from him, and thus the depressed plants' heads lay pointed in the direction in which the man had gone. A large hoofed animal, by reason of the semicircular sweep of its front feet, dragged backward the tops of high grass. Wherefore these tops would point toward the direction from which the animal had come.

That sticks or stones had been kicked out of their normal positions in the trail would appear from the unweathered, sharply defined contours of their former beds, from the non-appearance as yet of any attempt by these sticks and stones to reseat themselves in new position, and from the unweathered soil clinging to such of their surfaces as had fitted within their former resting-places.

Trees, plants, rocks beside the trail might, on their sides, record breaks or scratches of import correlative with these underfoot markings.

Foreign objects in the trail told their own story. They would include a bit of leather, a stone carried in a hoof and later dropped, a leaf or branch or flower that had adhered awhile to a boot, a spur, or a saddle strap and then fallen off, a piece of charcoal that had for some time clung to clothing and then been jarred away from its hold, sand that, collected upon the foot at a stream's crossing and thereafter drying had been gradually discarded, any leakings from the pocket of a coat or saddle or from a sack, anything that nature herself did not put upon the trail.

James Bridger from his horse's back saw an eagle feather upon the rocks. Realizing that such a feather always merited inspection, he stopped, dismounted, and found that attached to the butt of the feather's quill was a strand of buckskin. He needed no warning additional to that given by this dropping from a war-bonnet. One minute later and he had picked up the trail of a marauding Indian party.

James Dewing, travelling through a spruce forest in Wyoming, came upon a pathway among the trees. In the path lay a fresh leaf of an aspen-tree, a tree strange to that forest. Dewing dropped, crawled to one side, and found ambushed behind a log an Indian, to whose clothing was stuck an aspen twig with three leaves still adhering, and the attached stem of the one that had gone.

In the present Yellowstone National Park was a cliff of obsidian from which the local Indians, the Crows, quarried their arrow-heads. These heads were highly prized by the members of other tribes; and, in times of intertribal peace, were bartered in more or less sparing quantities to these outside Indians. There had been rumor of impending uprising among the Red Skins. James Bridger, wandering across country and traversing a wide ledge of exposed rock, strayed onto a line of obsidian arrow-points that, leaking through a hole in some carelessly carried pouch, had fallen onto the bare stone. There patently were too many of these heads for them to have come from any white man's curio sack, probably too many for the Crows to have spared in barter; and assuredly no peaceful savage would carelessly have portered so valuable belongings. Bridger reasoned that the Crow Tribe was very likely on the warpath. He soon found that his surmise was correct; for he, scouting around the ledge's rim, came in a few moments upon a discarded Crow moccasin and the fresh tracks of numerous ponies, but there was not a mark of any dragging lodge pole. When the savage went forth to battle, he left his tents at home.

Kit Carson in Colorado recognized, as coming from a certain sand-bar, grains of sand that, when drying, had gradually fallen from the hoofs of a horse which, having crossed that sand-bar, had been ridden onto ice. These grains of sand, many inches apart, guided the patient trailer two miles to where clear hoof-prints again appeared upon soft ground.

If a thieving Shoshone Indian had not included in his plunder a slowly leaking bag of copper rivets, he would have left no trail during the half mile that he walked in the swiftly flowing, clear waters of Wyoming's Pilgrim Creek.

The manure dropped by animals, and the clots of blood shed by a wounded quarry often offered valuable proof. The amateur trailer was apt to mistake for blood-stains the crimson markings imposed by frost on various kinds of leaves.

Birds and loose animals, disturbed by the fugitive and fleeing from him, not only revealed the fact of his motion, but also advertised its course. Crows were the most useful of these wild allies. They would fly promptly and to a distance upon a white man's approach, would rise as promptly upon Indians' coming; but were apt to tag behind the Red Skins' party, because the latter's distinctive odor suggested the certainty of future meals of discarded meat.

Crows, suddenly arriving from nowhere in particular, installing themselves in the tops of a group of trees, remaining thus aloft and constantly jabbering, meant not that they had convened for conversational purpose, but that an Indian camp was on the ground below the birds. Mere carrion would have called the birds to the ground, and eating would have stopped their caws.

Canada jays also would advertise the location of a camp.

A trailer, perched upon a hill and looking down upon a forest, could accurately chart the progress of an unseen traveller beneath the trees; and do so solely from the dartings of the birds and the hurried exits of the four-footed beasts.

Dave Rhodes of Montana, looking down into a wooded valley north of Jackson's Hole, Wyoming, remarked: "Here comes an outfit." He had noticed that, along an approximately straight line, not only successive birds had risen from the treetops but also some wapiti were hurrying from the woods. Presently four men rode into view.

Jim Scott, lying in a Kansan coulée with prairie-dogs all about him, saw the little animals one by one falling like tenpins and diving into their holes. He took the hint and still more fully hid himself. Twenty warriors presently came over the hilltop.

Every mounted trailer kept close watch upon the horse beneath him. The Range pony was alert to all movements, sounds, and odors; and, by his suddenly cocked ears, his quickly erected head, his sniffing, would direct his rider's notice to the quarry, or to some factor indicating its whereabouts. Sometimes the little brute's nose had to be held in order to stifle the whinny that was apt to hail the quarry's mount.

To avoid giving information to the quarry, the trailer often had to shun positions directly to the quarry's windward, lest scent drift on the breeze to a sensitive nose.

Hearing more rarely was important, and usually only when within fairly close distance from the fugitive; though the audible radius greatly could be increased by the scout's putting his ear to the ground. The steps of a moving horse, particularly when the animal was traversing hard ground and was travelling rapidly, could in this way be distinguished from quite far away, and distinguished so clearly as to disclose the identity of the gait the beast was using, *i. e.*, whether a trot, a lope, or a gallop.

At close range the kind of noise coming from breaking sticks told as to who was fracturing them. Horses, cattle, and white men, with their ruthless motion, produced sharply sounding cracks. Indians and all wild animals, however large the latter were, had a more stealthy step, and produced a slower, more crunching, and less insistent breaking noise.

Wet sticks and dry ones had, as compared with each other, quite dissimilar breaking tones.

Canvas or corduroy, when rubbed upon itself, upon rocks or upon tree branches, emitted a telltale sound. For this reason Indian scouts refused to include these materials in their clothing.

Sounds, particularly those from firearms, advertised to a trained ear the approximate position of the quarry; for the quality of the noise would tell the identity of its creator, and the quantity of the noise would evidence the distance it had travelled. In a matter of this sort the wind's direction and force were often factors for consideration, since the wind might be either an aid or a hindrance to the transit of sound.

With black powder (the only powder used till the decade of the nineties), no two rifles, even though of the same make and caliber, produced, when fired, sounds identical in character. Some occult difference in their steel differentiated their noises. And between weapons of unlike calibers, the difference in sound was very evident. If the trailer were familiar with the report of his quarry's weapon, a single shot from the latter would often indicate the fugitive's identity.

The trailer's sense of smell revealed to him the presence of neighboring Indians, wapiti, or fires, and also frequently permitted him to identify the ownership of objects dropped on the trail. Buckskin of Indian tan might, through long usage or rough treatment, change its appearance, but it never could rid itself of its characteristic odor. An excessive user of tobacco might have all his belongings so permeated with the weed's smell that his handkerchief or piece of cloth lying in the way would speak more definitely to the nose of the scout than to the latter's eye.

John Yancey, prowling through the Wyoming woods when the Indians were "out," saw a tiny bit of leather adhering to a tree. One look and one smell told that it was of Indian tan. No footprint appeared nearby, but inspection showed freshly broken bark above the bit of leather. What had happened was that an Indian, using treetops for a road, had come part way down to ground, but, on seeing Yancey, had climbed again.

The trailer's sense of touch had useful play in but two fields. Through that sense, there could, for the purpose of estimating age, be gauged the temperature of the manure which the fugitive animal had dropped. It also allowed one to ascertain, by feel at night, what one, in daytime, learned through the eyes, the trend of direction of the principal branches of the trees. These branches indicated the course of the prevailing winds, and thus a definite compass point. This latter phase had to do primarily with the exploratory function of scouting.

The discussion thus far has had to do only with ascertaining the identity of the trail of the quarry, and discovering the fact and direction of passage.

Ascertainment of the fugitive's distance ahead of the pursuer was a vital factor; for it not only determined whether the speed of the chase should be accelerated, but also often established whether correct diagnosis as to identity had been made. A footprint which had been assumed to have been that of a murderer of yesterday was suddenly proven to be three days old. Wherefore it was either not the trail of the quarry, or at least not his current trail.

Old markings were termed "old sign," and made a "cold trail"; while recent ones were called "fresh sign," and created a "hot" or "fresh" trail. Clearly visible sign made a "plain trail," indistinct sign a "blind" one. If the quarry's trail had been trodden upon by an animal or person, it was said to have been "fouled."

From the moment that a record was made, nature began to obliterate it. Its edges and projections were attacked by the wind, which carried against them sand, small sticks and stones or particles of ice; first rounded and later levelled them, and set about rolling debris into the little hollows; while possibly rain beat down protuberances, and washed flotsam into depressions.

The dust emanating from the scratching of a rock or of sun-baked soil was gradually dissipated. As soon as a branch broke, the clearly colored fibres at the point of fracture began to cloud from within and to collect dirt from without; the adjacent bark, if vital, began to parch; the leaves beyond the fracture commenced to wither; and, in some varieties of trees, sap gathered at the break.

From the moment that a plant was badly injured by being trod upon, there promptly set in around the wound rapid changes in coloration and in texture.

Blood clots tended to dry quickly, and to change their showy redness into inconspicuous black.

Temperature, the wetness or aridity of the ground, the humidity or dryness of the air, the velocity of the wind, the quantity and rate of change in the coloration and moistness of soil freshly exposed to weathering, the extent of the soil's normal willingness to cling together, the characteristics of wounded vegetation all came under the trailer's consideration; and usually he was able, from the appearance of "sign," closely to estimate its age. This conclusion as to age was reached through intelligent calculation as to the quantity of obliterative work that nature had done to the "sign" since its creation.

The quantity of melting or of freezing in and about a track that was impressed in snow or scratched upon ice told its story as to lapse of time. During frigid weather, drops of water oozing from a track offered clear evidence of the latter's freshness. Such drops would appear at a ford or drinking spot.

Upon a freezing day Tazewell Woody in Montana, breaking out from brush at a ford, saw upon the opposite bank a clearly defined imprint of a Sioux moccasin. Three drops of water were rolling down from the print's toe. Woody ducked, and a bullet went over his head.

Even upon dry soil, experts could reach close approximation as to age. It was only in windless, arid valleys that tracks were baffling to such men.

None of the foregoing is intended to suggest that the trailer made pretension to any knowledge of chemistry or botany. He merely kept his eyes and ears open, was intensely observant, and ever used common sense in making inductions from the very commonplace, very natural, and quite openly displayed matters that he observed.

There were other simple effects of nature's processes that gave definite information as to age.

Grass growing upon dry soil, and trodden-down but not severely bruised, would quickly rise to erect position when later wet by rain or dew. Grass growing in moist soil, and likewise stepped upon and fairly uninjured, would also promptly straighten and become vertical. But, in an arid country with a burning sun, herbage, flattened after the heat of the day had commenced, would lie for hours prostrate, much of it sullenly to wait for the coming of the next night's dew.

Dew, and still more markedly rain, by their action on the ground's surface, aided an observer in his gauging the age of tracks. The falling moisture wiped out the sharpness of all prior markings, and put upon the surface of the bare soil a smooth finish which recorded all indentations. Any cut upon that finish patently had been made after the finish had been created.

The edges of charcoal rounded under the slightest stress from wind or water, and placed almost a clock stamp upon the date of an extinguished fire. Still smouldering wood or steaming ground of course showed a more recently abandoned camp.

Frequently a footprint of the quarry merged with an imprint made by some other person or animal. If the trailer knew, as he often had reason to do, the exact age of the foreign track, his ascertainment as to which print was atop the other would give information of practical value.

The final matter to be taken into consideration during the chase was the psychology of the quarry. Persons or animals under pursuit had resorted since time immemorial to certain subterfuges for escape. These included entering running streams or other bodies of water, travelling for a distance in the water, and then returning to the land. These also included, for men, the ascent of trees, and the travel for a time through the treetops before returning to the ground and resuming ordinary method of locomotion. These also included, for men, placing their successive steps atop the bulges on the bases of the trunks of growing trees, and, by handholds upon higher portions of these same trees, swinging from tree to tree.

So much for the physical acts.

The mental element was the plan which nature since pursuit began had seemingly put in men and beasts pursued.

In approximately nine cases out of ten a human quarry would not follow a straight course for any considerable distance, but would subterfuge as follows:

In approximately nine cases out of ten he, if merely seeking safety and not hastening to a definite goal, would leave a stream upon the same side as the one on which he had entered. Whether he turned downstream or up it would depend upon the position of his pursuers or the physical appearance of the stream. If the pursuers were to one side of the quarry, the latter almost surely would, in the stream, proceed in the direction away from the side on which the pursuers were; but, if the pursuers were approximately to the quarry's rear, the latter, with almost equal certainty, would start in whichever direction a hurried glance at the stream's bottom suggested would give the speedier footing.

In approximately nine cases out of ten a man taking to the treetops would turn back upon the course which he had been following on the ground, and, unless hurrying to some definite spot, would ultimately leave the forest upon the same side as that at which he had entered it.

In approximately nine cases out of ten a man swinging from tree to tree would circle his way from his earlier course, and, on reaching the ground, would have reversed his initial direction.

The bear acted much as did the man. Dumb brutes other than the bear "doubled back" at streams only when the latter were of some size. Small watercourses seemingly did not strike them, as they did the bear and a human quarry, as being sufficient in size for manœuvres wherewith to deceive a pursuer.

The innate desire to deceive by doubling back was implanted by nature before the dawn of history; and still finds expression not only under the semiheroic conditions above described, but also among all children as they play games of pursuit. Watch a boy at his play and you can see what a murderer would do if chased.

One morning in the early nineties John H. Dewing, who would have been a very able Indian scout had he been an adult in the warpath days, was standing with Tazewell Woody in a hunter's camp near the southern end of Jackson Lake in Wyoming. There came to them a rider from Sargent's Ranch with news that, a little way to the northward during the previous night, one man had killed another, and that the killer was "wanted." The rider reported that, although the killer was horseless and probably the only pedestrian in the country, the rider did not know the characteristics of the killer's feet.

Woody and Dewing walked across the valley, and, within five minutes, had picked up a pedestrian's trail and ascertained that it was atop the tracks which horses of the hunting-camp's saddle band had made the preceding evening.

As Woody and Dewing followed this track, Dewing suddenly turned to Woody and said: "Mr. Woody, here's our man. First he saw our camp and circled it, and right here he is trying to make up his mind whether to double back or not."

What Dewing saw were human footprints which, at the beginning of a vista toward the camp, evidenced a sudden slackening of speed, a slight wandering about, and then a plunging rapidly upon a circular course centred upon the camp, and next a variation in length of stride and a twisting of the feet. Dewing guessed that this last phase meant that the killer had become dissatisfied with his direction, and had been looking to right and left to determine whether or not to leave the trail, and if so which way to turn.

Dewing was correct in his guess, for, less than one hundred yards farther along the trail, the man had gone off at a right angle and had headed directly for Jackson Lake. Obtaining the only boat upon that lake, he had rowed to its northern end and the foot of Mt. Moran, there left the boat, climbed across the shoulder of that mountain, struggled through the heart of the Teton Range, and so made his way to the railway in Idaho. Incidentally, the hurrying fugitive had, upon his journey, no food save a hawk which he shot with his victim's rifle and ate raw.

Through John Dewing's reasoning guess Tazewell Woody almost overtook that man; and, if he had been caught, Trampas of Mr. Owen Wister's "The Virginian," would not have had a real, flesh-and-blood murderer precede him over the very mountain route along which Mr. Wister, in his delightful book, later sent Trampas.

Trailers, following a quarry to the water's edge, would first scan the far bank for signs of egress; and, if seeing none, would look then at the stream's bottom for disturbed stones, bruised moss, broken sticks and whirls of discolored water, in order promptly to learn whether or not the water had been entered at all.

Trailers, losing footprints in the forest, would first scan adjacent trees for telling abrasions by a climbing fugitive. With or without those identifying signs, the psychological element had to be kept in mind until the normal trail should again appear upon recording land.

The trailer in his exploratory work was, through his previous close watchings of natural conditions, able to look down from the summit of any mountain he might have climbed, and accurately to diagnose the footing in all the valleys within sight. Accustomed to keep distances in mind and to realize their importance, he weighed the country's topography with a view to making no unnecessary steps. He would take short cuts along the tops of hills rather than undertake, as would many an amateur, longer journeys about the latters' bases.

Whenever he was on a hilltop, he studied the topography of the land below. He always had in mind sense of direction. In daytime the bearing of the sun, and at night that of the moon was never forgotten. Once "catching" the North Star, a brilliant planet, or a constellation; he marked the north, and thereafter the sky could cloud over for hours without causing him anxiety.

He knew the compass direction of the prevailing wind. Although, in certain sections of North America, moss upon tree-trunks grew most thickly upon the latter's northern sides, such was not the general rule; but, everywhere that the winds had a prevailing direction, the winds clearly recorded their own course. All foliage adapted itself to the situation, and extended its longer branches to leeward. Striations upon the snow or upon the ground mosses came from these same winds, and gave like evidence as to direction.

Pierre Duval, for six days, journeyed in a dense Far Northern fog across a country he never previously had seen, and came out upon the

Arctic beach within two miles of where he had wished. He had had no guide other than both the wind striations upon the moss and the leeward leanings of the dwarfed herbage.

Trailers, even the best of them, were not infallible. A quarry at times would perform an act so unprecedented as completely to delude his pursuer.

In this sort of ingenuity, there ranked, among all creatures north of the Mexican border, first, the Apache Indian, next, the Sioux Indian, the wolverine, the lobo wolf, and the coyote, and, next, a heterogeneous mixture made up of all other Indians, of the grizzly bear, and the more cunning white men.

Frank P. Fremont, late major U. S. A., relates the following anecdote.

Mounted Apache Indians having raided some Arizonan ranches, Fremont, then a lieutenant, started with a detachment of troops in pursuit; and, picking up the Indians' trail, followed it across a desert and into a forest. The trail, once amid the trees, showed that, every half-mile or so, the hoof-marks of three, four, or five of the Indians' ponies led off sharply to right or left. This sloughing, according to all previous experience of the army with marauding "hostiles," declared that the Apaches had definitely ended their foray, and were harmlessly dispersing for the sole purpose of quietly sneaking back to their reservation. Accordingly, the troops clung to the main trail until all of it had flowed away through these tiny, lateral leakages, and then the soldiers about faced, "back-tracked" through the forest and out into the desert. When they had marched several miles into the desert, they drew in all their outriders except a rear-guard; and, over flat treeless sands and under a withering sun, confidently jogged along, heads down, half asleep, bound for the fort.

The unforeseen element was that the Indians would violate a precedent of many years.

While the soldiers were far within the woods, unexpected things happened on the desert. The savages who had ridden off on those little sidings had promptly headed for prearranged concentration spots, one on each side of the main trail. Thus, without "fouling" this trail, there soon had been assembled two bands, each of some size. These bands then had moved out on foot into the desert by routes parallel with the trail, though at some distance from it; and, at an agreed time, had turned and marched toward each other, eventually to meet and to form across the trail a line, which bore to the trail the same relation as does the crossing of a capital letter T to the latter's stem. Next, except for a few of the Indians, each of the latter had dug directly in front of himself a shallow grave; and had crawled into it, with back up, and face and gun pointing in the direction from which the returning troops would come. Then the few excepted Indians had filled in the earth above the ambushing warriors, leaving however holes for breathing and sighting; had smoothed the ground's surface; and had fled.

The sleepy troops were jogging along. Suddenly, but a hundred feet ahead of them, painted, naked, whooping bodies, like devils on the Judgment Day, rose out of the ground and fired a volley. The soldiers did not break. They put the Indians back into the graves for a permanent stay.

Trailers may not have been infallible; but some of them were nearly so, and most of them were invaluable in their services.

CHAPTER XVII

LATER PHASES OF WESTERN MIGRATION

ORDER OF WESTERN MIGRATIONS—EFFECTS PRODUCED BY MINERS AND OTHERS—RANCHMEN PRINCIPAL CREATORS OF SPIRIT OF WEST—THAT SPIRIT—IMPRESS LEFT BY RANCHMEN.

HISTORY discloses that an affirmative public consciousness, an affirmative national spirit, occurs only among such people as are mutually engaged in active business affairs of however diverse sorts, and that, to exist, it must be founded on a lasting and overwhelming popular support of such principles as, deeper than mere matters of party politics, are socially and governmentally fundamental.

Before the gold excitement of 1848 but few whites lived beyond the far edge of the narrow strip which skirted the western bank of the Mississippi River. These few whites consisted of the scattered hunters, trappers, and Indian traders who, with blithesome contempt for distance, were wandering about the entire territory between that river and the Sierra Nevadas; consisted also of the scanty populations of California's and New Mexico's Spanish settlements, of an isolated group of ranchmen in southeastern Texas, of a pitifully small and astonishingly brave community in western Oregon, of the Mormon colony in Utah, and finally of a handful of expatriates who, quitting ships whaling or hide-droughing upon the Californian coast, had settled on its shore.

These few whites were too few in number, and, save for the people of Oregon and of the Spanish settlements, and for the Mormons in Utah, too widely dispersed, too differing in interests, and too individualistic to form even a local public consciousness; although the hunters, trappers, and traders passed down traditions which made an impress upon the consciousness of the entire West when that consciousness appeared.

The Oregonians and all their accretions of later years were merely a transplanted slice of New England, and, to this day in the year 1922, the peoples of coastal Oregon and of New England have been identical in thought, ideals, and action. The Mormons and the peoples of the various Spanish settlements each formed an isolated civilization, and were wholly self-contained.

The Oregonians, the Mormons, and the peoples of the Spanish settlements were not originators of the spirit of the West.

The next to invade the West were the miners, who, struck with the gold fever, began in numbers to make migration to California in 1849, to Colorado in 1851, to Oregon in 1852, to Nevada in 1859, to Idaho in 1860, to Montana in 1862, to Wyoming in 1867, to Dakota in 1875. But these miners, confining themselves to the circumscribed tracts of the ore beds, produced no general settling of the country.

Nor did they create a public consciousness. Once westward of the frontier, these miners, like the hunters, trappers, traders, and the expatriates mentioned above, considered themselves to be in a foreign land; regarded the territory in which they were as merely space from which wealth might be extracted; and restricted their ideas either to the labor in hand or to recollections of conditions "back home," in "the States."

These miners, self-cloistered in the areas of the orelands, gathered within those areas and about "rich strikes," like bees about a hive. They all stayed put where they were, and pecked away at the ground until the announcement that some one had elsewhere "struck it rich." Instantly some bearded, red-shirted, enterprising soul, seizing his shovel, pick, and pan, would desert his companions, and would "strike out" for the "new excitement," to be followed by a portion of the members of the "camp" just as a part of the inmates of a hive emigrate with a queen-bee. But this transit by the miners would mean merely a shifting from one settlement to another, the two identical in thought as well as in work.

This thought was limited largely to the contents of the ground and their extraction; and the miners' relations were with the earth rather than with people. The miners not only did not come into contact with persons living outside of the mineral belts; but also, as among themselves, had scant business intercourse. Their vocation, from its nature, required individual effort or at most that of small squads; and, from its severity, reduced life to digging in daytime and to sleeping at night.

Then too, natural desire to monopolize the results of eager, persistent, and successful search engendered secretiveness as to one's delving operations. Secretiveness, pursued on this point, tended to create uncommunicativeness in all important matters.

The miner carried with him to the West all the customs that he later followed there; and he changed them not at all except in so far as they related to the mechanical processes of procuring and refining ore, and save that he roughened his social manners.

He did found various towns, and he was the principal factor in their subsequent development into cities of importance and of multiple interests. Thus came Denver.

He did enter sleepy little Yerba Buena, a Mexican ranching hamlet lying upon the borders of a bay that had seen no ships except naval vessels, occasional Mexican coasters dropping in for trade, more occasional Yankee or Kanaka hide-droughers calling for hides or drinking-water, and equally rare Yankee whalers putting into port for either a refitting or an overhauling. True, he entered Yerba Buena; and, both directly by his local business and indirectly by the commerce which he induced, he converted a tiny, drowsy cluster of adobe huts into one of the cities of the world, San Francisco.

But he founded places, not the civilization which ultimately pervaded them.

He produced nothing except the structures in these cities and except extracted mineral wealth; and, as a class, has left no imprint beyond that of the recorded fact of his civic foundings, and that of a few phrases and of a picturesque memory. He for himself grew rich, and for us made Bret Harte and Mark Twain possible.

The miners were closely followed by their two providers, the merchant who sold supplies, and the transportation man, the latter portaging across the continent at first by wagon and later by railway train. The Western merchants, through the close of the nineteenth century, took on the color of their environments; and, until the comparatively recent urban development, were not sufficiently numerous to be a material factor in forming a public opinion. The transportation man, whether of the wagon or of the later railway, ever completely immersed himself in his immediate job, and customarily regarded the country he traversed not as the home of a populace but merely as a gap between terminal stations. These transportation men, who, with the army's aid, enabled the peopled West to be born and to grow, did not create or shape its spirit.

The superb Old Army was in the West, but officer and men dated their thoughts so generally from the city of Washington, kept their minds so much in national instead of local lines, tended so strictly to their military knitting, and lived so inside their own traditions that they left no imprint, although they primarily had made the West generally habitable.

The sheepmen, by the unadventurous nature of their animals, were withheld from the Cattle Country until it had been permeated by the raisers of horses and cattle, and its spirit had been crystallized. Furthermore, the sheepmen were too few in relative number, and were too much under the vituperative domination of the cattlemen to have been at any time a considerable factor. Among these sheepmen, were very able persons; but even these the Cattle Country said "smelt of wool," and so they were denied an influence.

Gamblers too were in the West, but they were of course merely incidental.

If the so-called spirit of the West was not made by any of the classes thus recited, who did make it? It had been formed in its entirety before the advent of the manufacturer, the professional man, and the farmer, so they could have played no part.

There is but one class left, the class composed of the rancher, the cowboy, and their fellow ranchmen. These men rode out into a vacant empire; met the traditions and the customs of the hunters, trappers, and traders, the primal pioneers; with unanimity adopted all of the traditions and the usable part of the customs; added to them; crystallized the whole into a code of compulsory usage, and actively embarked in the pursuit of a vocation by which they kept themselves in touch with all conditions of people and all four corners of the map. These men thus fulfilled the historical requirements for leave to create a public consciousness, and they performed the task.

If one wishes further proof, let him consider the present basic principles of the Far West. They stand forth in well advertised, clear-cut lore, even though in action they often be disregarded. They are the traditions of the open Range; and, when now transgressed, are so transgressed not by the ranchman, or by his children, but by some recent settler who knows not Israel, who has mistaken Elijah's mantle for a rag carpet. Mere living west of the Missouri River does not make one a Westerner.

If one desires still more evidence, then from his dictionary let him list all the words and phrases which have crept into popular use from any of the callings that were represented in the West before its spirit came. Let him take the words and phrases that were either invented or vitalized within each such calling. If he will ignore the numerous gambling terms (and logically they should be ignored), he will find the ranchmen to have been by far the largest contributors. But a few moments' search will give numerous expressions, like stampeded, bucked at it, caught in the noose, roped in, rounded up, rounded in, hobbled, hog-tied, corralled it, cinched it, it was a cinch, a lead-pipe cinch, ranch (in sense of home), cut it out, milling around, locoed, rattled, buffaloed, rustled, threw my hooks into him, throw the bull, horned in, butted in, bawled him out, to but a few verbal gifts from the miners with their now classic phrases, prospect around, good prospect, panned out, lucky strike, pay dirt, and struck it rich. Philologists assert that the best measure of the influence by one nation upon another is the extent of the modifications imposed upon the second nation's language.

The miner and the ranchman, though each living in the West, and thinking of the entire West as his own, did not conflict; for each dealt physically with only the sections for which the other calling could find no use. The miner, while beginning his West at the Missouri River, ignored the countless miles of flat lands, and pictured the country as, in part, a series of busy towns which, blocking the entrances to sombre gulches, filled the air with acid fumes, with the smoke of chimneys, with the ceaseless pounding of the stamps; pictured it also as in part a series of lonely canyons, within which isolated men either dug all day into rocky walls or stood all day upon a river bar and shovelled gravel into an ever hungry sluice-box; pictured it also as, in part, a wide surrounding area of uninteresting, oreless lands not worth investigating, of no advantage to himself, but of reputed value to the ranchman, and geographically a part of the West, in which the miner took such pride.

The ranchman, beginning his West also at the Missouri River, knew intimately every rise and swale throughout all the grass lands. He had no reason for entering the gulches and the canyons save to gratify curiosity or sectional pride. He thought in terms of sweeping stretches of open country, and had no instinct to found a city. However, as one of the exceptions, he did start Cheyenne upon its way.

Thus there were, coincidently within the geographical limits of the West, and each at heart claiming all of its territory, two Wests, that of the miner and that of the ranchman.

Such was the Old West.

What was the spirit of the West, of the Old West? It was a spirit that begat personal service and extreme self-reliance, which, in their exercise, were at all times, upon the instant, for however long duration, and without expectation of reward, as subject to the call of others, were they friends or entire strangers, as to the requisition of their owner. It was a spirit that offered a contempt for distance or danger as an impediment to duty or pleasure. It was a spirit that gave to a man an intense individualism, and not only a hatred of class distinctions save such as the West itself created, but also a bitter antipathy to all social usages in limitation of personal action except those which either were prescribed by universal fundamental law or were in the Western code. It was a spirit that nurtured an undying pride in the country of the West, a devoted loyalty to its people as a class, a fierce partisanship in favor of that country and its people, and a complete silence about and very generous forgiving of whatever wrongs any of the latter might have done.

The exhibition of these qualities was governed by the closely followed conventions which earlier pages of this book have attempted to portray.

Out of this spirit of the West, out of the forces which produced it or from the men who made it came three affirmative, continuing results. Of these three, two are patently of national importance and the third may ultimately prove itself to be so.

The first of these results was that Mason and Dixon's Line as a purveyor of sectional prejudices was never allowed to extend into the Cattle Country. It never yet has invaded where once the Range was open, and the lariat used to swing. Although Eastern emigration, obedient to nature's law, moved westward on parallels of latitude, although Texas had seceded and been in the Confederacy, although New Mexico and Arizona later were enpeopled dominantly by Texans, there was no North *vs.* South in the Cattle Country. Montana, Texas, and the States between met amicably over the cow's back.

The Texas Trail brought Southerner and Northerner of the Range together in intimate human contact, and fused them into the Westerner except in so far as the Texan reserved the right to pay obeisance primarily to his beloved Texas. Thus present-day Americans owe to the bygone man, atop a pitching bronco, thanks that the United States, for purposes of sectional prejudices, has but three divisions and not four.

The second result was a corollary of the first. It was an intense solidarity among all trans-Missouri River people; a solidarity still existent, and which, when the geographical centre of national population goes materially further westward than it now is, perhaps may speak dominantly at the polls. The West has not yet outgrown, gives no present evidence of ever outgrowing the example of the average cowboy. He had for his particular Western State and county an affection which, were he a Texan, was so strong as to make him call himself a Texan rather than a Westerner, but which, were he not a Texan, was not strong enough to prevent his terming himself a Westerner instead of a Coloradan, an Oregonian, or whatever. Nevertheless, and in any event, his ultimate, if not his primary, abject, blind, devoted allegiance was to the entire West, "God's Country." And, when the geographical centre of national population moves far westward, it will be politically well for the East if the then people of the one-time Cattle Country forgive the citizens who used to talk of the Alps instead of the Rockies.

The third result was that not only did Western democracy retain its vigor, unabated in quantity and unaltered in nature, but also it set itself affirmatively at work for the production of certain tangible results.

Although the methods of production and the tangible results produced were such as had been advocated by political socialists, the Westerner had no leaning toward socialism when he thus harnessed

LATER PHASES OF WESTERN MIGRATION

his democracy. His mind still functioned in terms of the neighborliness and of the willingness for mutual service that, in the early days, existed of necessity, and as a logical result, from both the scarcity of population and also the paucity of equipment for meeting untoward conditions. In this he was not inimical to the socialists.

But he still preserved his insistent demand for individualism, and bitterly resented any factor which might jeopardize its continuance. In this he was in diametrical opposition to the basic theory upon which political socialism rested.

Nor was any part of the Westerner's actuating motive a desire to dispense charity. He wished to benefit not the poor alone but the entire public, of which he formed a part.

With this attitude of mind, he was disposed to require that whatever institutions of higher learning, whatever hospitals, whatever orphanages, asylums, and other eleemosynary institutions might be locally needed be not left to the chance of private foundation or to support from private endowment. He took it for granted that he and his neighbors should get together and build and support a university, a hospital, or whatever, just as in primitive days he and his neighbors had joined forces when the round-ups called for collective efforts. Thus, save for the Rice Institute in Texas, and for various railway companies' hospitals, there are as yet, within the former Cattle Country and under private management, virtually no institutions organized for any of the purposes above enumerated.

The Cattle Country did not, of course, invent public foundation and public support, for the Eastern States already had institutions so set up. But these Eastern States were accustomed to additional institutions, all of private creation and, for their income, making no demand upon the taxpayer. It, however, remained for the Cattle Country wholly to omit from the public's reckoning all thought of private institutions in connection with plans for local betterments.

This omission did not come from any resentment against privately owned wealth. It did not signify any opposition to private endowment and management. It was not due even to scantiness of population. It was a direct inheritance from the enforced co-operation of the pioneer days.

It was not tinctured by any thought that Washington might provide at least a portion of the necessary moneys. True, the West had been accustomed not to pay for lands, grass, water, wood, or minerals, but rather to receive them as federal gifts; but the West had not yet awakened, as had some portions of the East, to the pleasing taste of federal cash. In the matter of its local institutions the West expected to foot the entire bill.

Perhaps the most picturesque task at which harnessed democracy
was set was that of installing and maintaining in various localities,
and for the gratuitous use of the entire public, camping-places, each
available for occupancy by numerous parties at a single time, and
many equipped with permanent cooking grates flanked by piles of free
wood. These camping-places were for the use of the entire public,
local or foreign, and not of only that portion of the entire public which
represented what the East amid its own population called the "general
public," which is to say the poor and also such of the financially more
well-to-do as at political meetings were given mere admission tickets
and not reserved seats. All Westerners, regardless of class or wealth
distinctions, used and still use these camping-places conducted under
the democratic doctrines of "for everybody," and "first come first
served," but nevertheless not requiring any more social intimacy than
the various camping-parties might care to have with each other.

These Western recreative spots stand out in contrast with most of
those within the East, a contrast which reflects adversely upon the East
unless its cause be understood. Heretofore such public playgrounds
in the East as have not consisted of mere roads have been devoted
largely to people financially unable to purchase recreation elsewhere.
That some persons have studiously avoided these resorts the West has
believed to have been due wholly to snobbishness, a word and a quality
detested in the Cattle Country. The West has ignored the other side of
the picture, and thus has overlooked the fact that the habitual users of
these places have commonly resented the attendance by such persons
as supposedly had means to go elsewhere and, by failing to do so, have
occupied space which otherwise a poorer man might have enjoyed.

However, whatever the causes, the East has not what the West has,
public parks filled with the spirit of democracy. That spirit in those
Western parks, that cooking grate flanked with piles of wood and
available to all who come, is neither more nor less than a perpetuation
of a little fire of sage-brush twigs which, built long years ago far out
upon the Range, heard its builder say "Light, stranger, light."

Not only was Western democracy thoroughly virile, but also, because
it was created and regulated by the public itself, it was thoroughly practical in both spirit and operation. In all this it differed much from the
laboratory democracy which cloistered political theorists have, from
time to time since America's founding, sought academically to purvey
to what they termed the masses.

The West but little welcomed such abstract prescriptions for social
betterment as on occasion detached theorists, however high-minded,

formulated and presented at long range to an ungrateful public. The West had no wish to be uplifted from afar, no wish to be uplifted by any one claiming superiority to it, no wish in fact to be uplifted at all. It was quite content with its own system of democracy.

This system, while starting with the American axioms that all men were created free and equal, and thus that a man might not acquire by inheritance an assured social position, declined nevertheless to admit that all men had to remain socially equal, but, on the contrary, ungrudgingly accorded to a man whatever position he by his individual worth had achieved. The Cattle Country thus recognized very distinctly defined social gradations. Brains, moral and physical courage, strength of character, native gentlemanliness, proficiency in riding or shooting—every quality of leadership tended to raise its owner from the common level. The aristocracy of the Cattle Country consisted of the likable element among the scouts, the ranch foremen, the "top" riders, the "crack" shots, the drivers upon principal stage routes, and the forceful ranch owners.

The West had such keen admiration for individual achievement that there were admitted to at least the fringe of this aristocracy such of the train-robbers as, not being "bad men," plied their vocation on bold lines, with conspicuous success, and with a tincture of chivalry.

The truth was that the West was so human and so masculine that it was somewhat addicted to hero-worship.

An Englishman's possessing a title of nobility or having close relationship with it did not in itself insure admission to the Western inner circles, though it universally made the man an object of curious interest. However, most of the English ranchmen of the type in question had so much innate social adaptability as, when in the country, to "travel on their own and not on their titles." Many of them were of great popularity, but they all, when absent from the country, were subject to be considered as impersonal absentees.

Nevertheless, all this is beside the mark, in as much as the West was made by its citizens and not by its guests.

The men who made the spirit of the West, who forbade Mason and Dixon's Line to extend, who harnessed democracy, wore "chaps."

Wherefore this book closes with the appeal that these bygone, virile, warm-hearted men of real idealism, of high courage and brave achievement, of maturest force and childlike simplicity, of broad tolerance if often of violent prejudices, these builders of an empire, may not, through the drama's stressing of their picturesqueness, be forgotten as to their bigness and be recorded by some definitive, historical treatise in the future as having been mere theatric characters.